The Rev. Dr Bruce A. Stevens is rector of an Anglican parish in Canberra where he also runs a private practice as a clinical psychologist. He obtained his Ph.D. at Boston University.

He lectures in pastoral counselling at St Mark's National Theological Centre, Canberra, and is a member of the Australian Psychological Society and the American Psychological Association. He is married to Jennie and they have four teenage children.

Dr Ian Harrison is a fellow of the Royal Australian and New Zealand College of Psychiatrists and is a consultant psychiatrist in private practice in Sydney. He was senior registrar in the Mood Disorders Unit and Eating Disorders Unit at Prince Henry Hospital, Sydney. He has recently completed a master's degree in psychotherapy at NSW University. He is a member of an Anglican church in the eastern suburbs of Sydney.

GW00691576

Other titles available in the Handbooks of Pastoral Care Series

GROWING THROUGH LOSS AND GRIEF
Althea Pearson
COUNSELLING IN CONTEXT
Francis Bridger and David Atkinson

Forthcoming Titles

FOR BETTER, FOR WORSE
Mary and Bruce Reddrop
FREE TO LOVE
Margaret Gill
FAMILY COUNSELLING
John and Olive Drane

HANDBOOKS OF PASTORAL CARE
Series Editor: Marlene Cohen

SETTING CAPTIVES FREE

*Models for individual,
marital and group counselling*

⁓⁓⁓

BRUCE A. STEVENS
with a supplement by Ian Harrison

HarperCollins*Publishers*

HarperCollins*Publishers*
77-85 Fulham Palace Road,
Hammersmith, London W6 8JB

First published in Great Britain in 1994
by HarperCollins*Publishers*
1 3 5 7 9 10 8 6 4 2

© Bruce A. Stevens and Ian Harrison 1994

Bruce A. Stevens and Ian Harrison assert the moral right
to be identified as the authors of this work

A catalogue record for this book
is available from the British Library

ISBN 0 551 02855-6

Typeset by Harper Phototypesetters Limited,
Northampton, England
Printed and bound in Great Britain by
HarperCollinsManufacturing Glasgow

FOR JENNY, ROWENA,
KYM, NAOMI AND CHRISTOPHER

CONTENTS

SERIES INTRODUCTION

The demand for pastoral care and counselling in churches has increased to record levels and every indication is that this trend will continue to accelerate. Some churches are fortunate to have ready access to professionally trained and qualified counsellors, but in most situations this onerous task falls to pastors.

Some pastors* are naturally gifted for the ministry of counselling. Some receive training before ordination and then seek to extend this as opportunity permits through the years. Others have the task of counselling thrust upon them. Most seem to feel some sustained demand, internal or external, to be competent in the field. This series aims to address some of the gaps frequently left in theological training. It is intended to offer support to those entrusted with responsibility for the care and well-being of others.

Comparative studies of healing agencies were pioneered in the United States. As long as thirty years ago The Joint Commission on Mental Illness reported that 42 per cent of 2,460 people canvassed would go first to the clergy with any mental health problem.

Of course there may be reasons other than overtly religious for a preference for clergy counselling. There may seem less stigma in seeing a pastor than a psychiatrist. Also, viewing a problem as a

*The term 'pastor' is used generically here, to include all who have a recognized pastoral role within a local church or Christian community.

primarily spiritual matter may preclude taking some degree of responsibility for it and for examining its depths. And, of course, clergy visits are cheaper! Unfortunately, there can be the additional reason that parishioners feel an inappropriate right of access to their pastor's time and skills. God's availability at all times is sometimes confused with ours, as is divine omniscience.

Being a front-line mental health worker can put a pastor under enormous and inappropriate strain. Counselling is becoming the primary time consumer in an increasing number of parish ministries.

Feeling unsafe and inadequate in any situation inevitably produces some form of self-protective behaviour, unless we can admit our inadequacy while retaining self-respect. Religious professionals who are under pressure to function as counsellors but know their skills and knowledge to be in other areas may understandably take refuge in various defences, even dogmatism. The term 'religious professional' is more familiar in some countries than in others. The clerical profession actually preceded all others, in status and in time. 'But what are we professional at?' can be a difficult question to answer. This is especially so when clergy are driven to believe that anything short of multi-competence will let God down.

Pastors may feel obliged not to appear inadequate in the area of counselling because of their confidence that the Bible contains the answer to every human need. And it does, conceptually. The difficulty is not with the Bible nor with the pastor's knowledge of the Bible. Neither of these should be in question. The concern is whether pastors have the additional ability of a clinician. Naming a counselling problem correctly - not the presenting problem but the real, underlying issues and their components - is a refined specialism. Making a faulty diagnosis, especially when God and biblical authority are somehow implicated, is the cause of much damage. Clinical terminology can be applied almost at random but with a surprising degree of assurance. Understanding the Bible, and understanding the complexities of clinical practice, are not one and the same skill. In 1985 a comparative study was conducted into the ability of 112 clergy to recognize 13 signs of suicidal tendencies. (Reported in the *Journal of Psychology and Theology*: 1989: Vol 17: No 2.) It was found that clergy were unable to recognize these signs any better than educated lay people and substantially less well than other mental health workers. This is no necessary reflection on the clergy. Why should they be expected to have this professional ability? Considering them culpable would only be just if they were to assume, or to allow an assumption to go unchecked, that their skills were identical to those of other caring professionals.

One pressure is that graduates of some theological colleges have actually been taught that ordination will confer counselling skills. 'We must insist upon the idea that every man who has been called of God into the ministry has been given the basic gifts for . . . counselling' (Jay Adams, *The Christian Counsellor's Manual*, 1973, Presbyterian and Reformed Publishing Company; Part One, Page 20).

Equating a ministry calling with being a gifted counsellor could be seen to involve some leaping assumptions. These are becoming more apparent as we distinguish what we used to call 'the ministry' from God's calling of *all* believers into ministry. As more work is done on what we mean by 'ordination' more clergy can be released into those areas of ministry for which they are clearly gifted and suited.

Belief that counselling skills are divinely bestowed in conjunction with a ministry 'call' will probably not issue in the purchase of this series of handbooks! Other pastors who believe or fear that neither counselling nor any other skills can be taken for granted, are possibly conducting their ministries under some heavy burdens. This series is written with a concern to address these burdens and to redress some erroneous equations that relate to them. Each author has extensive experience in some avenue of ministry and is also trained and experienced in some aspect of counselling.

These Handbooks of Pastoral Care are designed to aid pastors in assessing the needs of those who come to them for help. The more accurately this assessment can be made the more confident the pastor can be about the form of ministry that is required in each instance. Sometimes pastors will decide to refer the matter elsewhere, but on other occasions there can be a prayerful assurance in retaining the counselling role within their own ministry.

Marlene Cohen
Oxford, March 1994

PREFACE

St Paul wrote to the Colossians encouraging them to 'Be thankful' (Colossians 3:15). I find this easy as I approach getting this book finally published. I am grateful to the many people who have been my mentors, enriched my thinking with new ideas, supported me through friendship and with whom I have 'bonds of love'. I offer a Christian perspective to the counselling process, this would not have been possible without an initial experience of God's grace in 1973 and a sometimes 'stumbling in the dark' growth in understanding His ways over the last two decades.

I would like to give credit to my initial theological formation at the Alliance College of Theology in Canberra. I was deeply influenced by the godly lives of a number of the faculty, especially the Revd John Harvey and the Revd Murray Downey. The Revd Dr Richard Campbell of the Australian National University helped me to understand the 'rules' of scholarship. I remain indebted to the Australian College of Theology, especially the Revd Dr Stuart Barton Babbage, who allowed me to pursue post-graduate studies in the field of New Testament. In the months before I was ordained in the Anglican Church, I did a full-time quarter of Clinical Pastoral Education at Gladesville Psychiatric Hospital with the Revd Dr Milton Coleman as supervisor. This proved to be a turning point in my life as it stimulated an interest in Pastoral Psychology. I also received a lot of encouragement from the principal of St Mark's College of Ministry the Revd Canon David Durie who encouraged me in my journey into Anglicanism. I later lectured at St Mark's in Pastoral Studies and I have enjoyed the fellowship of other lecturers, especially the Revd Dr Jim McPherson and the Revd Dr Don Saines. We shared papers and encouraged each other to write for a larger readership.

My academic studies in Pastoral Psychology were continued at Boston University. I was a fellow at the Danielsen Institute, a mental health clinic of the university, where I was trained in clinical practice. Both Professor Merle Jordan and Professor John Maes, my supervisors in that programme, were also 'wise counsellors' in my writing of the Ph.D. dissertation. When I returned to Australia I had individual supervision in marital therapy with Mrs Leila Bailey of the ANU Counselling Service and in individual counselling and assessment with Dr Tom Sutton presently in private practice. Since 1988 I have been in a peer counselling group with psychologists Dr Malise Arnstein, Mr Ian Manton and Mrs Sally Guggenheim. This has been a source of support and clinical insight over the last five years. I also have appreciated lunches with Dr Don Lawrence, a psychiatrist in private practice, and our discussions about everything from multiple personality disorder to what is 'Christian' about counselling. Clinical insights from all these therapists have found their way into this book whether acknowledged or not. Although I have been amazingly fortunate in my teachers and colleagues, I think it is my clients who have taught me more than I can adequately say about being a counsellor. I have shared their pain, but they have inspired me with their courage and determination to overcome the most daunting of difficulties.

Various editors have published my writing over the past twelve years and encouraged me in this investment of my time. In particular my thanks go to Mr Gerald Davis, who has accepted over forty articles in pastoral care for the national Anglican newspaper *Church Scene*. This helped to form the foundation of this book and indirectly introduced me to my editor Mrs Shirley Watkins. When I first rang Hodder and Stoughton to ask about the possibility of writing a book, Shirley immediately said, 'Oh, you teach at St Mark's. I have read your articles in *Church Scene* and I have been thinking of asking you to write for us'. It was a wonderful first contact with an editor and potential publisher. Mrs Marlene Cohen approached me to write for this series with HarperCollins, and when difficulties became apparent with Hodder and Stoughton, I offered her the book. I very much appreciate her support and the warm encouragement of Mrs Christine Smith, the Publishing Manager of Marshall Pickering at HarperCollins. I have also benefited from comments of the Revd Dr Geoff Peterson who in reviewing the manuscript challenged me to better integrate my theological understanding with the clinical emphasis of the book and I am grateful for Dr Ian Harrison's contribution of a psychiatric supplement.

The Christian communities in which I have served – the Church of the Way, Canberra, St John's, Canberra, the Church of the Redeemer, Boston, St Paul's Millis, MA, and Holy Covenant Anglican Church, Canberra – have all extended to me the love of 'brothers and sisters in Christ' which is truly a miracle of grace. I am also grateful to Mrs Rosemary Kennemore, editor with the Bible Society, who has meticulously read and corrected this manuscript.

At the deepest level, 'Who I am' has been formed by the love of those closest to me, my mother June and my father Allen (now deceased), my brother Mark, relatives and family through marriage. I am most in debt to my immediate family: my wife Jennie and our children Rowena, Kym, Naomi, and Christopher. They have had to put up with the 'real me', especially my obsessive reading, alternated with writing on my Apple PowerBook. On them has fallen the cost of my emotional exhaustion after long hours in counselling or irritability after the demands of ministry. These five people, with whom I share my life, are God's greatest gift to me. It is only a small token, but I dedicate this book to Jennie, Rowena, Kym, Naomi and Christopher.

Bruce A. Stevens
Canberra, 1994.

INTRODUCTION

The counsellor is like a guide with a map. The Christian counsellor already has the most important map – that given by God in the Bible. I believe that all other maps are fallible. However, this is not to deny that there are many useful maps that can be placed alongside what we know from revelation. It is sad that Christian counselling, with so much to offer, has suffered from a self-imposed isolation. Yet counsellors who are mature in their biblical understanding can add to their effectiveness with modern therapy techniques and research from the social sciences.

I will outline some different styles of counselling which are relevant to the help offered by clergy, lay pastoral counsellors and Christian professionals who see a variety of people with different needs in their daily work. There is an old adage that to the person whose only tool is a hammer, soon everything will look like a nail. In a similar way it is very limiting to have only one style of counselling, so the chapters that follow will distinguish between individual, marital and group counselling. Case examples will be used to illustrate the distinct contributions that each style has to offer those in need of counselling. At the end of each chapter there are practical exercises to encourage the reader to think about relevant themes and to try out the skills mentioned. I will draw on the disciplines of both clinical psychology and pastoral care since I am an Anglican priest as well as a clinical psychologist with a private practice. Dr Ian Harrison has added a psychiatry supplement to introduce what that specialist medical profession has to offer.

Who do people turn to for help today? Very few go initially to mental health professionals. Instead they tend to approach medical doctors, clergy, lawyers, nurses, and teachers. Christians may seek help from other believers in the church. Perhaps most counselling is done in informal settings. For example, *Sonia has recently separated from her violent husband and she has the custody of two pre-school boys. Sue is a friend from church who is also a lawyer. Sonia has asked her to help with the property settlement and the paper work associated with the anticipated divorce. But Sonia had an additional agenda. She also needed a lot of emotional support and prayer as she tried to understand how God had allowed this to happen. Naturally, Sue's first responsibility was to offer competent legal services, but she also recognized that as a 'whole person' Sonia had other needs. She was not always able to separate these needs during their time together.*

Clergy and other professionals have severe limits on time. This book recognizes this reality and will give some guidance for the brief encounter as well as a strategy for short-term counselling (from four to six sessions). The main emphasis is on understanding the distinctive opportunities in individual, marital and group counselling. This may help some Christian counsellors to broaden their options for helping people. The recognition of the point at which to refer is equally important and this topic is also considered. It is always important to be aware of professional boundaries and the limitations of our knowledge.

Some professional people have had specific training in counselling. This can be part of a more specialized role such as alcohol counselling, youth work, chaplaincy, or grief counselling. But once skill is gained in one area it is possible to learn further skills and help others in need. *Betty is a lay counsellor in a large Pentecostal church. She has a Bible college diploma, but no formal training in counselling. She is gifted in helping others and has assisted many adult survivors of sexual abuse, but has had no exposure to the language of the professional field which closes the door to help from journals and professional texts. Her effectiveness may be increased if she has more exposure to psychological research and techniques used in secular fields - though she would naturally evaluate such information with biblical understanding. She may also consider forming a group as the best way to respond to the overwhelming need she has met in her church.*

In later chapters I will outline some of the theory of group development and introduce skills for leading therapeutic groups.

This book does not cover every kind of emotional problem. Instead, a number of common situations are used to illustrate the different styles of counselling. This includes the grief process, depression and assessing the risk of suicide, child sexual abuse, self-esteem and assertiveness. I have devoted four chapters to assessing and dealing with marital problems because this area causes such distress and will be a large part of the case load of the general counsellor. Also, in an attempt to bridge the gap between pastoral and clinical language, what might be unfamiliar diagnostic terminology from the American psychiatric manual DSM III-R (*Diagnostic and Statistical Manual of Mental Disorders* 3rd Edition revised) is occasionally used. There is also a discussion of the role of psychiatric drugs and what is involved in treatments such as ECT (electroconvulsive therapy).

Regardless of what we might hope to achieve, it has to be accepted that in the 'real' world there are all sorts of restraints on what is possible in counselling. Public services are not always available, financial limitations restrict access to other services and there are often long waiting periods to see a professional counsellor. In some rural areas distance may be a problem. *Angus is a priest in a remote parish. He has all the usual problems but he lacks access to specialist counsellors. A couple in the church came to see him with their fifteen-year-old son who had been caught stealing cars. Angus suspected that this was part of a broader family problem that had been 'in the making' for some time. It was now urgent and he needed to become involved.* Some general guidance can give him confidence and be important in resolving the difficulties while avoiding some of the more common pitfalls. An awareness of the systems approach that informs most marital and family therapy can also be useful if he has to 'go it alone'.

A listening ear with a reassuring pat on the shoulder and a comment, such as 'Don't worry', may be all that some people can manage. Indeed some professionals today might consider this adequate. But others, perhaps most of us, would recognize that there are increasing demands from those who seek help. We can all do better. Eugene Kennedy made the encouraging observation, 'In most emotional problems a little help is a lot of help.'[1] This book is an attempt to demystify what mental health counsellors are doing. There is no reason why gifted counsellors and clergy can not do more to meet the needs of those who are already entrusted to them in their normal professional lives.

CHRISTIAN COUNSELLING

There is a statue of the Venerable Bede in St Paul's, Jarrow. It was carved from the twisted trunk of an old tree. The wood was considered useless for building, but the artist used its knots and warps to good effect. As the image had been fashioned from the wood, so Bede had been shaped and used by God.

Christian counselling is not 'ordinary'. There is an element of transcendence. The wood of a twisted life can be shaped to become a tribute to the glory of God. The counsellor has the privilege of cooperating with God in this activity.

Christian counselling is part of the ministry of the Church. It is help in the name of Christ, but there are distinctions as suggested by Gary Collins:[1]

1 Pastoral care is the responsibility of all Christians to minister to one another. St Paul wrote, 'Bear one another's burdens' (Galatians 6:2). This mutual assistance includes intercessory prayer, teaching and guidance from the Bible, reconciliation, healing, nurture and the sacraments. This caring between believers happens as much in the coffee time after church services as in a visit by a pastoral care worker to the local nursing home.

2 Pastoral counselling is the central focus in this book. It is the spiritual and psychologically informed counselling offered by church leaders to help individuals, couples, and families to cope with crises and pressures of life. The traditional source of pastoral counselling has been clergy and members of religious orders; however in recent years gifted lay people have been recognized and some are called to serve in this way. The number of sessions is usually limited to dealing with the presenting problem (perhaps four to six) but can extend to months or even years. There is a reliance upon the insights of Scripture and the truths honoured in the Christian tradition.

3 Pastoral psychotherapy is generally longer term, perhaps twelve sessions or more. The goals are more focused on the dynamics of personality such as characterological changes, correcting developmental deficits and removing emotional blocks from the past. Although such changes can occur in pastoral counselling, it is not usually the goal of the counsellor. The therapist is usually highly trained with both tertiary degrees and a series of supervised mental health placements. Some clergy specialize in this area and complete psychology or social work qualifications. Others may undergo training to become Gestalt therapists or qualify as Jungian analysts. But it is more common that a Christian psychologist will work in a church setting or have a private practice that is recognized by the local churches.

Some Christians would question whether psychology has anything of value to offer the Christian counsellor. Jay Adams claimed that 'by studying the Word of God carefully and observing how biblical principles describe the people you counsel . . . you have all the information and experience you need to become a competent, confident Christian counsellor without a study of psychology'.[2] This makes sense only if one assumes that the Bible is a comprehensive textbook on psychology. In my opinion the absurdity of this position is illustrated by inserting doctor in this quotation for counsellor and medicine instead of psychology. It simply claims much more than Scripture claims for itself.

I believe that counselling in the Church needs to be much more aware of advances in psychological research and accepted methods of treatment. This is not a call to neglect our Christian distinctiveness, but to enhance such insights with the benefit of medical and psychological knowledge. As it has been said, 'All truth is God's truth'.

This book will not attempt to outline the various theories of counselling such as Freudian psychoanalysis, Jungian psychology, Rogerian non-directive counselling, existential, feminist, and other schools.[3] Instead I will be eclectic and draw on whatever resource seems relevant to the particular problem. In addition to the secular schools there are Christian approaches that have been popularized in recent years including those of authors Jay Adams,[4] Lawrence Crabb, jnr.[5] Gary Collins, Anne White,[6] John and Paula Sandford.[7] This list is hardly exhaustive, but these and other approaches have some following among Christians. None are universal in acceptance. Perhaps it is reasonable to conclude that each has some strengths and limitations. I intend to focus more on the different styles of counselling with individuals, marriage and family; and to stress when it may be appropriate to match a style with the presenting problem.

The Uniqueness of Christian Counselling

There are many varieties of Christian or biblical counselling. What is it that makes such counselling distinctive? There are various characteristics, almost generalizations, that can be said about all Christian counselling. I have sought to identify a number of these:

1 Beyond law and despair

St Paul was a pious Jew. He understood the burden of trying to live under the Law. The result is condemnation, 'all have sinned and fall short of the glory of God' (Romans 3:23). Christians believe that there is a moral order and the law reflects what God has ordained. There is no easy escape from the 'law within'. People experience 'falling short', even if they are not quite sure what was or is the standard. The result is feelings of guilt.

Guilt is a stumbling block to many modern therapies: as G. K. Chesterton quipped, 'Psychoanalysis is confession without absolution'. Although some therapies, such as William Glasser's Reality Therapy, emphasize responsible living, there is no freedom from genuine guilt without an experience of grace. St Paul rejoiced in the good news of Christ, 'There is therefore now no condemnation for those who are in Christ Jesus. For the law of the Spirit has set you free from the law of sin and death . . .' (Romans 8:1-2). In forgiveness there is transcendence.

Another prison is despair. Many people live out their lives with minimal expectations or a lack of belief in the future but Christians can anticipate what God promises. As the writer to the Hebrews expressed it, 'Faith is the assurance of things hoped for, the conviction of things not seen' (Hebrews 1 1:1). We have a basis for hope, even though we now see 'in a mirror, dimly, but then we will see face to face' (I Corinthians 13:12).

I was reminded of this reality when an agnostic sought me out as a Christian psychologist for help with his marriage. Even in despair he could reach out in hope to a God he was not sure existed.

2 Beyond reductionism

Psychological theories can almost be classified in terms of their limited focus: behaviour in Behaviourism, feelings in Rogerian counselling, thought in Cognitive therapy, impulses in classical Psychoanalysis, and interpersonal processes in family therapy. Some of these paradigms are simplistic especially in terms of what it means to be human. Is that uniqueness adequately conveyed by the parent-child-adult styles of communication in Transactional Analysis?

The biblical understanding of humanity created in the image of God is more holistic: 'Let us make humankind in our image, according to our likeness . . . so God created humankind in his image, in the image of God he created them; male and female he created them' (Genesis 1:26-27). The image of God not only preserves what is unique, but introduces the importance of relationships: 'our likeness' and 'male and female'. An individual was understood in a relational context that included family, neighbours, tribe, nation and certainly God. Therefore we are more than impulses, feelings, behaviour, thoughts, temperament, mood or psychopathology (cf. Psalm 8:4-5). [8]

This also raises the larger question of justice. Some therapies aim to help the individual to fit within what may well be an unjust system without looking critically at the big picture. In recent years feminist therapists have emphasized the importance of seeing pathology in social context, but then thousands of years ago the prophets burned with a similar passion. Amos refused to accept the token sacrifices; instead, the Lord required, 'Let justice roll down like waters, and righteousness like an ever flowing stream' (Amos 5:24).

3 Beyond confusion

It may well be that most modern individuals 'live on scraps' of meaning. There is no encompassing faith, no ultimate concern or unity of perspective. [9] Such world views are not very robust. A sense of personal meaning can be shattered by broken relationships, loss of job or business, life changes, sickness or tragic loss. The resulting confusion is understandable.

A person seeking counselling may have trouble integrating such experiences into a personal story: Why? Why me? Why now? The need for meaning is profound and yet it is not addressed in most therapies. Victor Frankl and existentialist writers have written on this theme, but this is not characteristic of the field as a whole.

The journey to make sense of what has happened may be lonely and a struggle each step of the way. The Christian counsellor is a fellow traveller. It is comforting to know that our Lord shares in this:

> *I will lead the blind*
>   *by a road they do not know,*
> *by paths they have not known*
>   *I will guide them.*
> *I will turn the darkness before them into light,*
>   *the rough places into level ground.*
> *These are the things I will do,*
>   *and I will not forsake them. (Isaiah 42:16)*

We will hear stories of brokenness. The plot may be tangled, emotions turbulent and dreams destroyed. We hear how God has been seen to be either absent or part of the story line. This is part of the meaning which the person tries to construct and the counsellor is invited to be part of this activity of writing a coherent story. As one theologian said, 'Any sorrow can be borne if a story can be told about it.'[10] The Christian pastor is also a bearer of stories, especially the story of God's activity in Christ, which through faith can provide a depth of meaning for the believer (Philippians 2:5-11).

4 Beyond alienation

The frequency of change in our society has meant that individuals, couples and families must increasingly rely on their immediate resources. This has led to a situation in which many people seek counsellors to fill needs once met by members of their own family or close neighbours. But this is only one aspect of the fragmenting of our society. The elderly live in isolation, the handicapped are out of sight in institutions and the mentally ill are invisible even in the midst of a crowd.

The mental health system is of little help in providing more coherence in care. In the trend towards specialization of services there is even more fragmentation with private practitioners, health assessments, psychological testing and various clinics. It is an all too frequent experience that people feel torn and confused by the various professionals in a long series of referrals. In this way it seems that treatment adds to a sense of alienation.

Clergy have an enormous advantage in this area. There are many people in the average church who can be called upon to provide genuine support. Churches are usually full of small groups and there are usually opportunities to be involved. In the mutuality of Christian community every member has some responsibility to 'Bear one another's burdens, and in this way you will fulfil the law of Christ' (Galatians 6:2). This also helps to keep some distressed individuals out of the mental health scene and the role of 'sick person' this might imply.

5 Beyond idols

The Hebrew prophets were the first to demythologize idols. They saw them as wood or stone and mocked the worshippers (*see* Psalm 115:3-8). However, as theologian Helmut Thielicke observed, 'Idolatry is an illusion, but the god gets a grip on us.'[11] The powers of our day are obvious: wealth, beauty, youth, health, success, fame, and glamour. These are the spiritual forces behind images of advertising and tokens of status. In the shadow of such idols we can see the demons of old age, poverty, sickness and worthlessness without a job or a position. Just to cite one example: a psychological disorder such as anorexia is usually entangled with media images of the 'perfect body'.

Merle Jordan has written about the work of the Christian counsellor as combating the power of idols. The counsellor uses his religious and biblical insight to 'confront those psychic structures, forces and images which masquerade as God.'[12] An individual's belief system is their 'operational theology' (p. 20). If self-concept is linked to a god-concept then psychopathology can be defined in terms of idolatry, 'when a person takes his or her identity from that which is less than the Ultimate Source of Being, then the sense of self is distorted' (p. 24). And this can lead to depression or other states of being out of touch with the self. The idolatrous relationship needs to be exposed, understood and renounced. As Jesus said to his disciples, 'You will know the truth, and the truth will make you free' (John 8.32).

6 Beyond illusion

If a counsellor speaks of personal beliefs it may sound patronizing or perhaps even proselytizing. Clearly any element of coercion or manipulation has no place in counselling which respects the autonomy of the person seeking assistance. The counsellor should adopt an open approach which allows the person in counselling to explore his or her own path.

However, it is not quite so simple. We live in a time of moral anarchy. Alasdair MacIntyre has described our society as one in which the language of morality is in grave disorder. We have inherited fragments of conceptual schemes which have lost not only their conceptual unity but their power of persuasion.[13] This is seen in the moral debates of our day, for example: abortion, bioethics, animal experiments and the environment. It appears that 'emotivism' is now prevalent. MacIntyre explained this as the belief that all moral judgments are expressions of attitude or feeling – it is all subjective. A good Roman Catholic may take the pill against the teaching of the Church and justify the action by saying, 'It feels right.' Such is the moral chaos of our day.

In contrast, many religious counsellors try to impose their categories of 'right' and 'wrong'. This can lead to an approach to counselling which restricts the freedom of the person to make appropriate choices. But on the other hand, can Christian counselling be 'value free'? This would seem to be impossible because our moral perspective is the way we understand issues that we encounter in counselling. Rather than chase the questionable ideal of such 'objectivity', I think that we should be transparent about our convictions but seek to encourage individuals to make their own choices. It is a difficult balance to find.

Another related difficulty is the way some counsellors will only be concerned with the therapeutic process. As MacIntyre noted, 'Truth has been replaced as a value by psychological effectiveness.'[14] The 'blinkers' are firmly in place. Yet Christian counsellors are often sought out because of a potential moral clarity. I consider that revealed truths are basic to what makes relationships work. One example of this is found in the words of the traditional marriage service. It may seem that faithfulness, honour, 'for better or for worse', and 'until death us do part' are outmoded, but such commitments enable a couple to stay together through some testing times. It is the depth of understanding of relationships in terms of what God desires as best for us that gives Christian counselling a sense of direction. And I believe that it makes good psychological sense since there is a realistic understanding of the shared frailty of human nature.

The task of integration is not easy. Henri Nouwen, a psychologist and Catholic priest, observed: 'One of our most challenging tasks today is to explore our spiritual resources and to integrate the best of what we find there with the best of what we find in the behavioural sciences.'[15] The temptation is to retreat behind professionalism for those well trained in the mental health field or to withdraw into an ecclesiastical ghetto for the church-based counsellors.

Just how 'Christian'?

What exactly is it about our counselling that is distinctly Christian? I would imagine that each counsellor who sees his or her work in terms of spiritual ministry might have a different response. So I can only answer for myself. What I see as most fundamental to my counselling is the invitation for God to be present. Since God is omnipresent, there is a sense in which God is always with us, 'invited or not', but there is also the important dynamic that God can be experienced in the process.

I have been encouraged by reading Wayne Oates's book *The Presence of God in Pastoral Counselling* where he advocated the importance of moving from dialogue to trialogue.[16] He explored the ways God can be present as Creator, in the stranger in community, in the darkness and both 'over-against' and 'alongside' the individual. Oates's treatment is not exhaustive but it is valuable in highlighting the various ways that God can be understood as active in pastoral counselling.

On the other hand I am not convinced that Christian counselling has to be particularly 'religious'. Most of my counselling is done in a suite of offices located in a medical centre alongside a paediatric surgeon, a sports medicine clinic and a pathologist. It is a secular setting and my clients are usually referred by their GPs. Some of them would not be aware that I also work as an Anglican minister with responsibility for a large suburban church. I do not generally pray with clients, but I do pray for them in the privacy of my daily prayers. I do not often quote Bible verses, but I do listen with sensitivity to the strivings of the spiritual life. I am not dogmatic about what should be believed but I have a bias towards traditional values and the expectation that an adult should assume responsibility in life. Nor am I moralistic in tone, but I am concerned when an individual makes careless and callous choices. What I am is a Christian who offers professional assistance and in that process I try to discern and cooperate with the divine activity.

Since I am not particularly directive in my style of counselling, I have sometimes felt a little defensive about more aggressively Christian approaches to counselling. I am rarely interventionist, though certainly quite active in both marital and group counselling. Some critics would question whether a seemingly tentative approach could be justified as Christian.

I would like to illustrate with an example of more non-directive counselling. Michael, a twenty-year-old man has made an appointment to see Sarah, a counselling pastor at a large Baptist church. After sitting down Michael begins:

> Michael: *'I just don't know where to begin. Everything is falling apart around me. As you know Jane and I have been 'going out' for the last three years. A few months ago we were considering becoming engaged.'*
> Sarah: *'Yes, I have known you both as leaders in the senior youth group.'*

M: *'Well, a month ago she went with Marcia overseas for a holiday. When they were in Cairo - in a cab - they had a bad accident. She has been in hospital ever since. Her condition is serious. I feel so helpless.' (He is crying)*

S: *'Everything is out of your control.'*

M: *'Yes, and somehow I keep blaming myself.'*

S: *'You blame yourself?'*

M: *'There is something you don't know. Jane and I have been sexually - together - you know what I mean.'*

S: *'Yes, I think I follow what you are saying.'*

M: *'But I can't get it out of my mind that God has judged us. He is punishing us with the accident because we didn't honour Him. And it really is my fault - I put pressure on Jane. I feel so terrible. But why didn't I have the accident? It doesn't make sense.'*

S: *'So you blame yourself and think that you should be suffering and not Jane?'*

M: *'That's right.'*

S: *'And the way you see it is that the only concern God has in this situation is to punish you both?'*

M: *'That has been what has been going through my mind since I heard about the accident. I can hardly sleep at night. I don't know what to think . . . maybe it is just that I feel so guilty.'*

S: *'That is a horrible feeling.'*

M: *'I don't know how I allowed things to get so out of hand. You know, ever since I made my decision for Christ - it was at a camp when I was sixteen - I have felt that God loved me - enough for Christ to die for me.'*

S: *'Yes, I believe that too.'*

M: *'I suppose it is this accident. Everything has become so confusing. Do you think that I have lost sight of all that? I mean God's love for me?'*

S: *'What do you think?'*

M: *'I think that I have been confused. I am thinking about verses I have memorized over the years. Texts like "There is therefore now no condemnation for those who are in Christ*

Jesus" (Romans 8:1). I guess that no matter what I have done or what we have done, there is forgiveness. When Jane gets better and she returns, I think we will have to talk about our relationship - and perhaps make some decisions.'

S: *'Would you like me to offer a prayer for Jane to recover quickly and for guidance for you both when you discuss your relationship?'*

M: *'Yes, I would like that very much.'*

This style of counselling gave Michael the space to explore the issues that led to his distress. A more directive approach would have responded to the possible questions raised. For example, after Michael said 'I feel so helpless', Sarah could have reassured him and possibly given a mini sermon on the value of intercessory prayer. She might not have listened to why he was blaming himself, or after his admission of immorality she could have demanded that he repent. All this might be justified from Scripture, but such interventions tend to block and close off the flow of the conversation. Usually the individual simply goes quiet. He may cooperate in a prayer but will not share the real cause of concern. Nor will he come to an adult resolution of what is the best course of action.

An incarnational approach

If we are to ask: In what way was God most present in human history? The answer would be to affirm that God was in Christ. This is affirmed in the theological truth of the incarnation. St Paul quoted what appear to be verses from an early Christian hymn to encourage the Philippians to have the same attitude as Christ:

> *Who, though he was in the form of God,*
> *did not regard equality with God*
> *as something to be exploited,*
> *but emptied himself,*

> *taking the form of a slave,*
> *being born in human likeness,*
> *And being found in human form,*
> *he humbled himself*
> *and became obedient to the point of death –*
> *even death on a cross.*
> *Therefore God also highly exalted him*
> *and gave him the name*
> *that is above every name (Philippians 2:6-9).*

If this is the way God was present, and we are to imitate his example, then this incarnational way of being can become a paradigm for the presence of the Christian counsellor in the counselling process.

Certain principles would follow. I would suggest that the above example of Sarah's counselling illustrates some important incarnational principles:

- that God's way is disclosed through human weakness
- counselling is a journey that acknowledges pain and suffering
- the counsellor limited her 'power' by not intervening at the first opportunity
- there was an aspect of modelling healthy attitudes and Christian maturity
- and a dependence upon the Holy Spirit as the way God works to bring about change.

Charles Gerkin has observed that the empathy of the counsellor is a kind of incarnation, 'to enter another's world requires getting inside the other's language world, with all the particularity and nuance that entails.'[17] This involves considerable knowledge of ourselves, especially our ingrained attitudes and past experiences that would lead us to be 'other' to the individual who is coming for help. Gerkin conceptualized Christian counselling as an encounter between two people within a 'horizon of understanding'.

We have an awareness of an 'ineffable mystery of a horizon that is both ultimate (beyond our knowing) and awesomely present (incarnate) in and through all events and processes in which we and our counsellees participate.'[18]

I have touched lightly on some important themes in the Christian tradition. At every point in the counselling process our perspective informs and limits what we see. As Christians we are part of a heritage which I have found to be enriching in the work of counselling. How I do counselling within this 'horizon' will differ from other Christian counsellors - but this diversity invites further creativity and I welcome it.

Exercise

Write an autobiography of your development as a Christian counsellor. What has shaped your understanding of the way God works? J. Robert Clinton suggests developmental stages in *The Making of a Leader*, Navpress, Colorado Springs, Colorado, 1988.

To read further:

Charles V. Gerkin, *The Living Human Document: Re-visioning Pastoral Counselling in a Hermeneutical Mode*, Abingdon Press, Nashville, 1984. This book is an excellent example of thinking theologically about what is distinctive about Christian counselling.

ESSENTIAL SKILLS

There are basic skills that are essential for every counsellor. The Christian may bring a distinctive view to the counselling process, but the essence of helping is surprisingly similar across theoretical perspectives.

These skills may look quite natural, but most experienced counsellors have had to learn them – sometimes with patience and surprising labour. It is like learning to ride a bicycle. At first the rider finds it all difficult and is very self-conscious with wobbly and uncertain progress. After a few spills the skill is gradually learned and soon becomes second nature.

I usually tell classes how difficult it was for me in the early years of my ministry. It must have been a case of a 'low counsellor IQ'. At parties or other inter-personal situations I would have to rely on my wife Jennie to fill me in on what was really happening. Gradually clinical training showed that I had an aptitude and helped me to develop the skills described in this chapter.

It is generally necessary to learn counselling skills through a training group or by working closely with a supervisor. I cannot place too much emphasis on this: there must be some feedback or the counsellor-in-training will tend to become inaccurate in practice. The skills can be described but reading about them is not enough. It is necessary to practise the more fundamental skills individually and then build on them to master gradually the advanced techniques described in the next chapter. This slow process involves feedback and correction. In most countries there are many volunteer programmes such as Lifeline, Red Cross, Parent Effectiveness Training, adult education classes and basic counsellor training programmes which can offer such help.

A good counselling relationship is like going on a journey with another person. At the end of counselling I sometimes say that it has been a privilege to share that part of the journey. It is an apt metaphor since we need to travel 'alongside', not 'ahead' or 'behind' or 'above'. We should share an experience of togetherness with mutual understanding and a realistic approach to working on the issues. Rather than focus on the right words or even an accurate response, it is more important to form an open and trusting relationship.[1]

The skills approach has been emphasized by many authors.[2] Gerard Egan's *The Skilled Helper: A Model for Systematic Helping and Interpersonal Relating* has been a textbook for training programmes for many years.[3] It was used in my own training in pastoral care skills in Clinical Pastoral Education. The basic skills include:

Attending

There is an intensity when a counsellor is fully present with another person in his emotional distress. Partly this may be thought of as attending to what is being said. The converse is a common complaint that someone, usually a family member, is not making the effort to listen. This may be obvious because he is reading a book, has one eye on the TV or appears eager to be somewhere else. The skill of attending includes showing in concrete behavioural ways that what is being said is being listened to. Rather than being passive, attending is an active process of communicating non-verbally the concentration of the listener. Egan listed some physical characteristics of attending:

1 *Facing the other person squarely.* This posture communicates involvement, 'I am with you.'

2 *Maintaining good eye contact.* When two people are deeply

involved in a conversation there is usually a lot of eye contact. This should be appropriate to the intensity of the interaction, but a high degree of eye contact invites the speaker to continue.

3 *Having an open posture.* An open posture is relatively relaxed. This helps to communicate, 'I am at ease with you and I can accept what you are saying.' This is the opposite of a defensive posture with crossed arms and legs.

4 *Leaning towards the other person.* It is a good idea to lean forward at times to emphasize the importance of what is being said.

The skill of attending encourages the person in counselling to open up and to share. The counsellor engages the other in a dynamic process of communication. There is an interpersonal tension in this depth of involvement. In effect, the body says what the counsellor is trying to put into words. There is a congruence of word and nonverbal messages.

'Listening' to nonverbal behaviour can also be considered to be part of attending. Nonverbal messages are ever present. Even when two people are sitting silently together the air is filled with messages. This form of communication is not always received consciously, but it is to some extent 'heard' and 'interpreted'. There has been research about the extent to which such messages are believed to be the real ones. It has been found that when the facial expression gives a different message to the spoken words, the nonverbal is more, credible. For example, a young woman has clenched teeth, tight and defensive posture and her foot is tapping restlessly. She says, 'I'm not angry!' What would you believe?

Nonverbal behaviour is important in communication, but it has some drawbacks. It is often ambiguous and can be easily misunderstood. The woman just described might have been very impatient. It is important for the counsellor to understand the context since this may give clues to the meaning.

Such messages can deny or confirm what is being said. They can also emphasize and add emotional colour. Such inflections punctuate the spoken message in the same way that full stops, question marks and exclamation marks punctuate the written language.[4] Non-verbal cues are important: facial expressions, bodily movements, voice quality and posture should be noted.

Another way to communicate attending is through minimal responses. These responses include nonverbal behaviour such as nodding the head. Verbal expressions such as 'A-ha', 'Uh-hm', 'Yes', 'OK', and 'Right' can also be considered minimal responses. These are a natural part of normal conversation. The person in counselling may be speaking continuously, but it is still important to reaffirm that the counsellor is listening. Such facilitators are ideal for this since there is an obvious attending with a minimum of interruption. There is, however, a risk of giving such responses so frequently that they can become distracting and somewhat intrusive. Once I had a student who said 'Yes' so often that it disrupted the normal flow of the conversation. But if the responses are too infrequent, the speaker may feel that the counsellor is not paying attention. It is a matter of balance and even pacing with the speed of speech.

Sometimes it is adequate to highlight a few of the words, e.g. 'So Mark crashed the car'. Some general comments function in a similar way: this includes 'I am hearing what you say,' and 'I understand how you feel.' Such reassurances add little of substance but can be encouraging. The most natural responses are usually the most effective.

Accurate empathy

There is nothing more fundamental to the counselling process than listening. True listening is described by Tolstoy:

Natasha, leaning on her elbow, the expression on her face continually changing with the story, watched Pierre, never taking her eyes off him, and seemed to be experiencing with him all that he described. Not only her look but her exclamations and the brief questions that she put showed Pierre that she understood just what he wanted to convey. It was clear that she understood not only what he said but also what he would have liked to say, but could not express in words. [5]

Listening is an active 'being with' or empathy rather than a passive stance. Listening without any verbal comments would be somewhat ambiguous. Thus the skill of listening includes the reply that shows the speaker that his concerns have been heard. This is the skill of accurate empathy. It can be broken up into different parts. The complete response includes both content and feelings:

1 *The reflection of content.* This involves indicating verbally that what has been said has been heard exactly. The skill is to capture the essence of what has been communicated in a brief and clear way. An example: *A thirty-year-old man: 'I had some difficulty finding a parking spot on the way here. And the smog is terrible today! (coughs) I have a cough that I can't seem to get rid of, it is all I can do to concentrate on being here.' Counsellor: 'There has been so much hassle just to get here that you find that it is distracting.'* This should be distinguished from parroting, which is nothing more than repeating the same words. Paraphrasing selects what is important. To some extent the selection is always a little arbitrary. There was, for example, no mention of the cough in the response. But nothing should be added to the content since that addition could become a distraction.

2 *The reflection of feelings.* Thoughts stay in the head, whereas emotions are in the guts. Geldard noted that feelings can be expressed in a single word, for example angry, sad, frustrated, miserable, relaxed, tense, happy or frantic. Thoughts can only be expressed with a string of words. [6] One of the most common goals of counselling is to help an individual to be more aware of and to own his feelings. Unfortunately, the most common response from friends and family seems to be: 'Don't worry, everything will be all right.' A quick reassurance tends to close off the emotions which seek to be expressed. There may be social taboos. For example, men may be discouraged from crying. Women are often inhibited from showing anger. However, the release of emotions, sometimes called catharsis, can be very helpful. The counsellor can give permission

for feelings, e.g. 'I notice that you have tears in your eyes.' (I usually have a box of tissues within easy reach.)

Responding to feelings: Teenage girl: 'I can't stand my boss, he keeps making sexual innuendoes.' Response: 'You are disgusted?' (Perhaps also angry). Although this response is short, and even selective, a brief response is less distracting and would allow the young girl to continue. However, it is important to do full justice to the feelings being expressed. I remember putting my daughter Kym to bed when she was four years old. She looked miserable and said, 'I have had a sad day.' I responded, 'I am sorry that you are feeling a bit sad.' With a tear in her eye, she said, 'Not a *bit* sad, *all* sad.' With her correction I saw that my 'a bit sad' had been shown to be inadequate empathy.

It is not so vital that every response should be absolutely accurate. Every experienced counsellor makes mistakes. Such mistakes are so frequent that misses in empathy can almost be counted in the average session. Sometimes I find myself making an inane comment. A few days ago I was about to lead a person into my office and I said without thinking, 'It has been a beautiful day.' The young man replied, 'Yes, in terms of the weather.' I recognized that my comment had missed. As counsellors we are human and make mistakes, but it is more important that we make the effort to understand. This will communicate an attitude of caring.

What is said can be very complex with content, emotions and behaviour. The response may need to be equally complex to reflect the various dimensions.[7] For example, 'I had a miserable day yesterday. My supervisor said my research was wrong and the experimental results proved nothing (an experience). I got angry (an emotion) and slammed his door (a behaviour) as I stormed out!' The counsellor might respond, 'It must have been upsetting to have your work so bluntly criticized. No wonder you exploded with rage.' Simply reflecting the feelings might add too much intensity to the emotional side of the interaction. A balance of both content and feeling responses is helpful – and these can be spaced out by minimal responses.

The skill of accurate empathy can be practised. Try writing out responses to the following remarks:

'When he gets clumsy, usually after having too many drinks, I get so embarrassed that I want to hide.' (shame)

'I was so mad when she left me that I wanted to break every plate in my flat. I just kept thinking about her and that guy . . . I thought about killing them both.' (intense anger, perhaps rage and the fantasy of homicide)

'Sexual fantasies keep coming into my mind. I try to fight them but nothing seems to work.' (frustration, perhaps guilt)

It may be that a number of different emotions are expressed.

'I know it is strange, but I keep thinking that people are following me and watching my house. I am beginning to doubt whether I am sane. I often cry at night because I think I can't cope.' (fear and suspicion, sadness, anxiety)

'I went to my daughter's graduation last week. She was one of the honours students. I could hardly believe she was my daughter, and I also got to thinking how often I had let her down in the last few years.' (pride and guilt)

This makes the task of accurate empathy more difficult because it will involve responding to a range of emotions.

The skill of listening is not too difficult. It is like watching a stream with debris floating past. The facts are the debris and the emotions are the water. It takes a little practice to be able to communicate that both have been 'noticed'.

In most cases the blockages to accurate empathy are in the counsellor. When there is growth in self-understanding, usually through peer interaction or supervision, we become more aware of our own difficulties. We can be:

- biased in how we listen. For example, we may find it hard to hear anger or sadness.

- have cultural filters. For example, about race or gender.

- have rigid models of how people should function, sometimes reflecting our understanding of biblical orthodoxy.

- have self-preoccupations which might be quite distracting.

Sometimes such a simple thing as curiosity will lead to a 'tug-of-war' for the agenda of the session.

A common counsellor anxiety or blockage relates to how to handle silence in a session. It can be uncomfortable and the counsellor may be tempted to fill the gaps with questions or comments that he or she wants to make. However, silence is an important aspect of the time together. For one thing it may help the person to formulate what is about to be put into words.[8] It may take a few moments to become aware of a feeling or an image that might have been repressed. In the last few months there have been a few sessions with my longer-term clients in which a period of silence has extended for five or more minutes. It was important later to explore together the meaning of the silence.

Listening can be an act of courage. The story is told of a mother whose seven-year-old daughter had an inoperable brain tumour. Both were in the kitchen preparing the vegetables for dinner. The daughter asked, 'Mum, will you and Daddy come to visit me when I am in the grave?' Her mother was flustered, and it would have been a natural response for many parents to change the topic, but she asked, 'What would you want us to do?' 'I think it would be a good idea . . . How soon will I die?' The mother replied that it was a hard question, one which even the doctors couldn't answer for sure. The young girl continued, 'When I get to heaven, I have a favour to ask of God.' 'What is that?' I want to ask him to make me into a boy.' The mother then asked, 'But how will I know you?' 'Just ask for Tim,' was the reply.

I have found that it takes courage to listen when being told about violence in a marriage, the shame and frequent disappointments of the child of an alcoholic parent, memories of sexual abuse, the struggle of a handicapped person, the horror of the rape of a teenager and the repeated rejection of gay men and women in our society.

Painful experiences can accumulate and the emotional load can become very uncomfortable. The repression of painful emotions such as sadness or anger can lead to clinical conditions such as depression. Once the pain is faced and the negative emotions begin to be expressed, I find that the person seeking help can begin to think more clearly and make rational decisions.

There is no more important skill than empathic listening. It is absolutely central to the counselling relationship. I have said to clergy in post-ordination training sessions that if they can just master the skill of accurate empathy, there will always be a line of church members wanting help outside their study door! There is such a scarcity of good listeners in our society that even a little empathy can mean a great deal.

Genuineness

Genuineness is something that can be observed. It is not so much a moral quality, though that is obviously important. Instead it is understood in a skills approach to counselling as part of the communication process. Another word for this is 'congruence'. To be congruent, counsellors must be themselves. As much as possible they should be integrated and non-defensive. In the words of Geldard, 'Everything must ring true.' Genuineness can be understood in this way:

1 The genuine counsellor does not take refuge in roles such as being a pastor. Academic degrees or membership in various professional associations may be important for credibility, but to hide behind a role is distancing and makes the counsellor less emotionally available.

2 Spontaneity is part of the interaction. The counsellor who is natural does not weigh every word but is free to engage in the helping relationship. This is not permission for being impulsive because professional counselling is a very disciplined activity, but it can still be natural.

3 The genuine counsellor is non-defensive. Whenever criticism of the counsellor is expressed, it is a test of this quality. For example, if a middle-aged businessman said, 'I seem to be getting nowhere in the counselling sessions. I think they are a complete waste of time and I don't think you are doing much for me.' A response like:

'You are the one wasting time' would be clearly defensive. But a response like: 'There has been very little of value here in these sessions, and you are concluding that it is not worth the effort. You are also thinking that I haven't fulfilled your expectations,' is empathic and manages to be non-defensive. It is also open to feedback. It helps if the counsellor has a robust sense of self-esteem and a clear understanding of his or her strengths and weaknesses.

4 Consistency is also an important quality. The genuine counsellor shows few inconsistencies. Egan explained, 'He does not have one set of 'notional' values (such as justice, love, peace) different from his 'real' values (influence, money, comfort). He does not think or feel one thing but say another.'[10] The counsellor would be naive to think he or she has no values that might intrude on the counselling work. It is best to acknowledge such values when asked but never to pressurize an individual in counselling to conform to an arbitrary standard. This would be an abuse of power and has serious ethical implications. Nor would the consistent counsellor dump negative feelings into the counselling relationship. Discipline involves an element of self-control and this provides 'safety' in the sessions. The phoney counsellor is betrayed through inconsistency.

5 The genuine counsellor is free and spontaneous enough to share of himself or herself. This should not be a form of self-indulgence; or even worse, a complete 'role reversal'. However, in an appropriate way, self-disclosure helps to build trust and mutuality.

Respect

Respect can also be considered a moral quality. But in a skills approach to counselling it is conceived in terms of counsellor behaviour. Egan listed the following qualities as indicating respect:

1 Being for the person. This is not a sentimental or saccharine quality. It includes the belief that an individual has potential and can attain realistic goals. Respect 'is both gracious and tough-minded.'[11]

2 The willingness to work with the person. This is a matter of commitment and can be seen in reasonable availability for appointments, flexibility over times, interest in the outcome, and follow-up.

3 Regard for each person as unique. Not only is this an important value but ultimately has a theological point, that each individual has value in reflecting God's creation. In the counselling situation the counsellor has no permission to make clones of himself or herself. I find it important to work towards the goals set by the individual and to support his uniqueness.

4 Respect for self-determination. This includes the assumption that the person in counselling has the resources to live more effectively and can make decisions about a worthwhile direction in life. Perhaps this reflects an element of 'free will' that I believe God allows us all.

5 Assuming an individual's good will. It is best to give the benefit of the doubt, a suspicious or cynical attitude destroys trust in the counselling relationship. I would have to be convinced beyond a shadow of doubt that a person is pretending in counselling, or not committed to change, or is only complying with the process because of family pressure. Even in such cases the counsellor does not blame or give up easily, but tries to understand such a reluctance from the other's perspective. Such reservations might be caused by repeated let-downs in childhood and later relationships. This does not invalidate the work of counselling; it sets the agenda.

6 Suspending critical judgment. Carl Rogers popularized the concept of unconditional positive regard. This does not mean that the counsellor has no values or agrees with everything an individual might do. But take the attitude that 'I accept the client as he is now, I value him as a person, I am nonjudgmental of his behaviour, and I do not impose my values.'[12] Over the years I have worked with a number of people whose sexual preferences are judged by society to be unusual. It was a challenge, for example, to begin to understand the hidden social life of the transvestite. Every counsellor has reluctance to work with some kinds of people,

whether it is the active homosexual, a violent spouse or a child molester. Perhaps we can learn to respect and grow in the ability to relate to a wider group of people.

An example of respect and acceptance is the teenager who came to see me because of pressure from her parents. Both were conservative Christians and sophisticated academics. They were very distressed when their daughter announced that she was gay in her sexual orientation. When I saw her she was concerned about her parents, but wanted to continue with her lover. Although I thought that she was not willing to face the full implications of that choice, I did not see any warrant for change at that time. She had every right to make adult choices in her life. I concluded, 'If you are satisfied with your choice, then it is your parents who have a problem. I will offer to see them.'

Concreteness

Vagueness is a hindrance to the counselling process. When a person in distress rambles or uses generalizations, it may be hard to understand what is being said. Compare: 'Sometimes I feel a bit tense,' with 'I am stressed at work. Just too many demands are placed on me by the new supervisor. I get tight in my stomach at the thought of going to work and by Thursday or Friday, I have pins and needles of anxiety most of the time.' This is more specific in details and more concrete. Such concreteness also helps self-insight.

Another concrete statement is: 'I broke up with Ann last week. I didn't think that she meant so much to me. I haven't been able to sleep. I feel so sad that I find myself fighting back the tears and I get morbid thoughts. I go to the pub most nights and I suspect that I am drinking too much.' This is specific in feelings (sad, to some extent worried), explains the situation (break-up with Ann) and describes behavioural reactions (tears, sleep disturbance, going to the pub and drinking more than usual). Although 'morbid thoughts' is not particularly concrete, the overall communication is very specific. In contrast, vague descriptions like 'I think that I have more relationship difficulties than most people' lead nowhere. It is hard to solve presenting problems in a verbal fog and almost impossible to find a path to effective action.

Concreteness can be encouraged by the way the counsellor responds to vague statements. The person says: 'Nothing seems quite right at the moment. I feel kind of lousy. You know you can never tell how others will react to you?' This is vague in that emotions are only hinted at, the 'you' of the reaction is not owned, and there is no indication what is the cause of the distress. If the counsellor responds with a minimal facilitator such as 'yes', the vague talk will probably continue and the counsellor will soon be 'half asleep'. If the counsellor reflects feelings in a more concrete way, 'You are feeling discouraged and perhaps a little depressed,' it may be more helpful. In this case the counsellor would have to know the feelings from other parts of the conversation. It is better to ask directly for more information, 'I do not follow you. What is worrying you about how people have been reacting to you?' But even this gentle confrontation assumes that there have already been a few empathic responses and that a measure of rapport has built up.

The best way to gain more concrete responses is through 'what', 'how' and 'with what feeling' rather than 'why' questions. 'Why' leads to endless speculation. Sometimes psychologizing leads to a form of pseudo-communication, while genuine insight is very different. Note the difference between, 'I think I have difficulty with men because of my oedipal complex,' and 'When Harry seems distant, I find myself reacting with rage because of my feeling of being abandoned. It is like when I used to try to get my father's attention when I was a child.' The difference is between the abstract nature of psychological jargon, which is not concrete, and the communication of personal feelings.

Without concreteness counselling loses intensity. Sometimes I find myself getting bored and have difficulty concentrating in a session. This is a good indicator that something is wrong and that more activity is needed in encouraging concreteness. The thread of what is important in the session may have been lost. It is not easy to find the right balance between allowing an individual to follow his own way and keeping on a path leading to growth.

The use of questions

There is a skill in asking helpful questions. Too often questions reveal only what the counsellor thinks is important. As Weinberg observed, 'An inappropriate question may betray some bias or preoccupation of ours, or indifference or stupidity. Such a question can sidetrack.'[13] It is not easy to frame questions that are helpful to the counselling process. It is wise for beginning counsellors to refrain from asking questions and concentrate on reflective listening. It is too easy to push the conversation along with questions. This leads to the counsellor becoming an interrogator. It can be intrusive and very controlling. This kind of pressure imposes the counsellor's agenda and easily misses what is most important. An individual will often skirt round the general area before coming to that which is of greatest concern. This can be a way of testing the counsellor's sensitivity. Too much pressure can cause the person in counselling to withdraw emotionally and never reveal the reason for seeking help.

It is important to understand the difference between a closed and open question. A closed question leads to either 'Yes' or 'No', whereas an open question encourages further exploration. There is a difference between the closed, 'Did you feel frightened?' and the open question, 'When your husband comes home drunk, how do you feel?' The best questions are open-ended. They are an invitation to explore further, 'Would you like to tell me more about that?' or 'How would you like to change?'

Sometimes a question can be used to slow the pace down: 'You just skipped over something that may be important. Could you tell me how you felt when your husband criticized your cooking in front of your best friend?' Questions are important in making an assessment. If, for example, the counsellor is hearing about anxious reactions, it might be an idea to ask whether the person has had panic attacks.

At a recent workshop for working with psychotic patients, we were encouraged to learn the skill of interviewing in a specific way to discover the pattern of breakdown which led to a psychotic episode. As part of the exercise we had to imagine our own story of such a breakdown and what had led to the hospitalization. I was asked to play the role of such a patient while my partner, a very experienced clinical psychologist, interviewed me. He asked me questions about the immediate events before the 'hospitalization' but in fact totally missed events which happened months before which I considered far more relevant. I experienced the frustration of trying to answer questions which were on the wrong track. It was a lesson for both of us about the danger of asking questions – even when we were both very experienced. Most of the information that is needed will tend to emerge naturally in the course of a session.

Summarizing

Sometimes it is important to gather up what has been said, to collect the main points and to give a summary. It is like paraphrasing but more succinct. The central themes which may include both facts and feelings are drawn together and reflected back to the person. It helps to get an overview of the ground covered. This can help the session to move along in a productive way. The individual can more easily absorb what has been said, both by himself and by the counsellor. To use Geldard's metaphor, the person in a dense forest sees nothing clearly. By summarizing, the counsellor helps him to see the trees and to find the path between them.[14]

This skill will be illustrated later. But it is enough to say something like: 'You seem to have been struggling in quite a few areas this week. The meeting was particularly stressful because you worried about your stammer. Your boss was harsh in the comment about the report that was a day late. It was so bad that you considered taking stress leave.' This kind of summarizing is an extension of accurate empathy.

Periodically a brief summary in a session can help the person gain direction and become more focused. I find that it is a good practice to give a more complete summary at the close of a session. This helps the person in counselling to get a grasp of what was covered and to consolidate any gains.

The basic skills of counselling can be learnt. But since they are skills it is important to practise them and gradually they will become more natural. It is exciting to hear students come back to a class and report on experiences using accurate empathy. Just a few days ago one of my students said, 'I tried just to reflect with a man I thought I knew quite well. I had thought that he was somewhat shallow, a very 'black and white' sort of person but I discovered a depth I hardly suspected. He spoke with great insight and I was fascinated to hear what he had to say.'

It is a common experience to find that with empathy the conversation becomes suddenly 'more real'. I would say that the skill of accurate empathy is not really mastered until such experiences become commonplace.

Exercises
If you are not currently in a training group it is possible to form an informal group to practise these skills. Join with at least two other people and practise the skill of empathic listening, sharing on the following topics:

- A close call when I was in a car.

- My proudest moment.

- An incident of intense frustration in the workplace.

- What I felt when my dog died.

The roles in the triad include the speaker, listener and

observer. At the end of say five minutes each person gives feedback and then roles change. It is best if an experienced counsellor can be present and act as a supervisor to this process.

As a theological reflection read through Jesus's encounter with the Samaritan woman at the well in John 4. Can you identify any of the skills outlined in this chapter? In what ways did Jesus go beyond the 'basics'?

To read further
David Geldard, *Basic Personal Counselling,* Prentice Hall, New York, 1989. This is an excellent introduction to the skills of counselling. There is a very practical emphasis which I found most helpful in thinking about what I do in counselling. Geldard is an Australian author.

Gerard Egan, *The Skilled Helper,* Brooks/Cole Publishing Company, Monterey, California, 1975. Egan was one of the pioneers in the skills approach to counselling. He was very clear in this first edition which I find better than the later editions. He has written many books which are worth reading.

ADVANCED COUNSELLING SKILLS

The skills that are explained in this chapter can help to deepen the counselling relationship and enable greater effectiveness. But it is absolutely necessary to have first mastered the basic skills. In particular, empathic listening will need to be accurate. It is important to practise the basic skills with other trainees, preferably under the guidance of a supervisor. Once proficiency is achieved, then a supervisor's guidance is usually necessary to learn the advanced techniques. Such skills are like a sharp scalpel, they can be used with surgical effect - either to wound or to heal.

Advanced accurate empathy

This style of listening 'hears' more deeply than what is directly expressed by the person. The counsellor response indicates not only the content and feelings as in accurate empathy, but suggests what might be implied from what has been said. This often makes it possible to explore new territory. For example:

> Female university student: 'I am confused (pause). I have enrolled in the honours philosophy course and it is very competitive. I have had some good grades but also some average results. I have tried hard in all that I have done but the logic course is a nightmare, and I hear from the other

students that the courses get even more difficult next year. It is all too much for me at the moment!'

Empathy: 'It is discouraging to put in such effort for mixed results.'

Advanced accurate empathy: 'It is discouraging to put in such effort for mixed results. Maybe it makes you wonder whether you have the ability to make it in the honours course?'

Here the counsellor probes deeper by taking into consideration the context, themes from previous sessions, and non-verbal cues. If the intervention is accurate and the timing is appropriate, the student might be able to move to deeper self-understanding.[1] In this case she can begin to address her own self-doubts and consider whether such reservations are realistic. This can also take place when unpleasant emotions are highlighted. This may include repressed anger, envy, resentment, bitterness, malice and self-pity. There may be only a minimal awareness of a deeper emotional turmoil. On whatever level the person in counselling is prepared to work, this skill of advanced accurate empathy helps her to begin to piece together the bigger picture.

This is a deeper form of empathy because the counsellor appreciates not only the present concerns, but 'reads between the lines'. Because it is such a powerful technique with the potential for deep insight, it should be used cautiously and tentatively.

Egan listed some of the ways advanced accurate empathy can be achieved:

- Expressing what is only implied.
- Summarizing concerns and pointing to where it might lead.
- Identifying themes such as dependency, poor self-esteem, self-depreciation, negative thinking, hostile interactions, etc.
- Connecting 'islands' of thoughts, feelings and behaviour. For example, the counsellor might see an association between tiredness and feeling depressed with a need always to perform better than other work colleagues.

- Moving from less to more. When a person touches lightly on a theme that might be of importance the counsellor can respond, 'You only mentioned in passing how you felt about your father's intrusiveness . . .'

Such a skill should not be used too frequently in a session. The advanced skills will place demands on the person in counselling and such interventions can increase the intensity to an uncomfortable level. A tentative person might flee from counselling. The proof of whether an intervention was appropriate is usually found in the response. If it was accurate and timely the response might be something like 'Yes, that's right!' and then further exploration of the path indicated by the counsellor. If it missed, then the momentum might be lost and emotion withdrawn. This is sometimes a subtle, but important, indicator of the interaction.

Counsellor self-disclosure

Sometimes it is helpful for the counsellor to share some personal experience. It is a skill in that the right balance needs to be achieved. On one hand the counsellor may share painful life experiences which can lead to a role reversal in which the 'client' cares for the 'counsellor'. In my view this is a breach of professional boundaries, and it is potentially damaging when the counsellor's needs take priority on the agenda. On the other hand, a counsellor may be so remote as to seem less than human. It may be hard for the client to imagine that the counsellor ever had to struggle with the common difficulties of life. Analysts in traditional psychoanalysis tried to eliminate any personalizing of the interaction and tended to prohibit such courtesies as a handshake. But today in most cases it is a mistake to be too austere.

Some therapists have argued for extensive self-disclosure as a means of modelling on the grounds that such a dynamic might help to develop trust. However, an overemphasis on any technique tends to have negative consequences. Counsellor self-disclosure about personal weaknesses may frighten the person in counselling if it is considered that the counsellor then seems less effective or able to help. There is also the possibility of diminishing gains with the overuse of any technique.

I have no doubt that some self-disclosure can assist the counselling process, but it must be used sparingly – perhaps rarely. It is always a therapeutic judgment as to when a counselling goal might be facilitated by self-disclosure. It is inappropriate if it is distracting from the topic of immediate concern in the session. It never must be an end in itself. Nor should it ever be a burden to the person seeking assistance. Compare the following.

> Young man: 'It is difficult for me just to get up. I find that it is all too much for me. I want to hide beneath the covers.'
> Counsellor: 'Yes, I know how you feel. When I was a student in my second year I wasn't sure I was going to make it and I was depressed for months at a time. But it all passed away.'
> Young man: 'Did you ever think of suicide?'

The shift of attention here should alert the counsellor that something has gone astray. The intervention has changed the agenda away from the original problem. There was too much disclosure and it turned out to be a distraction. A better response might be:

> Counsellor: 'I think that I know something of how you feel. I went through a period in university when it was hard to face the day. It makes things seem very grim.'
> Young man: 'Yes, it is an 'uphill battle', but things would be worse if I just gave up.'

This was more facilitating and the young man continued in the same vein. Here it was enough to be supportive with the message: 'I know how it feels and I am with you.' I tend to be sparing in my use of self-disclosure and minimal in the actual content. Individuals in counselling almost never ask for more about the matter disclosed. It is enough for me to walk alongside.

I remember one instance while training as a counsellor that my therapist used self-disclosure. I had told her about a painfully embarrassing incident in which I had made a mistake speaking in public. She shared with me briefly a similar experience when she had been flustered before an important university audience. I felt that she understood my experience and there was less shame in recalling my own failure.

Self-disclosure is a valid technique in counselling. As such it is potentially very helpful, but it is a delicate skill which requires both good timing and a sense of balance. The trainee counsellor should be very cautious with this intervention and carefully monitor the reaction of the person in the session.

Confrontation

Confrontation can be easily misused. Some aggressive individuals will use it as a vicious attack on the other person and then justify this action as being 'for their own good'. Even a counsellor can make the mistake of using confrontation in a way that is aggressive, punitive, or self-satisfying. When there is a dumping of personal feelings the result is usually destructive regardless of supposed good intentions. Encounter groups suffered a loss of reputation in the 1960s because of this kind of interaction – and they left a legacy of wounded people. Some Christian counsellors have equated confrontation with God's will. How could the counsellor go wrong quoting a Bible verse and demanding repentance? I believe that this raises many questions – not least of which is the possible contrast of roles of wise counsellor and prophet in the Old Testament.

The appropriate use of confrontation in counselling is a definite skill. It involves giving feedback about something the person is not seeing or fails to acknowledge. If such a task is not done with great sensitivity, it will be resented and the relationship will suffer. The following are aspects of an individual's behaviour that invite some challenge:

1 *Discrepancies.* The way I see myself may be very different from how others see me. *A quite attractive young woman saw herself as ugly. She found it inconceivable that anyone might have any sexual interest in her. The men in a therapy group gave her comments that confronted her self-image.*

It is common enough that nonverbal behaviour will not be congruent with what has been said, e.g. 'John, I know that you say you aren't angry, but you clench your teeth and you seem to tighten up like a spring.'

Sometimes the story seems inconsistent. *A counsellor saw a young couple for marriage difficulties. The husband assured the counsellor that he was no longer meeting the woman with whom he had had an affair, but he showed no grief in 'breaking up' and appeared to have little motivation to face the pain in the relationship with his wife.* This would be a very difficult confrontation and tact would be needed. And yet to ignore the evidence would stall any possible progress in dealing with the problems in the relationship.

2 *Distortions.* This may include self-defeating views of the self. *A middle-aged businessman said, 'I am hopeless, a failure, always weak and avoiding.'* Sometimes an individual will be in an emotional prison with 'should', 'ought' and 'must' beliefs. Behind such beliefs, which can masquerade as values, are inherited messages. These can come from parents but are not evaluated for current relevance. *A young man is a house husband. He cares for two toddlers who continually mess up the small living area of his apartment. This is intensely frustrating because he is convinced that the living room must always be perfect to receive potential visitors.*

3 *Games, tricks and smoke screens.* The ability to pick such manoeuvres comes with experience. An example is the 'Yes, but' game which an individual can use to defeat any attempt of others to help. Sometimes a person uses destructive ways to get desired results. *One example of this is a young woman who became engaged but tended to relate to authority figures in a seductive way. This led to problems of jealousy with her fiancé.*

I rarely come across such games in counselling sessions. This might be because of my emphasis on the client exploring his or her own situation as honestly as possible. When you never give advice it also avoids the 'Yes, but' game.

4 *Evasions.* It is natural to try to avoid painful truths. One way to attempt this is to blame others for whatever goes wrong. This includes the projection of 'It's all your fault!' (a common litany of couples in marital distress). Another evasion is endlessly repeating the same story with little insight or desire for change. This might lead to a confrontation that helps the person to be more concrete in what is shared in the session.

5 *Behaviour versus values.* There may be a conflict of values and action. *A deacon in a local Baptist church has fallen in love with a member of the choir. He says that he believes in the commitment of marriage, but wants to leave his wife without any attempt to solve their difficulties.*

Behaviour may be impulsive and self-destructive. For example, *a young homosexual male frequently gets drunk and engages in promiscuous sex regardless of the risk of AIDS.*

6 There may be issues that need to be addressed in the relationship with the counsellor. This might include conduct such as continually coming late to sessions or cancelling at the last minute. Some emotional themes will interfere with the progress of counselling; this includes dependency, passive-aggressive behaviour, disappointment, withdrawal and passivity.

It is essential that any confrontation be handled in a sensitive way. It is natural to be defensive if there is a threat to self-esteem and resulting feelings of shame. If an individual feels attacked it is inevitably counterproductive. There should be some protection in order for the person still to feel all right about herself or himself after the confrontation.

The skilled counsellor, after carefully assessing the motives for the confrontation, will proceed through carefully built-up accurate empathy. For example, 'John, you have struggled to cope with Annie's depression. Her unpredictable moods have been a source of frustration. This is especially testing since you want everything to be ordered in your home life. But I wonder whether your expectation that she "keep up her spirits" is realistic?'

It is also wise to make a confrontation in the most tentative way possible. As an example, 'Mary, you have gone more than the "second mile" in your relationship with Andrew. But as far as you have gone, it seems that you find it hard to forgive his affair with Sue last year. This is only my impression, but does it match what you feel?' This is highly qualified. Mary is free to deny that impression if it does not match her experience. Since the potential insight is offered so tentatively it is also easier for her to accept. Then she can go further in facing her reaction to the breach in the relationship with her husband. Compare this approach with the harsh, 'Mary, isn't it about time you put the affair behind you? Holding on to bitterness and resentment isn't helping you. After all, Andrew isn't perfect!' This is an aggressive comment with both blame and accusation.

I feel more confident in confronting individuals about potential strengths. This communicates 'I believe in you.' It can build up confidence rather than tear it down with 'frontal assaults'. The final criterion is whether she is now living more effectively. When a person is in distress she usually has a poor image of her strengths, and it is perhaps a safe bet that her resources could be more fully utilized. Although I have given a lot of attention to the role of confrontation, it is because it is so often misused, not because it has a large place in the helping process. If the other skills are done well, the entire helping process is challenging.[2] And the use of the other counselling skills is a far more natural process than the dubious tactic of trying to hurry things along by too much confrontation.

Immediacy

About twelve years ago in an open group in theological college a student was expressing considerable dissatisfaction with the establishment. The leader said to the student, 'When you spoke

I felt a blast of anger.' This was a very powerful intervention and the atmosphere of the group became tense. There was an element of confrontation, but it was more intense because the leader spoke from the impact he felt of the student's manner.

The skill of immediacy is similar. It is sometimes called 'You-Me' talk. This is illustrated by the following interaction in a therapy group:

> Female lawyer: 'Harry, I like the way you speak so clearly, but I don't hear you express much emotion. It seems so one-dimensional. I would like to get to know you better, but I find the lack of emotion is distancing.'
>
> Male computer programmer: 'Yes, Sandy, I think I know what you mean. Hold on . . . there, I did it again with 'think'. I want to be more in touch with my feelings. Like sadness when I consider how much I have missed in relationships. If you would help me I would like to do better in this group and perhaps also in my relationship with you.'

Recently a male client began to express frustration about not finding any satisfying relationships. He found that he had a need for intimacy which could only be met in counselling. He was hesitant in saying exactly how he felt, but with my support he said, 'It is almost like prostitution.' Now this might be somewhat threatening for the professional counsellor who may have some hesitation in receiving fees. I continued, 'You are acknowledging something that I have sometimes felt, like – am I a friend for hire? Although I think there are some differences, I would be interested in how you experience our relationship.' The encounter was quite liberating for the client (and for me!). The skill of immediacy can be used to deepen the counselling, especially when both the counsellor and the person in counselling skirt around the edges of 'taboo topics'. This collusion inhibits the interaction and the potential for growth.

This is a very delicate skill since it involves accurate empathy, self-disclosure and confrontation. It is helpful to 'clear the air' at times and it can facilitate growth in the counselling relationship. I sometimes find myself using this when confronted by a client for making a mistake in empathy. I might share some of the dynamics that led to my misunderstanding what was being said. It invites a mutual honesty and can be quite productive. There is a bonus in that it helps individuals to be more direct in their relationships outside the session. However, this kind of interaction is quite rare in everyday conversation.

Egan listed some occasions for the possible use of immediacy: different styles, trust issues, dependency, counter-dependency, directionless sessions, attraction (including sexual, but with extreme caution and only when it is raised by the person in counselling!)[3] I would imagine that an inexperienced pastor with aggressive tendencies might tend to overuse confrontation and avoid immediacy, since the latter puts too much of the self on the line. If there is to be a choice, immediacy should be preferred to confrontation. However, caution is the only sensible rule. It is a very delicate skill. Empathy, whether accurate or advanced, must be very accurate. The counsellor also needs to be confident and self-aware.

Jeffrey Kottler and Diane Blau have written a most helpful book about the common errors in counselling. It is called *The Imperfect Therapist* and they list the most common mistakes of the beginner as:

- Distracting mannerisms or facial expressions.

- Poor attending.

- Inability to follow and understand the comments of the person in counselling.

- The use of interrogation rather than open-ended questions.

- Frequent interruptions.

- Attending to the surface level of communication rather than deeper messages.

- Too much focus on the content of the session rather than the affect or process.

- Using excessive self-disclosure.
- Being too passive in style.
- Inability to tolerate silence.
- Appearing too friendly, seductive and informal.
- Making too aggressive confrontations.

However, it is reassuring to note that they conclude: 'If intimacy has been firmly established in the therapeutic relationship, if the client feels respected, accepted and valued, it is unlikely that any single mistake can unravel all the progress.'[4]

The advanced skills are very powerful techniques in counselling. The more basic skills should be thoroughly mastered in order for the advanced skills to be effective and not potentially damaging. I would recommend practising the skills under supervision with other counsellors in training. I found that being a participant in a therapy group was the best way to practise and learn the more demanding skills. It also helped me to address personal issues that would have contaminated my work as a counsellor.

Exercises

If you have formed a training group with a couple of other trainees, then you might try out the following topics:

(i) Advanced accurate empathy with 'When I feel most spiritually low,' and 'A conflict situation that I never seem to be able to resolve.'

(ii) Self-disclosure with 'My worst doubts.'

(iii) Confrontation with 'Personal strengths I never seem to use.'

(iv) Immediacy with 'What I have felt when I received feedback in this training triad.'

Remember to change roles every five minutes or so.

As a theological reflection read John 14:25-16:24. How does the Holy Spirit or 'Counsellor' (RSV) relate to the believer? How have you experienced God in your faith journey?

To read further

Gerard Egan, *The Skilled Helper,* Brooks/Cole Publishing Company, Monterey, California, 1975. This text explains the advanced skills of counselling. Highly recommended. I prefer this first edition of his popular book to the later revisions which became more complicated in terms of theory.

Jeffrey Kottler and Diane Blau, *The Imperfect Therapist,* Jossey-Bass, San Francisco, 1989. This helpful book encourages the counsellor to be more self-aware and open to learning from typical mistakes.

GRIEF

The skills of counselling are used to help people in situations of distress. The circumstances will vary, but there is usually some interaction between the capacity to be empathic and to have an overall theoretical context for dealing with presenting issues. This interplay of counselling skills and theory will be illustrated in the chapters that deal with case studies. In this chapter the focus will be on grief.

Loss can be seen as a part of daily experience. Ira Tanner made this point, 'Each day we grieve the loss of something, someone or some place important to us.'[1] There is an element of truth in this, since feelings of loss are so common, but in emphasizing this aspect there is the risk of trivializing more traumatic losses. Such losses that can overwhelm normal coping resources and can even put a 'pall' over the rest of a person's life. A more dramatic loss might include: the sudden death of a spouse at the age of thirty-five or an infant daughter through SIDS or a brother in an electrical accident. There are also losses that are not literal deaths but can be equally shattering: a messy divorce, a war veteran who lost his leg through amputation, an airline pilot forced to retire at fifty-five or an elderly woman struck by a bag snatcher in a local park.

Clergy have a natural entrance to situations of tragic loss. Often a pastor is asked to conduct a funeral and will be expected to help a family in the grief process. Even in our largely secularized society an individual confronting a major loss may want to explore existential questions about meaning, and it would seem that discussing such matters with a religious counsellor is well accepted. This has led to the specialization of many clergy in grief counselling – sometimes supported by the funeral directors.

The British psychiatrist John Bowlby researched the dynamics of attachment and loss.[2] He saw that emotional bonds are developed from infancy. Such ties usually relate to security needs: the nurture given by mother, protection from father, companionship from brothers and sisters. Intense bonds are usually formed with just a few close people, usually immediate family or relatives. The pain of grief is the result of breaking such bonds. It is like the strands of a rope that snap one by one. It is also common that an element of fear persists: a fear that related security and other needs might not be met in the future.

There have been many descriptions of the grief process. One of the first studies in the characteristics of grief focused on survivors of a tragic fire in Boston.[3] Elizabeth Kubler-Ross pioneered the stage approach to the grief process. Her five stages are well known: denial, anger, bargaining, depression and acceptance.[4] Unfortunately, stages or phases of grief imply a measure of passivity.[5] When I think of these models, I see the grieving person being washed down a stream on a raft, 'going with the flow' and so through the various stages.

J. William Worden has outlined a more active process in which the grieving person accomplishes four tasks: to accept the loss, to experience the emotions, to adjust to the new environment and reinvest in other relationships.

Task 1: To accept the reality of the loss

The first reaction to news of the loss is shock. A husband will say, 'It can't be true! Are you joking? My wife must be still alive.' Feelings of unreality are common. This may be so severe he experiences de-personalization when he feels like an observer looking at himself. The first task is to come to terms with the fact of loss: 'Mary is gone – dead – and will not return.'

The initial denial of death may range from a slight distortion to a developed delusion. *An example of the denial of death is the husband who kept his wife's body at home for three days before contacting anyone and asking for help.* A more common reaction is 'mummification' (Geoffrey Gorer). In this case the room and possessions of the deceased are kept ready for use when she 'returns'. *Queen Victoria, after the death of Prince Albert, told the servants to lay out his clothes and shaving equipment each day. She would talk to him as she moved about the palace.*

There is a normal resistance to dealing with the details that follow a death. There may be some reluctance to clear out wardrobes and send the clothes to a local charity. This may be something of a block if it persists for a number of years. Another form of mild denial is the minimizing of the value of the relationship, 'Harry and I really weren't that close.' I believe that spiritualism can be another form of the denial of death.

The absence of a body can make the acceptance more difficult. Many families who have lost sons and daughters in a war, especially in Vietnam, experienced the agony of holding on to a 'straw of hope' while trying to accept the almost certain loss. When someone is lost at sea the reaction is similar. *I once did a funeral service for a man whose seat was pulled out of a plane at 5000 metres. The body was never found. The widow had a church service in which I used a special collect instead of the normal committal prayer. I think that she found the service useful because it was tangible. It helped her to accept the death of her husband.*

Denial is an attempt to buffer the impact of loss. In the initial period it can give some time to enable the individual to accept the news and then slowly begin to understand what has happened. It is a psychological defence mechanism that should be respected. The counsellor should not treat initial denial as a citadel to be immediately stormed by the facts of the situation.

The facts soon become apparent. The hospital staff usually encourage the relatives to view the body and generally allow time for a more intimate farewell. *A couple in our church had a stillbirth and the nursing staff encouraged the mother to have the baby beside her in a cot for the first night.* There may also be an opportunity for a viewing before the funeral service. The reality and finality of death is also reinforced in the funeral service: the coffin sinking into the earth, the shovel full of earth, and the words, 'earth to earth, ashes to ashes, dust to dust'. [6] Christians have an expectation that extends beyond the 'victory of death' to the resurrection in Christ (cf. 1 Corinthians 15:35). I do not believe that this is a form of denial, but an acceptance of the limits of human life – and a recognition of a better source of hope.

Task 2: To experience the emotions of grief

There are various emotions that are part of the grief process. Perhaps sadness is the most natural feeling and yet crying is so frequently resisted. Sometimes the counsellor can give space – and even permission – for the bereaved to be sad. I remember helping a young man choose hymns for his father's funeral. When 'The Lord is my shepherd', was suggested he said, 'But that always makes me feel sad.' I gently reminded him that sadness was an appropriate emotion at a funeral.

Anger is also common and may be projected onto the physician, funeral director, clergy and, of course, God. The sources of anger may be complex. The obvious reason is frustration that nothing could be done to stop the death. But a less obvious cause might be the regressive experience of helplessness, separation anxiety and rage at being abandoned.

Guilt and self-reproach can be very painful. Although it is possible that guilt might be associated with past neglect, it is more likely to be a 'sin of omission' that is quite unrealistic. *A dutiful daughter leaves the bedside of her dying father to get a cup of coffee. He dies and she blames herself for not being there for him at the end. I have heard it said by nursing staff that a dying person often chooses such a moment to die because there is an emotional space for the 'letting go'.* It is helpful to distinguish between a personal responsibility and an unrealistic self-expectation. It may be important to encourage grieving people to be kind to themselves. I remember Dr John Maes saying to a class at Boston University, 'None of us ever loves perfectly.'

Anxiety stems from dependency needs. There is a natural question, 'How will I take care of myself?' It may also be due to a heightened sense of vulnerability to death. *When my daughter Rowena was four years old she saw a film about a person dying of cancer. She said later 'I am not going to die. I am going to keep my eyes open'.* This was her way of expressing her anxiety about death. C. S. Lewis described his feelings after losing his wife Joy: 'No one ever told me that grief was so like fear. I am not afraid, but the sensation is like being afraid.'[7] Other painful feelings may include: loneliness, fatigue, yearning, bitterness and helplessness. Positive feelings may also be present. It is not unusual for surviving children to feel relief or freedom when an aged parent dies after a long battle with an illness. Feelings are usually mixed and it can be quite a challenge to sort them out.

The absence of feeling or numbness is normal in the first hours following the news – or even the first few days. This is natural under the avalanche of feelings which can overwhelm a person. At an appropriate time a counsellor may help him to feel fully and begin to work through the feelings of loss. We can be aware that many bereaved people have difficulty with one or more of the emotions.

Although not everyone grieves in the same way, each person has to do their share of 'grief work' (Freud) or facing the painful feelings. Friends and family are not always helpful. It is common for them to say something like: 'There, there, don't let it get to you.' They may reward Stoic acceptance 'Isn't he handling it well?' Often the family will see their role in terms of distracting and cheering up. Since I came from this kind of background I can appreciate the cultural values. The example of the grief of King David is far more healthy. He mourned the death of Absalom:

'The King covered his face, and the king cried in a loud voice, 'O my son Absalom, O Absalom, my son, my son!' (2 Samuel 19:4)

The grief process can become stuck when an individual tries to 'keep a lid on things'. What is natural may become abnormal. Anger can turn into self-blame and depression. Sadness is often buried by alcohol abuse or excessive work. Anxiety can be artificially calmed by tranquillizers. The ways of avoidance are legion.

Task 3: To adjust to the new environment

The effect of a major loss is not always obvious. It may take a while for a widow or widower to appreciate fully the extent of the change due to the death of a spouse. After three months he may begin to come to terms with such things as raising children alone, cooking and managing the household finances or coming home to an empty house. But it is more than a list of tasks to be done. The loss of a spouse may mean the loss of a companion, sexual partner, audience for bad jokes, bridge partner, bed warmer and a person with whom to argue. At the onset of bereavement it is seldom clear what adjustments will have to be made.

Some people resent having to learn new skills or to take on roles previously filled by the spouse. But this challenge needs to be faced. Different strategies may need to be adopted to deal with the demands of daily life. This third task can be aborted by surrendering to helplessness and becoming more dependent on family and friends.

A problem-solving approach may initially be helpful. What needs to be done today? What has highest priority for this week? Are there bills to be paid? Can other family members help with specific tasks, e.g. a fifteen-year-old daughter might help with mowing the lawn. However, there are times when it is both necessary and difficult to get the grieving spouse to slow down!

There is a therapeutic maxim that an individual who has suffered a recent loss should be discouraged from making any hasty life-changing decisions. Sometimes a grieving person will impulsively try to do such things as selling the family home and moving north, quitting a job or retiring early ('take a package' in public service language), or rushing into another relationship to 'replace' the lost partner. It is better to live life as 'normal' for at least a year.

One potential benefit of successfully meeting the demands of this task is that a grieving person may experience a rise in self-esteem. A new sense of competence and joy may come from learning to perform in different roles. Sometimes a somewhat 'downtrodden' spouse will blossom at this point rather than wither. There is something invigorating about facing challenges, as José Ortega y Gasset once said, 'We cannot put off life until we are ready. The most salient characteristic of life is its coerciveness; it is always urgent "here and now", without any possible postponement. Life is fired at us point blank.'

Task 4: To withdraw emotional energy and reinvest it in other relationships

This task is often misunderstood. A grieving husband may lament, 'Am I supposed to forget Mel after spending nearly forty years with her?' The withdrawal of attachment from the deceased may be seen as disloyal. It is as if enduring anguish is the only way to honour the memory of the dead person. However, this severing of the bond is part of the grief work. Freud emphasized this in his classic paper 'Mourning and Melancholia' (1917). And as he said a few years earlier, 'Mourning has a quite precise psychical task to perform: its function is to detach the survivor's memories and hopes from the dead.' [8] This may take quite a while, certainly months and even years. Sometimes it seems as if relatives and friends will give permission for only a few weeks of obvious grief and then wonder why Bill isn't getting over Joan's death! Time is needed. There is no fixed schedule, but some losses, such as the death of a child, will certainly leave a wound that may bleed for years. Anniversaries of the death, birthdays, family celebrations and holidays tend to bring back the memories and lead to an upsurge in the feelings of loss. Last year an Advent sermon on the sadness of Christmas was appreciated because this celebration is a time when adults tend to notice 'who is not with us this year'. The pain of grief through such seasons can be likened to 'the rise and fall of waves hitting against the shore.' [9]

There may be considerable anxiety in facing the challenge to reinvest in other relationships. A widower might lament, 'But if I love another person I could get hurt again.' Indeed, this fear may be rationalized by the romantic notion that 'marriage is for life' rather than 'until death us do part'. It sometimes seems as if life has ended for the mourner as well. This may be the most difficult task of all but some engagement with life is necessary, some willingness to find value in making new friendships and renewing old relationships – it is the risk of loving.

I once did a funeral service for a man who had died from cancer a year before he had planned to retire. The timing was difficult for the widow. She was uncertain about whether to go on with their plans and move. Although the relationship had been tense at times, they shared numerous activities. They had both been active in a local bowling club playing mixed doubles. It was a difficult step for the widow to return to the club, but gradually she was able to go along and began to play in competition with other male partners. Her progress was marked by the change from my initial ease at finding her at home to, in time, almost never seeing her when I called. She successfully completed the fourth task.

It is hard to say exactly when mourning is finished. Robert S. Weiss observed: 'What does achieving recovery mean? It means once again being able to do some perfectly ordinary things. Being able to feel good if something good happens. Being able to feel hopeful about the future. Being able to give attention to everyday life. Being able to be cheerful.'[10]

Case study of Anthony

The four tasks of grief counselling apply to many common counselling situations. Such tasks are of relevance to any significant loss and not just to the death of a spouse. The grief following the break-up of a marriage is one of the most common problems that a person will bring to a counsellor.

Anthony was worried that he was not coping very well with the separation from his wife Sally, ten months previously. He was a forty-one-year-old police inspector, well over six feet tall with a quick and agile mind. He remembered his parents having a volatile relationship but managing to stay together (most of the time!). There was some tension in the wider family background. I noted that his maternal grandfather had died under suspicious circumstances, supposedly 'accidental' but it was a matter never discussed in the family. One of his uncles was alcoholic.

Anthony was the unwilling partner in the separation. When he had rung his wife Sally, while away on a three-week course, she had said, 'Don't bother coming home. I now have a boyfriend.' His GP was concerned about symptoms of depression and referred Anthony to me. A mental check against the signs of depression suggested that there were some positive indicators:

- Some sleep disturbance. About three times a week he woke early and although he could get back to sleep after about an hour he did not feel refreshed in the morning.

- Lack of energy and lethargy. He felt he was going 'through the motions'.

- Mild suicidal thinking but no specific plan. When closely questioned he did not think that there was any risk that he might injure himself.

- He could be irritable at times, but he did not lose his temper at work.

There were enough signs to indicate a mild depression, and a reasonable initial hypothesis was that it was related to the grief process. Since there are some similarities in symptoms between grief and depression it is easy to confuse the two. J. W. Worden distinguished grief in that: 'There is not the loss of self-esteem commonly found in most depressions . . . and if the survivors of the deceased experience guilt, it is usually guilt associated with some specific aspect of the loss rather than a general sense of culpability.'[11] With this in mind I found that Anthony had no trouble with feelings of guilt; his self-esteem had suffered a blow but it was not 'terminal'. I concluded that it was a reasonably straightforward case of grief counselling.

Another question that needed to be answered was the degree of Anthony's vulnerability to loss. The following are possible factors in assessing this:

1. Who was the person lost? An aged uncle will be mourned, but the grief will be less intense than for a parent who has lost an infant from cot death.[12]

2. The nature of the relationship. This is central to the concept of grief as a broken bond. How necessary was the relationship? Was there a high degree of dependency, for example a wife who has never learnt to drive and always depended on her husband for transport.

3. The kind of death. The usual categories are natural, accidental, suicide and homicide. Greater difficulties are associated with unexpected and unnatural death.

4. Previous losses. How has this person coped with other deaths? This is a reliable guide as to how that individual might react in the current situation. It is a good indication to see that previous grief work was completed, rather than left as 'emotional baggage' to be carried into the present. Are there healthy models for handling grief in the family?

5. Personality variables. This includes age, gender, level of self-esteem, strengths, values and religious beliefs. What coping strategies are usually employed? Has there been a history of psychiatric treatment? Conditions such as chronic depression or a vulnerability to psychotic episodes might be aggravated. The loss may put enormous stress on coping abilities, and for a fragile individual it may be overwhelming and a breakdown can occur.

6. Social support. Does this person have a close family or network of friends? Involvement in a community such as a church is usually a strength. There may also be a high level of support in

an ethnic community. Sometimes there can be very helpful rituals associated with mourning. One example is the Jewish practice of unveiling the headstone on the first anniversary of the death.

Anthony had many strengths. He was very successful in his job and he had friends who were able to communicate on a feeling level. There was no history of mental illness and he had always functioned well under pressure. It appeared to be a straightforward case of grief counselling and I estimated that it would take six to eight sessions.

In the first two sessions Anthony reviewed his relationship with Sally. They had dated for about two years before drifting into marriage. Anthony had a difficult year in 1988. He would come home from work quite irritable. Sally tried to be supportive but he found her concern claustrophobic. One of the 'hot issues' was whether to have children. She wanted to begin but he was reluctant. Gradually Anthony was able to see how he had contributed to the deterioration in the relationship; it wasn't simply her fault for 'throwing me out'.

Anthony then began to speak of some of the tense periods he remembered from when he was a child. His father and mother had separated for three months while his mother had a brief affair. Could it be that a family pattern was recurring in his generation? He was also becoming more aware of his feelings. Since he was initially inarticulate about what he felt, we simplified the labelling of feelings to 'sad, glad, bad, or mad'. He could identify these with some reflection and then began to make more subtle distinctions.

Gradually he began to be aware of the depth of his anger. He found that he could ventilate this by taking a bucket of golf balls and going to the driving range to hit them as far as possible. Sadness was a more difficult emotion. It began as 'mild regret' but later he was able to acknowledge the depth of his pain. This helped him to recall times when his father would put him down as a child. He felt that the marriage became 'another failure'. He wondered why he could not balance this sense of failure with his success in the police force. Then he began to confront some phrases from childhood such as 'Don't lose control'.

We were able to list as his strengths such things as intelligence, experience in life, appearance, social skills, good friends, 'not devious', having a moral standard, sociability and a capacity to care for others. This seemed to be realistic and a good sign of progress in counselling.

He was able to cope with the milestone of the court session for granting the divorce. In legal terms it was only necessary for his wife to be in court but Anthony chose to be present as well. It was a poignant moment when he reflected, 'Where was everyone who drank to our health and happiness when we got married?' It was something of an anti-climax. 'It was over in two minutes. A quick funeral, I guess.' It is helpful for the reluctant spouse to make as many choices as possible. Sometimes there is more opportunity in this last phase. This helps to counter the prevalent feelings of powerlessness. Since it had been Sally's decision to leave the marriage, he could at least decide how it ended for him. As he said, 'I was there at the wedding; I wanted to be there at the death as well.'

It might have been helpful to Anthony for the church to have offered some kind of ceremony to mark the end of a marriage. Such a need for a ritual might have been a factor in his desire to be there at the family court. I was present at a service designed to help a recently divorced woman in her grief and to enable a process of 'letting go'. I thought that it was very healing. The service also affirmed that God could be part of that experience. It is not uncommon for divorcees to feel excommunicated by the church.

In a later session Anthony thought about the kind of women that he found appealing. He noted that they were generally 'dark, good-looking and with high energy'. He took the risk of going out with someone else. She was not like Sally, 'more easy-going and relaxed'. At first he was worried that he might be 'using her', but then he saw that he was appreciating her for her unique qualities.

Anthony came to see me for a total of eight sessions. One was a follow-up session two months later. He had made excellent progress. He talked more freely about being able to feel his pain. He was able to maintain the momentum and the healing continued in other areas of his life.

Case study of Claire

Claire was a nineteen-year-old secretary in a local public-service department. She was referred to me by a supervisor because of emotional stress. He felt that it was beginning to affect her work performance. About three months previously her uncle had died in a car accident and she found it hard to get to sleep at night. Uncle Bert had been very close to her. She was able to express her emotions and cried easily in my office. For most of the first session she talked about how devastated she felt after his death. I was mildly surprised at the depth of her feeling. I routinely 'prescribed' that she make up a grief journal at the end of the session, saying, 'I would like you to get an exercise book and write the story of the losses you have faced in your life. Start from as early as you can remember. Include such things as moving to a different school, friends you lost, any relatives or pets that died – no matter how trivial it might seem now. And make sure that you write how you feel about the loss, experience the emotions as fully as possible.'

The next session began with her relief:

Claire: *'I was surprised at how I felt much better after last week. It was as if something was taken off my back.'* (She smiles at me) *'Did I use too many of your tissues?'*
Me: *'A small cost to pay for getting the burden off your back.'* (empathy and continuing the gentle humour)
C: *'I rang my father last week; it was Friday, after I saw you. I am really worried about him. He hasn't got Mum to look after him any more.'*
Me: *'You care about him but it is really out of your control?'* (accurate empathy)

C: 'Yes, but I feel like there is a black cloud hanging over me.'
Me: 'Somewhat ominous?' (missing in my response)
C: 'No, it is more like I feel too much and it is hard to penetrate the cloud.' (manages to correct me and keep on the right path)
Me: 'So it is important for you to face what you feel about your father even if it is difficult.' (summarizing and empathy)

It may have seemed like a rambling session, for she then went on to her first boyfriend. 'He dropped me when he didn't get what he wanted.' She then talked about a more serious relationship which lasted nearly three years. However, it did not survive when she moved to take up her present job. It was one of a series of losses. She was getting more involved with her Grief Journal. She found that it was surprising how many small things had touched her in a significant way.

In the third session she was able to reflect on how her family handled grief. 'Mostly through withdrawal, I guess.' One example was the break-up of her parents' marriage. They had separated three years before and the divorce had become final a couple of months before she came to see me.

Claire: 'Dad was involved with another woman. My mum just couldn't put up with it any more.' (tears)
Me: 'How did it affect you?'
C: 'I just cried for a day or so, but then I pulled myself together. I had to be strong for Mother and I didn't feel too much after that.'
Me: 'So you didn't allow yourself to feel more than a little sadness?' (accurate empathy and focusing on the task of feeling)
C: (sobs and is unable to speak).

The fourth session was the last. Claire was feeling a lot better. There were still times of sadness, especially when she thought about what she was writing in her journal. She realized that she had not spoken about her uncle since the first session and said, 'I guess that losing him was not the most upsetting thing. I was more sad about losing my parents.'

I replied, 'They are no longer there together. That is quite a loss.'

Although this was an instance of delayed grief, it was nevertheless a relatively simple case of grief counselling. The problem here is quite common. It was more of a difficulty in the way Claire handled losses in her life: the presenting difficulty of grieving the death of her uncle was the climax of a series of losses, the most important being the divorce of her parents.

Sometimes the grief process is more pathological. In *Great Expectations*, Pip lamented the design of Miss Havisham, who had been jilted at the altar, in raising the beautiful Estella for purposes of revenge:

> I knew not how to answer, or to comfort her. That she had done a grievous thing in taking an impressionable child to mould into the form that her wild resentment, spurned affection and wounded pride found vengeance in . . . But that, in shutting out the light of day, she had shut out infinitely more; that in seclusion, she had secluded herself from a thousand natural and healing influences; that her mind, brooding solitary, had grown diseased, as all minds do and must and will that reverse the appointed order of their Maker.[13]

Such a case of grief that is unresolved is called a 'complicated bereavement' in the diagnostic manual of the American Psychiatric Association (DSM III).[14] Perhaps it is better to think of the abnormal grief in terms of chronic, delayed, exaggerated and masked grief reactions:

1. *A chronic grief reaction* is prolonged, excessive in duration and without resolution. The bereaved recognize that grief has continued for a number of years and yet it is unfinished. The wound is still bleeding; there is little or no scar tissue.

2. *Delayed reactions* are initially inhibited, suppressed, and postponed. There may have been some expression of grief, but it was insufficient. At some time in the future there may be an

excessive reaction to a small stimulus such as watching a sad movie or the death of a family pet.

3. *Exaggerated grief* contains serious symptoms of psychological distress. This may be quite disabling, for example, when a dependent widow becomes agoraphobic, a reactive depression turns into a suicidal crisis, or a schizophrenic begins to hear voices again.

4. *Masked grief* may result in physical symptoms. These may include: headaches, lower back pain, ulcers, even symptoms resembling the sickness of the deceased. Alcohol, reckless spending, drugs and overeating may become compensating addictions.

It is not easy to deal with such complications. It is a specialized form of grief counselling, perhaps better called grief therapy. There may be conflicts around separation. 'The greater the underlying conflict, the more resistance there will be to exploring thoughts and feelings previously too painful.'[15] A counsellor engaged in grief therapy will still keep in mind which of the four tasks have not been completed and this will provide a focus for the work. When the tasks are finished it is possible to give permission to stop grieving and to say a final goodbye.

A case study from the Bible

It is natural that the question of meaning should enter into the grief process. The suffering person asks from the depths of anguish, 'Why?' Even with the non-believer the question so easily becomes, 'Why, God?'

This is the question asked in the Old Testament Book of Job. The central character is Job, a righteous man, who was accused by Satan and tested by God. In a series of tragedies he lost his ten children, servants, prosperity, community esteem and finally his health. His wife advised, 'Do you still persist in your integrity? Curse God, and die.' (Job 2:9)[16] Three friends came to visit. They expressed their sorrow by raising their voices, weeping, rending their robes, throwing dust on their heads and sitting in silence for seven days. 'No one spoke a word to him, for they saw that his suffering was very great.' (Job 2:13) The three counsellors were not hypocrites who came to gloat, nor fools to offer empty words, but friends who conveyed a traditional view of suffering.[17]

Eliphaz explained that there was a moral order. 'Think now, who that was innocent ever perished?' (Job 4:7) All humans are imperfect, 'But human beings are born to trouble just as sparks fly upward.' (Job 5:7) So not even the righteous can complain if they find themselves in distress. Suffering may also be a discipline from God, a way of shaping character. 'How happy is the one whom God reproves . . . for he wounds, but he binds up; he strikes, but his hands heal.' (Job 5:17-18) All the friends assumed suffering to be the result of sin. Bildad observed, 'Surely the light of the wicked is put out . . . the light is dark in their tent . . . their strong steps are shortened, and their own schemes throw them down . . . by disease their skin is consumed . . . they have no offspring or descendant.' (Job 18: 5-7, 13, 19) Zophar spelt out that Job was a sinner, 'Know then that God exacts of you less than your guilt deserves.' (Job 11:6)

Job refused to have his suffering trivialized. He resisted simplistic formulas and exposed empty arguments. He saw the irony in a situation where the healthy tried to theologize about suffering. 'Those at ease have contempt for misfortune.' (Job 12:5) Sometimes it is easy for Christians to be like Job's comforters and use our theological words to oppress rather than to give comfort.

When God finally spoke to Job he changed the subject. 'Where were you when I laid the foundation of the earth?' (Job 38:4) There appears to be no answer to the why of suffering. Instead God revealed Himself and Job responded,

> I had heard of you by the hearing of the ear, but now my eye sees you; therefore I despise myself, and repent in dust and ashes. (Job 42:5-6)

It is not enough simply to mourn the loss. Job illustrates that there is a need for transcendence.

This suggests a distinctive role for Christian counselling. Bruce Rumbold of Whitley College in Australia observed, 'The client's major mode of transcendence can be recognized, and supported, supplemented or modified... counselling involves hearing the stories of people's life and assisting them in both telling and reframing it, not only exploring loss but strengthening their capacity for positive transcendence.'[18] Loss and transcendence are not opposites, but complementary aspects of human existence.

Ultimately it is a question of meaning. Almost every individual who has suffered a tragic loss will ask the larger questions. This is equally true for Christians. We can not neglect the centrality of the cross in this matter. If God has suffered in Christ then the question really becomes, 'Why does God allow Himself and His creatures to suffer?'[19] This does not trivialize the question, but it does assure us that God is not merely an observer in human suffering but a participant.

Many people need help with dealing with losses. It may be a job, health, place, role in society or the Church, or the death of a family member. In this chapter I have outlined Worden's four tasks of working through the grief process. Grief counselling is usually reasonably straightforward, but when it is more entangled with personality factors it is better left to an experienced mental health professional.

Exercises

Write a grief journal of losses you have suffered in your life. Reflect on the way your family handles grief - are you any different? Have you completed the four tasks with major losses you have faced?

Can you identify different styles of handling grief in the Bible? Take Jeremiah as an example (see Chapter 9). Do you think that God suffered grief in the death of His Son? 'God so loved the world that he gave his only Son, so that everyone who believes in him may not perish but may have eternal life.' (John 3:16)

To read further:

Francis Macnab, *Life After Loss*, Millennium, Newtown, NSW, 1989. Macnab is a popular Australian author. This book is quite useful. He has an excellent section on hurrying along the grief process and dealing with obsessional thoughts.

Beverley Raphael, *The Anatomy of Bereavement*, Hutchinson, London, 1984. A classic text by an Australian psychiatrist. Superb and comprehensive in theory. A very careful examination of the different kinds of loss (e.g. loss of spouse, bereaved child, death of a child, growing old, disasters, etc.)

J. William Worden, *Grief Counselling and Grief Therapy*, Routledge, London, 1983. Essential reading for the grief counsellor. He explains the four-task approach in this brief book. Also he gives an overview of grief therapy with cases of abnormal grief.

INDIVIDUAL COUNSELLING

Amanda has come to see Roger, a Christian counsellor attached to St Monica's parish. Amanda complains of feelings of panic while waiting in line at the bank or at the local supermarket. She asks why prayer has not helped? Where is the peace that God promises to his followers? Roger agrees to see her for five or six sessions.

The most common formal counselling is 'one-to-one' or individual counselling. This style is more supportive and generally less threatening. There are many advantages such as privacy, an exclusive focus on the person in distress, and the space to explore fully the issues that are of concern. It is more nurturing than other forms of counselling. It can give an opportunity for what analysts have called a 'corrective emotional experience'[1] where the relationship with the counsellor is found to be healing in itself. Some of the common elements include: restoration of morale, release of painful emotions and developing an explanation that makes sense of previous events.

Individual counselling is best suited to specific problems which can provide a focus for the counselling sessions. This can include almost any personal difficulty such as mild depression and symptoms of anxiety, low self-esteem and difficulties in close relationships.[2] Sometimes the difficulties will present as part of a picture of problems in the spiritual life. There is a natural expectation that clergy will be available for counselling with a spiritual focus, but there is also a willingness for believers to seek help in other areas as well. The process may not be as formal as outlined here, but the principles of disciplined counselling still broadly apply.

In this chapter I will examine some of the elements of the counselling process within the context of working with an individual.

The first interview

There is a sense in which this interview begins with first contact. It is usually by phone so I will notice the tone of voice: How urgent? Is there some desperation? This will influence how quickly I respond. Usually, setting a time for the first session, even if it is a few days away, will reduce anxiety.

The first session sets a pattern for future work. After a general greeting, I may ask how they came to see me. The referral source is always relevant and I usually write a note to acknowledge that the person did come to see me. It is worth noting the title of address whether Dr, Mr, Pastor, Rev., Father or the familiar Bruce. The choice of title carries some connotations about how the relationship is viewed and initial expectations. I also notice appearance and other non-verbal cues: eyes, facial expression, whether the clothes match or are appropriate, which emotions are expressed or avoided. I might begin with an open-ended question such as 'You said on the phone that you were feeling depressed . . .' This allows the person to express the problem in his or her own words.

The ambiguity of the situation is helpful. Michael Basch observed about learning how an individual attempts to order his world, 'You have to give him a chance to work at ordering with you; he should not be presented with a series of preconceived questions that relieve him of the tension of having to adapt himself creatively to you and to the session.'[3] The way a person presents himself is as important as the problem that brings him to seek help. In this way I begin the process of assessment. It is important to check the level of risk which may include suicide, psychosis, violence or even homicide. I try to get a sense of what work needs to be done and whether I am a reasonable choice of counsellor. If not, a referral will be made. A word of caution about the first session: The anxiety is usually very high and symptoms may look more severe than in later sessions.

It is helpful to consider, 'Why is this person seeking help now? What has caused the present crisis or motivated the request for assistance?' The reasons will vary: a wife has found out about her husband's affair, a teenage son has run away, a bad work report has led to feelings of worthlessness. Such reasons may not be directly expressed, but will be an important part of the picture.

I also keep handwritten records on cards and record such details as the address and phone number (both could be vital in a suicidal crisis). I code the name on the card and this assures confidentiality. It is best to keep such records in a locked filing cabinet or enter the details into a secured file system in a computer.

The 'must' of the first interview is to make empathic contact; 'ultimately there can be no replacement for showing that we care.'[4] Without this bond the first session is usually the last. A biblical example of lack of empathy was Job who was tormented by the well-meaning efforts of his friends and lashed back, 'Miserable comforters are you all' (Job 16:1).

At the end of the session it is helpful to give an overall impression of how you see the problem and some indication of how many sessions might be necessary to see some improvement.[5] Indeed, saying that it may take four sessions lessens the expectation of a 'magical cure.'[6] I try to be realistic in commenting on the nature and complexity of the presenting problem. I usually emphasize that the person will be helped to find his or her own solutions to difficulties. Answers are not provided, but assistance is given to solve whatever difficulties are present. It is helpful to leave the person feeling that an important step has been made in helping himself or herself affirm what has been done, highlight any insights gained, and possibly give some practical means of dealing with presenting symptoms. In this way something can be taken away from that first session.

Assessment

Accurate assessment is an important part of the early process of counselling. If the counsellor can ask sensible questions it tends to be reassuring rather than intrusive. There is a feeling of security, 'I am in the hands of a professional.' It also helps to clarify whether there is any risk of suicide or other self-injury.

It may be helpful to have a clear outline of areas that might be covered. The following outline is quite comprehensive, even for mental health professionals, and there is no need for most counsellors to investigate in such detail. However, 'knowing what to leave out' is a choice that can only be made with an awareness of the whole picture. Once an assessment is made I can be more relaxed and allow the person space to follow his or her own agenda.

Evaluation Outline

1. *Referral:* source and reason for the referral.

2. *Identifying data:* name, address, phone number, age, sex, marital status, race, religious allegiance and general appearance. Non-verbal cues can be noted. Also related questions such as 'Does this person look or act their age?'

3. *Complaint:* the reason in the person's own words for seeking help. What are the motivating factors? Why now?

4. *Current symptoms and level of functioning:* This includes a history of the troubling symptoms. Is there a cycle? Any impairments in work, sleep, appetite, decision-making, interpersonal relationships, etc. Try to distinguish the effects of short-term stress from personality factors.

5. *Previous mental health treatment:* this can include institutions, number of admissions, duration of counselling, medication, name of counsellors, success or otherwise of treatment.

6. *Addictions:* Drug or alcohol abuse? Heavy smoking?

7. *Legal history:* any antisocial behaviour? Trauma from accidents, war, etc.

8. *Developmental history:* date and place of birth, abnormalities during pregnancy, birth, postnatal care, bed-wetting in childhood, adolescent rebellion and running away from home, etc.

9. *Academic:* age started school, school or other phobias, absences, attitudes towards peers and teachers, shyness, truancy, expulsions, tertiary experience and qualifications.

10. *Sexual history:* age of puberty, early dating patterns, age of first sexual activity, significant relationships, present level of libido, sexual disorders, any deviant sexual behaviour? The sexual attitudes of parents also have an effect on the development of a sexual self.

11. *General level of maturity:* is there any obvious dependency? Impulsive behaviour?

12. *Occupational history:* age began work, type of jobs, reason for changing positions, competence, work relationships, stability under stress, absenteeism, promotions, any military service.

13. *Medical history:* genetic problems, disabilities, operations, dates of hospitalizations, allergies, most recent physical examination and result, any current medication.

14. *Marriage history:* include de facto relationships, any separations, pregnancies before marriage. Quality of the marital relationship and level of satisfaction. Number of children.

15. *Family history:* is recorded by using a three-generational genogram. This shows all members of the family, relationships, birth order, names, occupations, etc. (*See* Chapter 9 on marriage counselling for details on how to draw a genogram.) It is also important to record any evidence of family pathology, e.g. mental illness, suicide attempts, depression, criminal behaviour, violence, sexual abuse, gambling and other addictions.

16. *Religious history:* who has been baptized? What denominations? Who have been practising their faith? Are there tensions about

religious belief in the family? What have been the major events in the person's faith journey?

The following additional areas are for the mental health professional to consider:

1. *Mental status exam:* Normally this is carried out by a psychiatrist or clinical psychologist. It assesses the presence of more serious mental illness. The following areas are covered: appearance, general behaviour, talk, mood, content of thought, abnormal beliefs and interpretation of events, abnormal experiences, cognitive state, estimate of intelligence, assets and strengths.

2. *Psychological or neuropsychological testing:* A referral for a medical examination or specialist report on an area of concern might be indicated.

3. *Initial diagnosis:* using the five-axis format of DSMIII-R.[7]

4. *Psychodynamic formulation* of the presenting problem.

5. *Initial treatment plan:* including goals, frequency of sessions, any family members to be seen. It might be important to consider whether another professional should be consulted and perhaps brought in as a co-counsellor for a session or two.

Although it is not really as necessary to be so comprehensive except when making a written assessment or a psychological evaluation for legal purposes, I still find it valuable to have an overall outline. If, for example, an individual presents with an eating disorder, specific questions can be asked about the problem: how long has the behaviour been present? diets? medical and hospital treatment? fluctuations in weight? present weight? friends or family members with eating problems? messages from parents about food? It is also helpful in the diagnostic phase to be very concrete when the person responds with vague descriptions. For example if told, 'I have been feeling a bit blue lately,' the counsellor might respond, 'You sound like you might be depressed. How have you been sleeping?' If told,

'I drink too much sometimes,' 'How many glasses? When? How often?'

The purpose of making an assessment is to get the best possible 'map of the territory' to guide the work of counselling.

Making progress in counselling

A new phase begins when the assessment is complete. The person has felt some empathy and senses that the counsellor has something of a 'game plan'. At a session there is less awkwardness and more ease in the greeting. He or she knows where to sit and quickly settles down to work. The deepening of the relationship is known as the 'working alliance'. It is basically a joint commitment to work on the issues that motivated the counselling. Joseph Sandler, writing within the psychoanalytic tradition, spelt this out: the alliance is 'based on the patient's conscious or unconscious wish to co-operate and his readiness to accept the therapist's aid in overcoming internal difficulties . . . there is an acceptance of the need to deal with internal problems.'[8]

An example of a good alliance was the relationship formed between a priest and a passive, dependent young man who had difficulties separating from his parents. A spirit of camaraderie began to develop with the clergyman seen as 'big brother'. The young adult began to examine his low self-esteem and over-dependence upon his parents. Where did this come from? Why was it necessary? Attitudes and behaviours were identified. Little by little a sturdier sense of self developed and he moved out of his parents' home. Each act of independence was followed by a surge of anxiety, but gradually he learnt to tolerate the discomfort. Later he was pleased that he was able to lead a more self-directed life.

The alliance is not always tranquil. One of the insights of psychoanalysis is that the client will often act out difficulties within the counselling relationship. Weinberg added that the people will 'cease being our allies at some time. They ask us to do too much, blame us for what goes wrong, refuse to speak to us. The harmonious alliance is honoured more in the breach than in the observance.'[9] In my experience this observation is accurate for longer-term psychoanalytic treatment, but it is rarely a problem in short-term counselling. There is usually a willingness to work on the presenting difficulties in counselling. It is also possible to think of the alliance more in commercial terms. Empathy, support and understanding 'put money in the bank'. Each confrontation or unwelcome insight involves a 'withdrawal of funds'. It is a rare therapeutic relationship that can tolerate an overdraft for long!

In earlier chapters I emphasized the skills that are necessary in counselling. These skills can be learnt through involvement in volunteer programmes such as Lifeline or Red Cross. I would advise such a course as a beginning point for anyone interested in training as a counsellor. At the very least it is essential to get objective feedback on accuracy in reflective listening. It is also helpful to join some kind of therapy group since this helps a counsellor-in-training both to work on his own issues and learn the more advanced skills. A three-month course in CPE (Clinical Pastoral Education) is an excellent way for clergy and church workers to improve their ability in counselling.

Careful listening is absolutely central to the helping process. It encourages the individual to think aloud about a situation, suggesting that solutions are within reach. As Gelder observed about the role of the counsellor, 'He encourages the patient to talk about emotionally painful subjects rather than avoid them, to review his own part in any difficulties that he ascribes to other people and to look for common themes in what he is describing. At times, the therapist helps the patient to look back on his life to see how present patterns of behaviour began. He asks him to consider whether behaviour that served a purpose in the past is continuing to the present, although no longer appropriate. Finally, he encourages the patient to consider alternative ways of thinking and behaving in situations that cause difficulties.'[10]

It is usually very appropriate for the person in counselling to explore the situation as fully as possible. Important decisions may have to be made. I usually refuse to give 'solutions' even when they might be requested. I believe that it is far more important to maintain the focus on the possibilities of the situation. The counsellor can encourage speech in a general way and then use summarizing statements to help the person focus on specific choices to be made. When a decision has to be made it may be helpful first to consider the most unlikely or least preferred options and then move to what is more likely. This leaves a smaller range for more careful consideration. [11]

This can be quite agonizing. I once saw a young man from the church that I served who was deeply torn between choosing to stay in a 'safe' relationship and wanting to revive a past romantic fling. He was living with a very supportive woman but the relationship had always been a little dull. She met quite a few important needs and he was wise enough to be able to value her role in his life. The dilemma came because he had had an affair with a married woman three years earlier and now that she was divorced he was tempted to 'look her up'. In session after session he thought about the advantages and disadvantages of every possible course of action. Gradually he became more aware of issues from his childhood and that his inability to make firm decisions was part of his emotional 'baggage'.

It seemed inappropriate for me to give advice about a life decision he had to make. In order for him to focus on both sides of the choice, I usually took the 'devil's advocate role' and questioned whether he would be strong enough to live with the decision. This was taken to the point of suggesting that he alternate his decisions from day to day. He would decide to leave and live with that decision for a day and then the next day decide to stay and again live with that choice for a day. In this way he was able to think through the situation more clearly and to gauge how he felt about both options.

It is wise to consider the consequences of each potential choice. Perhaps some grief work will need to be done in letting go of one possibility. There may be no need to make a quick decision and the process can sometimes be slowed down. Sometimes it is appropriate, as Geldard advised, to give permission to remain stuck for a while. [12] This can take some pressure off and facilitate a more sensible path of action.

Reframing is a technique that is used by many counsellors. An individual in distress will usually have a negative outlook. Sometimes it is possible to offer another more positive perspective from which to look at a familiar situation. Some examples I have used:

- A young woman saw her mother as controlling. It was suggested that the mother was not only concerned for her daughter's welfare but frightened for herself.

- A couple were locked into heated and destructive conflict. It was suggested that they cared so much for each other that they both wanted to stay connected and unresolved conflict was the only way they knew how to manage it.

- A middle-aged woman was hurt by her husband's sudden announcement that he was leaving. She felt rejected, but rather than her seeing the situation in terms of his being indifferent, it was helpful to see that he felt too intensely and had to escape from feeling entangled in the relationship.

- An older man had received a promotion. He was fearful of the public-speaking component of the job. This was reframed as 'blocked excitement'. (Gestalt therapy term for anxiety.)

There are many possibilities in the 'art of reframing'. [13] Sometimes there are deeper spiritual understandings. For example, a young Christian came to understand that a hurtful disagreement in her beach mission team was a test from God to probe her leadership capacity.

As a person progresses in non-directive counselling there is usually a growth in self-awareness. This includes the ability to experience a broader range of feelings, perhaps contain better negative reactions, reflect more deeply on actions and relationships. A good deal of what is said in a session has been known all along but rarely spoken out loud. As one young woman said to me, what she said in the session was, 'at the back of my mind'. The putting of thoughts into words is very useful. It is the means 'whereby we detach ourselves both from the world about us and from the inner world of our own emotions and thoughts. It is by means of words that we objectify, that we are able to stand back from our own experience and reflect upon it.'[14]

This has been called the 'observing ego' – the ability to observe oneself critically. Naturally such self-awareness is part of maturity but it is enhanced in the counselling process. There is a greater refinement of self-understanding: feelings are better labelled, impulses seen for what they are, fears explored, difficulties clarified and new behaviours are 'tried out'. This can be seen in the following goals:

1. To become more aware of life as it is truly experienced, especially the emotional life.

2. To clarify past experiences, present awareness, and future goals.

3. To experience more personal freedom and fulfilment of potential.

4. To accept responsibility for thought and action.

5. To become aware of the spiritual dimension in life and for the Christian to grow in spiritual maturity.

As Weinberg summarized, 'The essence of psychotherapy is to enable the patient to appreciate how he has been keeping himself the same – and how he can change.'[15]

A general distinction can be made between supportive counselling and healing wounds from the past. Most crisis counselling needs to be supportive. An example of this is a clergywoman who was called on her hospital bleeper at 2 a.m. When she arrived at the hospital she found that the eighteen-year-old son of a regular parishioner had been involved in a serious car accident. The hospital staff were pressing for a decision about whether to turn off the life-support system. This was a time for her to listen with sensitivity and assist the couple to think clearly. There was a later opportunity for grief counselling.[16]

Supportive counselling is characterized by empathic listening, reassurance, suggestion (used sparingly!), allowing temporary dependency, explanation and advice. A counsellor might explain what will happen with the medical tests and what the findings might mean. This is more a case of 'what will happen' and 'how to cope'.[17] Some of these techniques break the normal rules of counselling but are necessary in a short-term crisis. However necessary such interventions are in a short-term crisis, allowing dependency is inappropriate when an individual is capable of managing for himself or herself.

Compare this to another scene. A lay counsellor is sought out by an attractive woman in her early twenties. The presenting problem is an inability to form lasting relationships with men. She has become aware of a destructive pattern: she quickly becomes irritable on the first date and cringes from any touch from the man. When she speaks of her family of origin, she becomes angry at her father who was frequently violent and terrorized her as a child. This is not an acute crisis, but a chronic problem with roots back into the past.

There are various forms of counselling that seek to address past wounds. The work of uncovering is a slow process which I would liken to an archaeology of the psyche. It may bring out feelings long forgotten: a resentment is acknowledged, a sadness faced, a jealousy explored, and a rage expressed. Sometimes the person begins to feel the pain for the first time. The pieces may begin to fit together, 'Now I can see why I have been so restless at work.' Often there is a joyful sense of discovery, 'When I get mad at Sally I think that it is really my mother who I am angry with!' And, 'Is this what I have been trying so hard to avoid seeing?'

Insight is not always welcome. In one of the *Peanuts* cartoons, Linus asked, 'Charlie Brown, do you want to know what is the trouble with you?' Charlie answered, 'No.' They stared at each other. Then Linus said, 'The trouble with you is that you do not want to know what is the trouble with you!' This is equally true in many counselling situations. It is sometimes called a defence when the individual resists the insight offered by the counsellor. It is important to be aware that a defence usually hides a deep vulnerability and that should not be stripped away without some other garment to hide the nakedness.

Stating the obvious can also be demeaning. It may also be resisted if, like Charlie, the person is not ready for the insight. I would prefer to think of the counselling process as one of gradual clarification and deepening of understanding, as J. Mann wrote, 'The therapist recognizes that a host of important feelings, ideas and conclusions lie scattered in the preconscious mind of the patient. The carefully listening therapist hears bits of important data and makes equally important observations of behaviour at a number of points . . . The patient cannot keep track of them, engaged as he is in a highly emotional piece of work, the therapist does keep track, brings important bits together, and presents them as a unified concept.'[18]

Insight can be gained at a number of levels. The reflecting of emotions can lead to insight; and the patient may realize, 'Oh, I am that angry.' The next level is simple description of what is experienced, 'It seems that you are depressed about what happened at work.' The counsellor's observation can be more searching. 'This difficulty has really got you down and you wonder if there is any point in going on.' Sometimes the insight is linked to past experience, 'When your boss at work says, "Be careful", it is an echo of what your mother said long ago.' It is also a useful guideline for counsellors that formulations based on a theoretical framework are not presented 'cold' to the person, but revealed piecemeal in the form of comments about the origins of behaviour and feelings as they emerge in counselling.[19] There is no benefit in saying something like, 'Your desire to spend time with your mother is just a manifestation of the oedipal complex.' This would probably be nonsense, but even if the counsellor believed it, he would have to prepare carefully for such an interpretation.

The most important thing about an insight for the person in counselling is in making a self-discovery. Then it is owned. It is felt deeply. Irvin Yalom explained it: 'The problem in therapy is always how to move from an ineffectual intellectual appreciation of a truth about oneself to some emotional *experience* of it. It is only when therapy enlists deep emotions that it becomes a powerful force for change.'[20] In the spiritual realm, I would think that the revelation of a truth through reading the Bible is a higher form of insight – and it shares the strong experiential 'a-ha'.

It is sometimes helpful to encourage the writing of an autobiography. This is like a journal exercise. It is a way of re-examining the past and eventually forming a bigger picture. *Recently a client said how she was surprised, through writing in her journal, that she hated her mother even more than her father. Her father was violent and abusive, but her mother neglected her. She was forced to look after younger siblings, and now she saw that she had lost her childhood.*

In longer-term psychotherapy there is an important developmental dimension that I will mention in passing. Sometimes a distressed person will lack basic competencies that should have been learnt in childhood. When there is such a deficit, which is commonly called a 'developmental arrest', the counsellor can pay attention to that developmental area. Although it sounds patronizing, the counsellor re-parents and encourages the counsellee to grow along that trajectory into a mature adulthood. Michael Franz Basch listed the following areas:

1. Affect/cognition. This would include the capacity to feel and label emotional reactions.

2. Attachment. This is seen in the ability to feel safe in relationships, in effect believing, 'I am loved.'

3. Psychosexuality. This includes being able to relate in a mature way sexually to others. Intense conflicts in the area may lead to impotence or frigidity.

4. Autonomy. Maturity in this is basically the ability to 'stand on one's own feet' as an adult. Unhealthy dependence upon a spouse is an example of a degree of failure to mature.

5. Creativity. Not all of us are artists or composers of music, but

it is obvious whether an individual is in touch with the creative side of his or her nature.

6. Other. Basch is modest enough to acknowledge that there may be other developmental sectors of the personality.[21]

I would certainly add the spiritual dimension, which I think can be stunted by unbelief and lack of willingness to be open to what God reveals. In some people, for example, saints in the Catholic and Protestant traditions, there is a remarkable transparency to the nature of God. It would seem that such people display spiritual maturity.

I recently saw a very distressed couple. Their fourteen-year-old daughter had left home and was presently living in a youth refuge. This was a very frightening situation with a lot of risk for the adolescent, but the mother was reacting in an extreme way. She was in a state of panic and she would fly into a rage at anyone who attempted to help. At one point she said, 'It would be better if Kirsty was dead. I can't stand the thought of her being there and I can't see her!' This was more intense than the feelings of rejection that might be expected; it was a problem in the developmental area of attachment. The mother was suffering the terror of a four-year-old girl left in child care against her will. If I was to make any progress in this crisis situation I had first of all to soothe the panic and then later address what had been missed in childhood.

This brief introduction cannot begin to indicate the diversity in the practice of counselling. Shorter treatments tend to be more structured, whereas longer, more psychotherapeutic approaches encourage the client to say anything that comes to mind. There are differences in the activity level of the counsellor, the role of interpretation, the attention given to matters other than events of daily life (e.g. fantasies, dreams, creative expressions such as paintings, the strivings of the spiritual life), and the role of what might be unconscious in the relationship with the counsellor. The dynamics of counselling are present in every session and I will now indicate some elements that counsellors from various schools agree are important.

Some dynamics in the counselling process

There are unseen dynamics in every human interaction. Freud noticed an element of projection in his *Studies in Hysteria* (1885). 'The patient is frightened at finding she is transferring on to the figure of the physician the distressing ideas which arise from the content of the analysis.' He further understood transference through reflecting on the failed case of Dora (1905). 'A whole series of psychological experiences are revived, not as belonging to the past, but as applying to the person of the physician at the present moment.'[22] The essence of this insight was understanding the transference of emotions from the past to present experiences in counselling.

Something of this reality of *transference* can be seen in the way some parishioners refer to clergy. Is he a good or bad 'father'? Women clergy carry the same overtones from the experiences of parishioners with their mothers. Is this based in reality or fantasy? People will coopt the clergyperson to play psychic roles repeating childhood patterns. But it is an example of a more general dynamic that is present in most intimate relationships. *Mavis, who was the adult child from a family with a violent father, said, 'I can't understand men, I keep thinking that my boss is abusive in the smallest details, but none of the other employees seem to have any difficulties.'* As analysts have said for years there is a tendency endlessly to *repeat* in the transference rather than to *remember*.

Counselling usually begins with a honeymoon period. This is the *idealized transference*. The counsellor becomes the 'good father' or the 'all-caring mother'. Although it is somewhat unrealistic, it is helpful to the counselling process in that it encourages a high level of trust and builds the foundation for the working alliance. The person in counselling will make far more intimate revelations than might normally be expected. In most cases the relationship settles down and a more realistic image of the counsellor is developed. If there is an extreme of idealizing then it will tend to be unstable. The counsellor will inevitably fall off the pedestal and then be devalued. Normal idealizing should not be initially challenged, even though it can be quite uncomfortable to the novice counsellor.

Negative transference is a more difficult matter. In mild forms it can distract from the course of treatment. This may include flashes of irritability, thoughts of counsellor coldness and attempts to prolong interviews through a need for dependency. A more developed reaction through negative transference may lead to flight rather than staying and working through therapeutic issues. Also of concern are dramatic gestures such as threats of suicide.

The negative forms of transference need to be quickly recognized and addressed. If this distortion is allowed to develop then the work of counselling will suffer. *One example of a negative transference was with a highly successful business executive. We were close to the same age and he initially seemed to see me as a 'big brother'. However, he often spoke of his disappointment in his inadequate and weak father who was a cab driver. Gradually he began to miss sessions and arrive late when he came. With the help of supervision I recognized that this behaviour related to internal conflicts about his father: I had become 'father' but would I also be 'weak'? When I confronted him we were able to work through the issue and treatment proceeded.*

The emotional reaction of transference is a 'here and now' lens to see emotional events of the past. If a young man over-explains his every action, then it may be a clue to past experiences of his integrity being doubted. If a woman expects to be cross-examined after a date, then it may raise the hypothesis that she had a similar experience in adolescence. A child may cringe after a lifted voice – almost expecting a violent assault. A list of such examples could be endless. In traditional psychoanalysis, the analyst interpreted the transference. However this ability was the result of long training, personal analysis and a highly disciplined approach to treatment. It is not advisable for counsellors who lack such a rigorous training to attempt such interpretations. Even analysts, who have the opportunity of numerous sessions per week, move at a 'snail's pace'.

The other important dynamic is the transference experienced by the counsellor. This is called *countertransference* in which the counsellor experiences a reaction to the person in counselling. It is equally unconscious and becomes a kind of 'blind spot'. Some common countertransference responses include:

1. A tendency to see people as very needy and dependent upon our support.

2. A fear of intimacy when the person in counselling expresses affection, warmth, and gratitude. (After growing up in an 'unemotional' home, this has been an issue for me.)

3. A difficulty in accepting compliments.

4. When a counsellor finds himself 'falling in love' or thinks obsessively about a counsellee outside sessions.

5. A bias towards a sub-group of people such as racial groups, older women or children.

Since the counsellor is the source of this distortion and it colours the counselling relationship, it is a potentially very destructive process. It is important for him to develop his sensitivity to such countertransference or his work will suffer.

I am sometimes surprised by the strength of countertransference feelings. I remember having something of a father transference with an older clergyman. His first wife had died and he was marrying again. When I was at the wedding the priest said 'If anyone . . .' and I had a strong impulse to object. How could my 'father' marry anyone else than my mother! Such is the logic of transference.

In counselling sessions I have learnt to monitor closely my emotional reactions. These may include such feelings as irritation, boredom, anger, sadism, erotic attraction, benign fatherly concern, disdain, etc. This may be potentially important information about that person's interpersonal style. My reaction to a female client may be typical and others who live or work with her may feel similarly. *A young woman related to me in a seductive way and I speculated that it might be an indication of her style in dealing with authority figures.* Experience has helped me to be more aware of my normal style in a session. If, then, I notice any deviations in how I react, it may be an indication of a transference. Michael Basch concluded, 'To some extent it helps to be aware of one's therapeutic style and to recognize that if one's mood is atypical, it may well be a signal that a personal complex is intruding on the work . . . Most important, of course, is the therapist's own experience in his own treatment. He is likely to recognize the remobilization of his unconscious conflicts if he has worked on them in a therapeutic situation.'[23]

There are various ways we can learn to deal with counter-transference. I found that in training in the USA, there was an emphasis on the importance of the trainee being in counselling for his own issues and allowing time for adequate growth. I had a year of Rogerian-style counselling at a university counselling clinic and I followed this with working on more unconscious issues with a Jungian analyst. I believe that these experiences were most important in my development as a therapist.

I have also seen psychology, social work and theological students who have wanted to resolve conflicts that were disturbing their clinical work. *One example was a woman student in a master's programme in clinical psychology. She is an adult child of an alcoholic father. She recognized a pattern of co-dependency that was affecting her work in an out-patient alcohol treatment programme.* It is my impression that the best private practitioners have all had periods in counselling for personal issues.

Another important resource is supervision. When I returned to Australia and began to work as a psychologist, I took the initiative and continued individual supervision with two senior psychologists. One was excellent with individual cases and the other was an expert in family therapy. I now share cases with a peer supervision group of privately practising psychologists. We meet fortnightly and all take turns to present. This has worked well for some years. Sometimes I am made aware of a bias in the counselling process and learn to make adjustments. One early learning experience was of insensitivity to women's issues relating to power – more usually lack of it – in society. I should also add that professional associations recognize the importance of supervision before full membership is granted.

Termination

Woody Allen has often joked about his decades in analysis. When a friend asked how it was going, he replied, 'Slowly.' There is usually an appropriate time to end counselling. It is called termination.

There are unique aspects to each phase of counselling. At the end there are usually mixed feelings. This may include sadness at the loss of the relationship. There may also be conflicting feelings of anger, regret, disappointment, pride, satisfaction and gratitude. It is helpful to acknowledge and examine such feelings. I also find it valuable to review progress. This can be as simple as asking what changes have been experienced in the course of counselling. This is not to imply that all issues have been resolved, but the crises should have passed and new patterns of coping acquired. All this can be affirmed.

I also allow myself to be seen as more of a real person in this stage. This counteracts any idealism remaining from the initial positive transference. Such idealism is unrealistic and it should not remain as the lasting impression. A reference to my wife and family, mention of a time of doubt or failure or even a relationship difficulty reveals that I have not got every aspect of my own life together - I am human as well!

When is counselling over? It is usually a mutual decision based on treatment goals. Has the person achieved what motivated him or her to seek help? Is there a sense of closure? Is there a healing of wounds? Are the symptoms no longer disabling? For example, can a person who sought help for depression now sleep through the night? Is there an integration of the issues raised into the narrative of the journey of faith? Normally there is some indication of satisfaction over the progress made. This may mean that goals have been achieved and the counsellor can begin to think about the possibility of termination.

The period of termination is in proportion to the length of

counselling. A brief period of four sessions may end with fifteen minutes discussing the gains made in the past month. On the other hand, counselling that has lasted more than a year may require a month or more to work through the feelings of termination. It may also be necessary to taper off the sessions to fortnightly, monthly, quarterly and then 'on call'. The door is always open to return.

A final comment on the opportunity of termination. It is not uncommon for the relationship to deepen in the final few sessions. Some people fear 'enmeshment' and with the end in sight reveal the most intimate of details. This may also happen at the end of a session with only five minutes left. There is security in the limit of time available. It is a matter of judgment whether to extend the number of sessions in the light of what has been revealed. In general, I am reluctant to do this since there is usually the opportunity to return later for more work. Nevertheless, termination is 'the end' and because of the unique dynamics it can be an important opportunity for growth.

Referral

One of the best indications of professional competence is knowing one's limits. I would not see a thirteen-year-old boy who was having trouble with school attendance. He would fall outside my areas of competence. He is too young when I specialize in working with adults and his problem has an educational aspect. I would tend to refer him to a school psychologist. There are also some areas with adults where I would hesitate. At the moment, I would not take on a difficult case of anorexia since I do not think that I have had sufficient experience with eating disorders. Other counsellors specialize in such problems and would be able to offer considerable expertise.

There are times when it is dangerous to misjudge this and not refer people to qualified professionals. A person may be suicidal and need antidepressant medication from a GP. I have occasionally seen individuals who are schizophrenic and need to be under the care of a psychiatrist. If I work with them it has to be in tandem with the medical professional. Sometimes there are other good reasons to make a referral: the counsellor or client may be moving out of the area, there may be difficulties in the time availability or cost factors and on rare occasions the counselling may be stuck.

Eugene Kennedy has written, 'Referral represents a moment of decision at which, for the greater good of the client, he or she is transferred for help to another professional person. This should not come as a total surprise to the client; counsellors can easily and honestly make this a possibility right from the start. Referral fits the context of the counselling in which the helper is open and honest with the client.'[24] I sometimes find that there is a need for neuropsychological assessment or a medical examination. At times it is necessary to have additional support from a self-help group such as Alcoholics Anonymous or other community organizations. A referral can help the person to get in contact with such groups.

A colleague, Dr Malise Arnstein, gave the following guidelines on making a referral:

1. Be careful to state the limits of your knowledge, skill and ability in being able to help the individual. In what role do you feel comfortable and competent?

2. Give some indication of the severity of the difficulty. Is it important enough to warrant attention now? What does he or she think needs to be done now? What will he or she do if things continue to deteriorate?

3. Ask the person if he or she wants help?

4 Give information about other sources of help or where he or she may be able to find out more information.

5. When suggesting the names of other counsellors, try to give the names of two or three people in the field and discuss the pros and cons of each. For example, one person may be easy to reach but not very experienced in that area, whereas another may be

difficult to contact but very highly regarded for such work. Some indication of costs may also be helpful.

6. If he or she is uncomfortable making the first contact, then would he or she prefer that you were to make the first appointment? In some extreme cases it may be necessary to take the person to the appointment.

7. Invite him or her to let you know how satisfactory the contact was with that professional.[25]

It is a common practice to phone the professional to let him know that he might get a call. When he or she makes contact it is professional courtesy to receive some acknowledgment back. I generally write a note after the first session and later when the counselling has ended.

Referral also raises some potentially uncomfortable feelings. The initial counsellor may feel that he is abandoning or getting rid of a troublesome individual. Sometimes this can indicate counter-transference issues and the counsellor should engage in some self-examination. Only with self-honesty can the counsellor avoid sending mixed messages. There may be similar feelings for the person seeking counselling. If he or she feels rejected then it should be explored with some sensitivity. The obvious risk is that the referral will not be successful.

Once work has begun with another counsellor, the initial referrer should not interfere. He or she might return to complain about the new counsellor, but it is best to encourage the taking of such issues into the new relationship. Unless there is a report of professional misconduct, it is advisable to trust the colleague to judge what is best. It is best to be supportive while maintaining a 'hands off' attitude.

Counselling is more art than science. There is a need for skill but in very good counselling there is something more. It is hard to express and yet it transcends the ordinary. For the Christian counsellor the distinctiveness would be conveyed with such words as 'gift', 'healing' and 'divine presence'. Jesus spoke of such a reality,

'When the Spirit of truth comes, he will guide you into all the truth'. (John 16:13)

In this chapter we have considered some of the dynamics of the counselling process. This awareness is built upon the important skills such as accurate empathy. In the following chapter some of this will be illustrated in a case study and discussion about depression.

Exercise

Write an account of a recent session in which you were the counsellor. Include background details, an extract of the conversation as you remember it (this is called a verbatim) and list the issues that you feel are important. Are there any theological or spiritual dynamics? Arrange to see an experienced counsellor and use this as the data for supervision.

To read further

Gary Collins, *Christian Counselling:* A comprehensive guide, rev.ed., Milton Keynes, England, Word Publishing, 1989. This is a comprehensive book by a Christian psychologist. It has a lot of useful material to guide counselling believers on specific problems such as anxiety, anger, guilt, interpersonal issues, etc.

John and Paula Sandford, *The Transformation of the Inner Man,* Plainfield NJ, Bridge Publishing Co., 1982. This book is written by Christian counsellors and addresses issues of inner healing. I thought that their images were vivid and generally helpful, e.g. inner vows, hearts of stone, bitter root judgments, etc. It is a good example of a Christian approach to an 'uncovering' style of counselling.

Michael Basch, *Doing Psychotherapy*, New York, Basic Books, 1980. This book was written by a leading secular psychoanalyst. It is a superb 'inside look' at the dynamics of counselling from a Self Psychology perspective. It has excerpts from a training counsellor and an experienced supervisor. This is one of the most useful books I have ever read.

George Weinberg, *The Heart of Psychotherapy*, New York, St. Martin's Press, 1984. Again a secular therapist. Very useful book on the practicalities of professional counselling.

DEPRESSION

Depression has been called the 'common cold' of mental health and it often motivates a person to seek counselling. It is more than 'feeling a little blue', since it can lead to considerable anguish and pain. Sometimes the anguish is so overwhelming that the only way out seems to be suicide. In spite of the problems caused by depression it is not widely understood – especially in the Church.

Some devout Christians would equate being depressed with a failure in the practice of their faith. Biblical texts are sometimes used to justify this attitude, for example, 'Rejoice in the Lord always.' (Philippians 4:4) Some who would want to be 'living the victorious Christian life' tend to emphasize being 'up' and make no allowance for 'low' periods. Although it is quite appropriate to pray for healing from chronic depression, a few will get the impression that it is their lack of faith that is to blame – sadly the guilt escalates and the cycle repeats. Yet heroes of the faith like Elijah, Jeremiah, Martin Luther and C. S. Lewis all struggled with despair. In fact the Church does not always care in the best way possible for those who are depressed; too often the advice is 'cheer up' and spiritual help may be limited to 'pray more about it'.

In recent years there has been a great deal of research on depression. Some significant advances in treatment have proved to be very effective. This chapter outlines the clinical nature of depression and suggests some ways of responding to this common difficulty.

Recognizing the Symptoms

Generally, these can be classified in four categories:

1. The *mood* is one of misery. He does not feel better in the presence of good company or enjoy normal activities. Feelings may include sadness, anxiety, despair, guilt, and self-blame. There may be some irritability and a sense of not being able to meet everyday demands. A loss of energy or feeling lethargic is often part of the picture.

2. *Thinking* is usually pessimistic. Consideration is often limited to the negative aspects of the situation. He may suffer a lack of confidence and have thoughts of failure. The past carries unreasonable guilt and self-blame. The future is seen as ominous, bringing the worst of all possible outcomes. Hopelessness and thoughts about suicide are common. Poor memory and difficulty in concentrating are frequent complaints.

3. Changes in *behaviour* may include a decrease in activities, sluggishness, social withdrawal, tearfulness, over-dependence upon people and outbursts of anger. An increase in the use of drugs or alcohol is typical. Depressed people may 'move in slow motion', talk slowly and even appear to think in a sluggish way; alternatively some people are very agitated and restless. The physical appearance can be distinctive with a downcast expression, long mouth, vertical furrowing of the brow, shoulders bent, and a downward gaze.

4. *Physical health* may be affected. Disturbed sleep patterns are a reliable sign of depression. This includes delay in getting to sleep, broken sleep and early-morning waking (two or three hours early and not being able to get back to sleep). Some people sleep excessively but report waking unrefreshed. A loss in weight may be caused by a decrease in appetite. Alternatively 'binge' eating may lead to a sharp increase in weight.

Other difficulties may include aches, pains, gastrointestinal problems, loss of interest in sex, menstrual irregularities and feeling ill.

It is somewhat rare, but depression can be so severe that psychotic symptoms can occur. These can include delusions such as 'I have cancer no matter what the tests say', and hallucinations where voices in the mind confirm feelings of worthlessness. The depressed person can end up in a stupor (i.e. motionless and mute).

Diagnosis

Mental health professionals sometimes distinguish between:

1. A *reactive depression* which is considered to be the result of a loss, trauma or a series of personal problems. The period of depression depends upon the nature of the cause and may last a few days, weeks or even longer.

2. An *endogenous depression* refers to internal causes. It is more puzzling and causes may be difficult to determine. It is likely that there is a physiological dimension to the problem and anti-depressant medication is commonly prescribed. While there are no obvious triggers, counsellors have found that unresolved problems and stress contribute to the mood disorder. Among the characteristic signs that have been cited are: early-morning wakening, feeling better as the day progresses ('I feel better after my morning cuppa'), loss of interest in sexual activity and some women report menstrual irregularities.

DSM III-R is the diagnostic manual of the American Psychiatric Association. It is used internationally to standardize the diagnosis of mental illness. The following criteria are listed for assessing a Major Depressive Episode. With such a depressed adult at least five of the following symptoms will have been present for a period of at least two weeks:

- Poor appetite and significant weight loss when not dieting. Alternatively, increased appetite and significant weight gain.

A weight change of one or two pounds per week or ten pounds per year would be considered significant.

- Depressed mood.

- Insomnia or hypersomnia.

- Psychomotor retardation or agitation.

- Loss of interest or pleasure in usual activities, and/or a decrease in sexual drive.

- Loss of energy or fatigue.

- Feelings of worthlessness, self-reproach, excessive or inappropriate guilt.

- Complaints or evidence of diminished ability to think or concentrate, such as slowed thinking or indecisiveness.

- Recurrent thoughts of death, suicidal thoughts, wishes to be dead or a suicide attempt.[1]

Such a depression may last a year or so without treatment. Approximately six per cent of the population suffer from depression with this severity at some time in the life cycle.[2] I suspect that this figure is a quite low estimate, but it may reflect a very strict reading of the criteria and the degree to which the symptoms are present during the two weeks. *I have seen an elder in an independent Baptist church for a number of years. He has what he calls 'sub-clinical depression' and although he does not make all the criteria listed, his life has been very restricted by short periods of intense depression.*

I would imagine that a large percentage of the population are significantly troubled by symptoms related to depression. The anguish of severe depression is considerable, people who suffer terrible physical pain rarely commit suicide but depressed individuals are commonly at risk.

Example of the assessment of depression

'Sally' came to see me for counselling because she had recently separated from her husband for the fifth time in three years. She was a forty-year-old mother of two teenage children. The impression she gave was of an expensively dressed, slightly over-weight woman, extroverted and apparently easy-going but her humour was hollow and her smile had a brittle quality. My impression was that she was 'almost attractive'. I asked her the standard questions for depression.

Counsellor: *'How are you sleeping?'*

Sally: *'Not very well, I haven't for years.'*

C: *'Do you have trouble getting to sleep or is it waking early?'*

S: *'I often wake at about three a.m. but most of the time I get back to sleep.'*

C: *'After how long?'*

S: *'Maybe an hour or two. My doctor has given me some mild sleeping pills, but I rarely take them.'*

C: *'Have you lost or gained weight in the last year?'*

S: *'Gained.'*

C: *'How much!'*

S: *'About nineteen pounds over the last two years. I am looking more like the "before" in a Weight Watchers' ad. If I could only become the "after".'* (briefly laughs)

C: *'How do you feel about yourself?'*

S: *'Rotten. I hate the way I look. I keep blaming myself for everything that happens to the family – even things that I have nothing to do with. I go to Mass regularly, but I still feel cut off from God. I am not sure I am making any sense. I can't seem to concentrate any more. I hope this isn't confusing you.'*

C: *'I think I can follow you. Is your self-esteem low?'*

S: *'Yes, very.'*

C: *'Have you ever wished you were dead?'*

S: *'You mean being suicidal?'*

C: *'Yes.'*

S: *'I tried to cut my wrists when I was sixteen. My mother was very worried and I spent three months in hospital. I suppose I was being silly at the time. I haven't tried anything since then but I have been tempted. Especially lately.'*

In spite of her 'cheerful' appearance 'Sally was very seriously depressed. The depression was somewhat masked and may well have led her GP astray. She was positive on most of the diagnostic criteria of depression. It must be emphasized that such objective criteria are more important than any visual impression. Her history was also relevant. Since there had been a suicide attempt, she was at a greater risk for another attempt. There was also a suspicion that she was abusing alcohol. When I asked directly about her drinking patterns she was evasive. In a note to her doctor I suggested that she be assessed for anti-depressant medication and listed the relevant criteria.

Somer clergy or pastoral care workers will decide to refer to a mental health counsellor at this point. However in isolated places such a referral might not be an option. In addition a lack of finances may be a barrier to professional treatment when there is no local government health clinic. In such cases the less experienced counsellor will have to learn quickly and try to help the distressed individual. This is the quickest way to gain experience!

Assessing the risk of suicide

There is no possible way to be absolutely certain about the risk of suicide. But it is important to be aware of factors that increase the risk and this may help the counsellor make an informed judgment.

When a depressed person admits to thoughts about suicide, it is important to question carefully whether he has a specific plan, whether the means are available (e.g. sometimes a supply of sleeping pills is hidden away), and whether he is living alone. To what extent is despair dominating the mood?[3] In dealing with the potentially suicidal person it is advisable to get the address and phone number, since that information may prove to be vital in a later emergency. Briefly, the following factors increase the risk:

1. Any prior attempts at suicide, especially with more violent means such as firearms.

2. Any treatment for psychotic episodes in which there is a loss of the sense of reality. Quite a few mentally ill people with diagnosis such as schizophrenia or manic depression will attempt suicide and many succeed.

3. Alcohol or substance abuse. In parish ministry I have conducted funerals for a number of suicides; all had been alcoholics.

4. Friends or relatives who have attempted or succeeded at suicide. Teenagers and young adults sometimes 'copycat' suicides.[4] Suicide may be a theme that runs through the generations of some families.

5. There is a greater risk with patients with a chronic debilitating disease and a poor prognosis. A positive test for AIDS might lead to such a crisis.

6. The statistics indicate that males tend to commit suicide at a greater frequency than women. This is probably because males tend to use more violent means.[5] It may be surprising, but the risk also increases with age.

7. A role crisis may lead to an attempt. Examples of this would include the loss of a job, exclusion from a peer group and a broken relationship.

The counsellor should be alert to what is implied. One example of this is metaphors.

One trainee therapist conducted an intake interview with a young man who said, 'I am seeking a peace deeper than sleep.' She correctly challenged him, 'You mean that you are thinking of killing yourself.' In this instance she forced him to face the reality of what he intended to do.

We should be cautious about removing any barrier to the self-destructive act. *An elderly parishioner once said, 'I want to end it all, but God would send me to hell if I did it.'* It was not the time to straighten out a questionable theology!

A final thought on assessing the risk of suicide. Sometimes an individual who has been suicidal will appear to brighten up. It is easy to conclude that the danger has passed. However, the risk may then be at its highest. George Weinberg advised, 'The jeopardy may be greatest just as the depression begins to lift. While the person was numbed by heavy melancholy, he found it hard to do anything, even to kill himself. Feeling slightly better, he may now have the clarity and the energy to go through with it.'[6] The thought of 'ending it all' or of ceasing existence may be very appealing. It can become the only hope for a despairing person.

Causes of depression

There have been numerous attempts to explain the causes of depression. Some of the physical factors that have been linked with depression include influenza, glandular fever and certain endocrine disorders. There may also be a genetic factor since severe depression can have an inter-generational pattern. More recently biochemical explanations have been produced. Psychological theories about what causes depression come from a variety of sources including Freud and psychoanalysis, Seligman's theory of 'learned helplessness' and cognitive psychology.[7] Gender factors in depression have been explored in a recent study, *Women and Depression: Risk Factors and Treatment Issues*.[8] Although there are various arguments for and against these theories, the positions are not necessarily mutually exclusive. The major focus here will be on more accessible aspects of treatment.

Treatment of depression

A medical doctor, after a diagnosis of depression, will often prescribe some form of anti-depressant medication for the depressed patient. This medication includes both tricyclics (brand names such as Tryptanol and Sinequan) and monoamine oxidase inhibitors (Nardil and more recent medications such as Aurorix). Sometimes medication alone is judged to be a sufficient treatment. In very severe cases electroconvulsive therapy (ECT) may be recommended. This can be most effective. There is some fear and a great deal of misinformation about it.

The best results in counselling appear to come from *cognitive therapy*.[10] Counselling should certainly be included in an overall treatment plan since this is an attempt to treat the causes rather than to mask the symptoms.

Dr Aaron T. Beck developed the cognitive approach to the psychological treatment of depression at the Mood Clinic at the University of Pennsylvania Medical Center. He argued that reactive depression is not primarily an emotional disorder so much as a result of negative thinking. The natural progression is from events to thoughts about what has occurred, to emotional reactions and then to behaviour. Thus the feelings of depression are not spontaneous but arise from personal meanings given to events in life.

David Burns has popularized this therapy in *Feeling Good* and his recommendation illustrates the logical steps in this process, 'Every time you feel depressed about something, try to identify a corresponding negative thought you had just prior to and during the depression. Because these thoughts have actually created your bad mood, by learning to restructure them, you can change your mood.[11] Burns listed nine common forms of cognitive distortion:

1. *All-or-nothing thinking*. Everything is seen in absolute terms. If a sprinter runs second in a race, he might conclude, 'I am a total failure.' Other people are either 'black' or 'white', wonderful or terrible, for or against me, good or bad. Everything is polarized.

2. *Overgeneralization*. A single event is seen as part of an overall negative pattern. It is a case of 'here we go again'. One mistake, or defeat, or unpleasant event becomes a prescription for the future. 'Damn! I dropped the tray. I will always be a clumsy idiot.'

3. *Mental filter*. The exclusive focus is on a single negative event

and the whole picture is ignored. This effectively dismisses anything positive in the situation, 'I have two freckles on my nose, I am ugly, ugly, ugly!'

4. *Jumping to conclusions.* A negative interpretation is made without any real evidence. This includes 'mind-reading' which is a form of jumping to conclusions: 'When I see you sitting there I *know* that you are angry with me.' Another variant is called 'fortune-teller' when it is anticipated that everything will turn out badly and this conclusion is then taken as an established fact.

5. *Magnification or minimization.* This is a 'no-win' situation in which the importance of bad things is exaggerated while personal assets are minimized: 'You think that I am clever just because I got into the class for gifted students. But I can't keep up in the physics stream. Most of the time I don't even think that I belong.' Closely related to this is 'catastrophizing', in that whatever can go wrong will go wrong!

6. *Emotional reasoning.* This is the mistake of confusing feelings with facts. An older man lamented, 'I feel so guilty that I must have done something very wrong.'

7. *'Should' statements.* This is a case of unrealistic self-expectations. The words 'should', 'must' and 'ought' commonly occur in thoughts and conversation: 'I must get this right' (and everything depends upon it!).

8. *Labelling.* Instead of admitting a mistake or error, he blames himself and attaches a negative label: 'I missed that shot on the seventeenth hole, I am a born loser.' Such language is usually highly coloured and emotionally loaded.

9. *Personalizing.* He takes responsibility for everything that goes wrong: 'It's all my fault.' If a member of the family is in a bad mood, 'I must have caused it.'

Beck labelled this kind of thinking 'automatic thoughts' and it is perfectly natural for a depressed person to think this way. The central work of cognitive therapy is to identify such thoughts and to change them.

Australian authors Susan Tanner and Jillian Ball have written an excellent self-help book called *Beating the Blues.*[12] It gives a much fuller outline of treatment, together with straightforward exercises. Tanner and Ball give the following steps:

Step 1   The client is taught to make a daily diary. This record is used to note situations in which he felt 'down', identify feelings, automatic thoughts that accompanied the mood, why these are distortions, assess the strength of feelings and the degree of belief in the negative thoughts. This can be tallied in columns and sometimes graph paper is useful for recording the number of occurrences.

Step 2   The person is taught to recognize faulty thinking in each automatic thought. This may include identifying patterns such as 'black and white' thinking, setting unrealistic expectations, seeing only the negative, mistaking feelings for facts, etc.

Step 3   The next step is to challenge the thoughts by questioning the logic of the assumptions. This is a critical process and involves gathering evidence to prove or disprove the assumptions, looking for alternative explanations and trying to put the situation into a wider perspective. It is like having a 'mental debating team'.

When a young army corporal received his first 'less than glowing' report, he felt that it was the end of his career in the services. After some counselling he became familiar with challenging his distortions and he was able to put up an alternative case: 'I have been promoted early. I have been given the toughest assignments and in every case so far I have exceeded the expectations of my superiors. I haven't adjusted well to the computer systems environment here, but I am sure that I will find my skills better suited in my new posting.'

Step 4   More positive thoughts about the self are encouraged. In contrast to having the automatic negative thoughts, he could keep repeating such thoughts as 'I am a worthwhile person, I may not be perfect, but I am loved by my family and can be happy about my uniqueness, etc.'

Step 5 Other thought control techniques can be used such as: thought stopping (e.g. imagine a stop sign to halt an unwanted train of thoughts), and distraction (e.g. go and visit a friend or watch a movie). It may be helpful to rehearse with a counsellor or friend how a difficult situation might be handled. Another technique that is useful is to have a period of worry or sadness each day, about half an hour is usually sufficient. By facing worries and upsets they may be pre-empted and kept from intruding at other times in the day.

I have also employed a reframe technique that changes the context for thinking about an event. After making an embarrassing slip of the tongue, I might think 'I am allowed three slips of the tongue per day; this was the first.' If it's a bad day and four mistakes were made, then it is the one day in the month I am allowed to make that many slips!' This is also helpful for parking tickets and speeding fines – they still cost the same but the self-recrimination is less.

The cognitive strategies about right thinking can easily be used with a supportive style of Christian counselling. Jesus emphasized the importance of a right 'heart' (e.g. Matthew 5:28). This would have included thoughts that govern inner attitudes. The apostle Paul wrote specifically about the need to transform our thinking, 'Do not be conformed to this world, but be transformed by the renewing of your minds' (Romans 12:2). The importance of reading and meditating on the Scriptures cannot be overemphasized. This provides an opportunity to allow our minds to be shaped by grace – by what God has done for us in Christ. Paul also advised, 'Finally, beloved, whatever is true, whatever is honourable, whatever is just, whatever is pure, whatever is pleasing, whatever is commendable, if there is any excellence, and if there is anything worthy of praise, think about these things' (Philippians 4:8-9).

Sometimes a believer will feel so guilty, usually as part of a depression, that he will believe that he has somehow committed the unforgivable sin and fears that he has blasphemed the Holy Spirit by thinking some unworthy thought against God (Hebrews 6:4-6). This usually has an obsessive quality accompanied by persistent anxiety and fear of being damned by God. It is usually sufficient to consider this as a case of depression and assure the person that God forgives all our sins in Christ (I John 1:9; 2:1-3).

It is timely for the distressed person to think carefully about his relationship with God. If he had sinned in such a way and was forsaken by God, he would hardly be so full of the conviction of his sin, since this is a unique ministry of the Holy Spirit (John 16:8-11).

Another resource for those burdened by guilt is sacramental confession. This should be used for genuine guilt rather than false guilt: 'I missed the seven a.m. Eucharist last Tuesday.' Over the centuries many devout believers have found it gives reassurance of forgiveness and reconciliation. In non-Catholic traditions it may be possible to find other ways of consoling the penitent believer, perhaps by reading scriptural promises and a prayer together.

Some styles of biblical counselling are overly confrontational.[13] Sometimes it amounts to the blinkered approach of seeing all psychological distress as the result of sin. The inevitable result of this logic is to restrict the cure to repentance. Some sincere people will repent and repent but with no lasting relief. This can be quite destructive for those with tender consciences. Even more common are endless petitions such as 'Oh, Lord, please heal me.' It almost goes without saying that some understanding of the nature of depression would help the Christian counsellor.

Example of Nick

Nick, a Ph.D. student, had recently begun to attend a Christian group on the local university campus. He had spent the last two years gathering his research data, but he had a problem with procrastination. Over the previous few months he had begun to be more aware of his negative thinking. After about six counselling sessions he became very familiar with the tenets of cognitive therapy.

Nick: *'But I can't seem to get the results the team had hoped for. It was to be a real breakthrough.'*
Counsellor: *'But some of your hypotheses had been confirmed?'*
N: *'Yes, that is true enough. It's just that unless it is completely*

right, I feel that nothing has been achieved. It will never get
finished, everyone will think of me as a failure and I'll have to
leave the university.'
C: *'Hold on! Haven't you made some jumps in your logic?'*
N: *'Yes, it is just as we have talked about. All the traps again. I*
have magnified, catastrophized, overgeneralized and read the
"crystal ball" again. It is no wonder my feelings are rotten.'
C: *'How would you challenge such thoughts?'*
N: *'I suppose that it is more accurate to say that it is original*
research and my supervisor is pleased with my progress. I have
good skills in writing and the deadlines will be met as they have
in the past. Just because I feel this way does not mean that
everything is hopeless and my scholarship is about to be
cancelled.' (He laughs and smiles for the first time in the session)

Nick later joined a Bible study group in his residential college and
gradually became more active in a local Anglican church. It is often
overlooked that there is a great benefit in belonging to a church.
It is a healing community that is unrelated to government mental
health facilities. Even for those quite crippled by the effects of
depression, the normal interaction is with people who are not in
a present crisis and have no history of mental illness. There are also
psychological gains in participating in the sacraments, experiences
of worship, and in taking the opportunity to serve others. It is
reassuring to me as the rector of a parish to see such improvement
by participation in the life of the church.

A case study in Postviral Syndrome
Usually counselling is not so clear-cut. Depression may be part of
a more complex picture. Physical complications such as chronic
pain can add to the distress and contribute to despair. Moods can
be mixed. Severe depression can coexist with anxiety problems.
The following case study is an example of this overlapping.

Jonathan was twenty-five and a recent graduate in architecture.
He had been briefly engaged but was now single. His mother

brought him to the first session. It was obvious that he was very upset. He appeared to be tense and quite agitated. Initially he seemed to be in some danger of a psychotic breakdown. Although it is good to be cautious, I later realized that he was one of those people who look much worse in the first session. He was intensely focused on symptoms which both he and his mother believed related to Postviral Syndrome following glandular fever. He was very dependent upon his mother who brought him to the first few sessions. His father, a senior partner in a prominent law firm, was described as somewhat intimidating and emotionally distant from the rest of the family.

The GP had prescribed medication for both the depressive and anxiety symptoms, with Prothiaden and Valium. In the first few sessions we focused more on his activity level. He agreed to chart his activity (scale 1-100), assess his mood (scale 1-10) and level of discomfort from anxiety (scale 1-10). The daily scores were placed on a graph. He proved to be very diligent in this homework exercise. He had some slight obsessional tendencies which led to high compliance. I was also delighted when his improvement was almost immediate. He began walking in the local park and this activity built up to a number of kilometres per day in the next few weeks. About three months later he was able to tolerate returning to part-time work and then he built up the daily hours. The main thrust of counselling was to support him, assist the exploration of feelings and help him to be more aware of interpersonal dynamics. He was gradually able to become more assertive and it was a great triumph when he was able to confront his father on an important issue.

It is worth noting that in counselling, depression will often improve 'spontaneously' as the person gives attention to pressing matters. The example of Jonathan and his recovery over the period of about a year was such a case.

There is an important role for clergy and lay leadership in helping depressed people. Sometimes it will be primarily supportive in association with out-patient or psychiatric help at a local hospital.

In the various parishes I have served there has usually been at least one person who has been kept from suicide by the loving support of a network of parishioners. In general, the help has been mostly practical such as inviting the individual for dinner or helping with shopping. There is also a 'front line' role in counselling the depressed in our congregations. A nondirective and empathic style of counselling will generally help a depressed individual. I find that people with moderate or mild depression will usually improve quickly. There is more need for caution with severe and chronic depression. In all cases the risk of suicide must be carefully assessed and this will be a factor in the decision of when to refer.

Exercises

Share with a close friend or with others in a training group a time in which you felt very low. Did you have any thoughts like 'I would be better off dead'? What did you find helpful in what the others said? Did you talk with other Christians? Was it of any benefit?

Read through the 'Sermon on the Mount' (Matthew 5-7). Can you identify anything Jesus said here that would be relevant to a depressed Christian?

To read further

D. Burns, *Feeling Good: The New Mood Therapy*, S & W, Melbourne, 1980. This is a popularization of Beck's important concepts of cognitive therapy. It is an excellent book, perhaps more suited for readers with a tertiary background.

S. Tanner and J. Ball, *Beating the Blues: A Self-Help Approach to Overcoming Depression*, Doubleday, Sydney, 1991. Very readable for people of all backgrounds. The authors are Australian. The exercises are straightforward and helpful.

INCEST

A few years ago a cartoon appeared in a magazine. It showed a large crowd standing around an open manhole. From the drain, the tentacles of a giant octopus were coming out and dragging helpless victims to certain doom. The crowd watched passively. Two men walked past and one said, 'It doesn't take much to draw a crowd in New York City'. In the past, incest has been hidden beneath manholes of secrecy, but like the tentacles of the octopus, it has touched the lives of many people.

It is difficult to estimate the incidence of incest in our society. The Kinsey Report in 1953 documented a five per cent rate among women, but this was largely ignored by a society not ready to face the implications. Today the issues are more likely to be discussed, but the statistics remain difficult to assess. One of the main problems is finding a definition of incest that researchers can agree upon. Incest is one part of the more general category of sexual abuse[1] which includes date rape, a stranger who exposes himself masturbating, voyeurism or a 'peeping Tom', obscene phone calls, gay bashing and sexual harassment at work.

Wendy Maltz defines sexual abuse: it 'occurs whenever one person dominates and exploits another by means of sexual activity or suggestion.'[2] Although incest is certainly sexual abuse, the scope is much narrower. The following definition has been suggested: 'the involvement of dependent, developmentally immature children or adolescents in sexual activities that they are unable to give informed consent to, and that violate the social taboos or family roles.'

Most women have experienced sexual abuse in some context. It is now relatively common for women to report experiences of sexual exploitation in their family-of-origin, but full sexual intercourse with close relatives is more rare. The most recent estimates that I have heard is that between 20 per cent and 30 per cent of all women have had unwanted sexual contact with a male before their eighteenth birthday, 8.5 per cent to 15 per cent report sexual contact with a close family member and 1 per cent to 4.5 per cent report being sexually abused by their biological father, adoptive father or stepfather.[3] It is hard to be more precise, but survivors are now seeking counselling in greater numbers.

The Bible is an honest document. In it there is an accurate portrayal of the complexities of family relationships including illicit sexual activity. The daughters of Lot took the initiative, 'Come, let us make our father drink wine, and we will lie with him, so that we may preserve offspring through our father' (Genesis 19:32). Among King David's children there was an incident of incest rape. Amnon schemed to seduce his sister Tamar. He pretended to be ill and when she came to him, 'He took hold of her, and said to her, "Come, lie with me, my sister." She answered him, "No, my brother, do not force me; for such a thing is not done in Israel; do not do anything so vile!" . . . But he would not listen to her; and being stronger than she, he forced her and lay with her' (Samuel 13:11-14).

There were specific prohibitions in the Law about incest. This was spelt out in terms of the sanctity of family relationships (Leviticus 18:6-18). The people of Israel were to be different, 'Do not defile yourselves in any of these ways' (Leviticus 18:24). The biblical guidelines leave the reader in no doubt about what was not permitted.

The taboo against incest has been more or less universal.[4] In our society the issue is more openly discussed but there are factors that make it confusing. The young are seen as sexual objects in advertising and in the media. R-rated movies promote rape myths such as 'she really wants it' and 'no' means 'yes'. Pornography is even more blatant and gives permission for deviant sexual practices. We live in a society in which there is greater diversity in sexual relationships and noticeably less moral restraint from traditional authorities such as the Church. The nuclear family is fragmenting into 'variations on a theme'.

The nature of abuse and risk factors

Although there are many varieties of incest the main focus in this chapter will be father-daughter incest. From clinical experience it is possible to list the factors that increase the risk:

- Alcoholism or alcohol abuse by the father.
- A sexually unresponsive mother.
- A mother incapacitated by illness, depression, mental illness or frequently absent.
- An eldest daughter who adopts the role of mother in caring for younger siblings.
- A father with a psychopathic personality, psychosis, or mental retardation.
- A previous history of incest in the family. [5]

Father-daughter incest is common, but it is not the only kind of sexual abuse in families. I have seen survivors of uncle-niece intercourse, grandfather-granddaughter molesting, brother-sister relationships, stepfather-stepdaughter sexual activity, abuse of adopted children and homosexual molestation. The effects are traumatic even years later. The developing sexual self is fragile and easily damaged by such abuse. This is highlighted by Peter Horsfield. 'Most sexual assaults are not random incidents against which one can take precautionary action: most sexual assaults are calculated exploitations of trust relationships. They are generally premeditated and well planned and in many cases are carried out by men whom the woman or girl and society have looked on and trusted as a protector. This compounds the effect by undermining the woman's sense of trust in trust relationships, in social institutions and in her own judgement and undermines her sense of security and safety even in familiar environments.'[6] It is an abuse of power and trust.

I have not encountered a case of mother-son incest. It appears to be relatively rare. However, when it does occur it may be disguised as care taking (e.g. inspecting genitals or still wiping the backside of a twelve-year-old boy). Full sexual intercourse would appear to be even less common.[7]

The nature of the abuse tends to vary with the age of the victim. When men are the perpetrators it appears that fondling and oral-genital contact are most common with pre-puberty children. Sometimes digital insertion and even anal penetration occurs. After age twelve vaginal intercourse is preferred. The duration of abuse varies from a single incident to infrequent encounters to years of sustained abuse.

Younger children are usually compliant with adults and tend to take what is said on face value. Initially a young child may not be aware that it is sexual activity. The perpetrator may want to play a 'game'. Sometimes the sexual advances are disguised as affection or as part of a 'special relationship' (which may be highly valued by the child as the only attention received). The emotional aftermath may be very confusing and can include the mixed feelings of guilt, anger, fear and regret.

The nature of sexual abuse varies. It may be gentle from the 'nice' father or relative, but the results of this can be even more insidious because of the resulting confusion. Very young children may play along with the game before they know that something is wrong. Children may agonize about how much they can resist. Bribery may then become part of the coercion and this can leave a legacy of guilt. Some children are passive, 'I felt nothing', 'I pretended to be asleep', or dissociating, 'It was as if I floated on the ceiling'. When a girl reaches her early teens she may discover that it is perverse but feel powerless to do anything about the abuse. There may also be mixed feelings especially if there are some pleasurable feelings or even orgasms. Clearly the result may be unwarranted guilt. If the girl resists such advances then the result may be violence and rape. This can be a reason behind some teenage 'acting out' which can include rebellion, running away from home, promiscuity, early pregnancy, substance abuse and suicide attempts. At least such behaviour enables some teenagers to get help by coming to the attention of school counsellors.

The psychological effect also tends to differ with the age of onset of the abuse. Incest in infancy or when a toddler is comparatively rare but the physical trauma can be so severe as to disrupt a sense of physical integrity, of a separate self and of basic trust. Preschool children tend to cope through denial and dissociation. It has been reported that 95 per cent of people suffering from multiple personality disorder report sexual abuse between three and five years of age. The average age of the first incident of incest is between seven and nine years of age. In this period the abuse inhibits the development of self-competence and increases the feelings of guilt and shame. In adolescence incest disrupts the development of sexual identity and the normal formation of opposite-sex relationships. Adolescents who become victims after puberty tend to be comparatively less injured in psychological terms.[8]

Signs

There has been a lot of debate on the topic of what constitutes legal evidence for child sexual assault. A child's testimony now requires other support. Some element of caution is warranted since there have been cases of discredited and even fabricated evidence. This has been especially common in custody battles. However, the following would be considered 'hard signs':

- Injuries to vaginal, urinary or anal areas.

- Venereal diseases such as herpes or syphilis.
- Genital warts.
- Compulsive masturbatory activity in pre-puberty children.
- Sexually explicit language and overtly sexual games by young children (after excluding the possible influence of X-rated videos).

Since family secrecy is usually such a high barrier, 'spontaneous' reports by children and adolescents should be initially given every benefit of the doubt. Testimony should be considered credible until proved false. It is equally important that the accused be seen as innocent until it is proved beyond all doubt that he or she is guilty. I have seen the cost in human terms when accusations are made without adequate grounds.

It is natural for a child to both love and depend upon parents – even when this trust is betrayed. This means that there will be impossible dilemmas around family loyalty for most victims. The abusing parent may demand secrecy but the child needs help and understanding. A child may fear the split-up of his parents if the incest is known and then will legitimately worry about 'Who will look after me?' It is not uncommon for the victim to face family hostility when the 'secret' is revealed.

Incest victims tend to construct their own meanings about the abuse. The most common reaction is self-blame. 'This can only be happening because I am such a bad person.' This leaves a legacy of guilt and self-hate. There are, of course, profound spiritual implications.

Family dynamics

There is no 'typical family', but there may be common features. *A number of years ago I saw a woman in a counselling clinic in the USA. She was most distressed at the recent discovery that her ex-husband had been sexually abusing a number of her daughters. She had married an academic and he had a very successful career. The marriage had been troubled from the beginning, but they had managed to 'keep up appearances' as a happy family with a wide circle of friends and had been active in the local Methodist Church. She had been divorced for three years. She was gradually adjusting to single life and at last finding some self-respect. Now everything seemed about to collapse. She felt an array of emotions: intense anger, a sense of being betrayed, guilt for not being more protective and rejection as a woman.*

This case had some familiar themes. Incest is equally prevalent in the professional and middle classes as in lower socioeconomic classes. Nor is active participation in a church a barrier. Too often abuse is hidden behind a veneer of respectability. The wife was distancing emotionally and the husband felt emotionally deprived. Unfortunately he felt entitled to seek affection and nurture elsewhere. He may not have begun with sexual intent but even affection tends to be sexualized in our culture. I am not trying to excuse the father. Incest is a criminal offence and the responsibility for setting appropriate limits is always with the adult. However, he should not be made a scapegoat in the treatment process. From a family systems perspective we can see other dynamics in the incest family. For example, the mother might be encouraged to examine her role in neglecting the sexual side of the marriage and failing to see suspicious signs that might have been present.

It is also too simplistic to dismiss the abuser as a pervert or sick person. The offender is rarely a paedophile, or a molester of children, even if the abuse is with a young child. The paedophile is usually more sexually immature and tends to see himself at the age of the child with looking and touching the most frequent activities.[9] The incest offender is more adult in sexual orientation, preferring a mature sexual partner and in erotic fantasy will imagine that the child is an adult.

The first priority in treatment is to guarantee the safety of the victim. The counsellor cannot allow himself or herself to be part of a conspiracy of silence. Mandatory reporting is usually a legal requirement. Sometimes this has led to the removal of a child from the family. For a number of reasons I think this can be a mistake.

If the child leaves there is a natural tendency for the family to regroup and exclude the child, in effect saying, 'It is all your fault!' The victim can be blamed for 'lying' or for 'telling'. There can be a resulting attitude of 'We're getting along fine now' and less motivation to work on the issues with the father still part of the family. There is also the risk of the father abusing the next sibling in line after the daughter is removed. It is better to place the blame on the offender, symbolically removing the guilty party, rather than having the child leave with the uniformed police as if he or she is being taken away to jail. There is considerably more leverage for the therapeutic process if the family want the father to return.

It is common for the family to disintegrate after the discovery of sexual abuse. The mother's denial will finally break down and the incest becomes the 'final straw'. However, if the couple decide to work on their relationship, then there may be a need for individual, marital and family therapy.[10] Sometimes group therapy for offenders is helpful. The TV movie *Something About Amelia* (1984) gave a realistic picture of the effects of incest in a middle-class family. There was a positive outcome to treatment. My only reservation was with the removal of the thirteen-year-old daughter from the home rather than the father being forced to leave.

I should emphasize that the child or adolescent should never be blamed for being seductive. It is healthy and natural for a child to be affectionate in families and this should not be mistaken for a sexual advance. It is also appropriate for developing teenagers to 'try out' their sexuality on their opposite sex parent with innocent flirting. It is natural to want to be admired and affirmed in the gender identity. Current awareness of abuse may, however, have produced an adverse climate in that some fathers are now reluctant to hug their daughters or to show any affection for fear of misunderstanding.

Return of the memories

The victim may repress the memories after the period of abuse and 'forget' what happened. Often this inner barrier breaks down in the adult years and frightening memories may motivate the person to seek help.

The disturbing memories will slowly return. There is no need to hurry this healing process. As Dr Judy Herman, author of *Father-Daughter Incest*, [11] advised her patients, 'You will get your memories when it is safe.' I have found that a gentle, non-intrusive interest is sufficient. There is no need for the counsellor to 'hear all the details', but there should be an understanding that he will listen to whatever needs to be shared. It seems to work out in practice that some survivors will want to share everything, while others simply want companionship while the private memories return.

It is wise also to be cautious at this point. There is some recent evidence that memories can be 'created', especially if counsellors communicate expectation of childhood sexual abuse. I believe that it is important to get other evidence before confronting relatives or making charges. [12]

Survivors of incest commonly present to counsellors as adults with symptoms such as depression, low self-esteem, impulsive and self-destructive activity, recurrent nightmares, dissociating and depersonalizing experiences. Relationship problems are almost the norm, with difficulties in trust and intimacy, lack of mutuality, passivity with a pattern of 'being taken advantage of', and sometimes explosive anger. Traits such as impulsiveness and lack of self-respect lead to revictimization. I have begun to appreciate that for many of us our sexual self is the most damaged part of our human nature. [13]

Additional risk factors

There are three factors that can add to the risk of the sexual abuse of children: blended families, alcohol and involvement in Satanic cults.

1. The breakdown of the traditional nuclear family has led to a

great diversity in what is considered 'family' in our society. One result of a higher divorce rate is the number of reconstituted or blended families. As if there were not plenty of difficulties, there can also be sexual tensions between stepfather and stepdaughter or between stepmother and stepson. To some extent, it is the attraction of a younger version of the mate and the natural taboo is weakened by an absence of blood relationship. I would still think that incest is an appropriate label for such sexual activity. The relationship between Humbert and his stepdaughter was the subject of the novel *Lolita* by Vladimir Nabokov. The recent scandal of the relationship between Woody Allen and Mia Farrow's adopted stepdaughter, Soon-Yi, is also an example of the difficult issues of complex family relationships.

Karin Meiselman has made some suggestions to minimize the danger in blended families: strengthen the sense of family bond, call parents 'Dad' and 'Mum', perhaps adopt stepchildren and ensure that the sexual needs of parents are met in the marriage relationship.

2. Alcohol is a common factor in incest families. The abuse of alcohol tends to increase impulsivity and reduce moral inhibition. Alcoholics sometimes have an unhealthy sense of entitlement and this can extend to the attitude that 'I have a right to meet my sexual needs.' There may be a misguided sense of 'ownership' of those in the immediate family. Some alcoholic fathers are violent and physically abusive. Unfortunately this can lead to rape of both the wife and children.

3. There has been a recent increase in awareness among mental health professionals of the abuse of children in the rites of Satanic cults. This is now called Ritual Abuse.[14] The stories of horrific abuse include incest and other atrocities. The victims suffer not only the damage to the sexual self through incest but the lasting effects of the ritualized trauma. This 'stone is being overturned' and health professionals are addressing the issue in its clinical dimension. I hope that Christian counsellors will give

a lead in recognizing the spiritual danger of this manifestation of evil. Perhaps clergy can offer healing rituals to survivors.

There are also certain common precursors of sexual abuse. David Finkelhor has proposed a model of four:

1. The offender has some motivation to abuse the child or adolescent sexually (e.g. abuse when the offender was a child, misattribution of arousal cues, excitement through child pornography).
2. He has a lack of internal restraints (e.g. impulse disorder, alcohol intoxication, senility, psychosis).
3. He has to deal with external constraints (e.g. social isolation of the family, lack of supervision, wife away from home, cramped sleeping conditions).
4. He must undermine or overcome the child's resistance to the sexual activity. I am encouraged that school programmes are now helping children to say 'no' to adults and to assert that 'This is *my* body.'

Treatment with offenders can address these areas and hopefully reinforce the barriers.

A case of sibling incest

Mary, a young female police constable, had just moved to Canberra from Brisbane. She came to me with some concerns about the pressure her de facto was placing on her to have 'his child'. She was also troubled about flashes of irrational anger which she felt might hurt any future children. She had a history of unstable relationships and the present 'live-in' was 'a bit of a problem'.

As she spoke of her childhood it was obvious that she had been impoverished not only by a lack of money but by emotional deprivation. She had attended fifteen schools before her twelfth birthday. There was no sense of approval from her parents. Her father was frequently violent. When she was in her teenage years her mother repeatedly called her a slut. She could remember few friends since her parents assessed them as 'not good enough'.

In the first session the following inter-generational diagram (see Chapter 9 for an explanation of the symbols) was drawn:

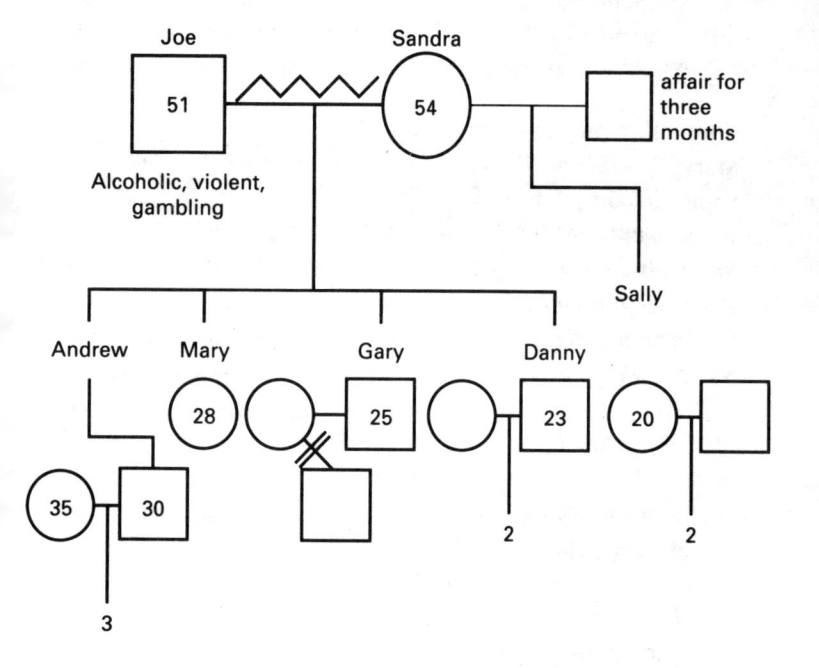

I also noted that she was very depressed with the following indicators:

- restless sleep, waking at 3 a.m. and then having difficulty getting back to sleep,
- less energy at work,
- guilt feelings generally related to past relationships,
- low self-esteem,

- gained three kilos in the last three months,
- complaints about being more irritable,
- and some suicidal ideation.

I was concerned and made a note to refer her back to her GP for assessment for antidepressant medication.

I then asked her a series of standard questions associated with intergenerational themes. These included:

> Counsellor: *'Any child sexual abuse?'*
> Mary: (hesitating) *'I am not sure. . . What would you call a passionate kiss from my father?'*
> C: *'Sexual abuse. How old were you?'*
> M: *'Thirteen. I was being driven home from a school dance. I think my father had had a few drinks.'*
> C: *'Anything else?'*
> M: *'Not with Dad.'*
> C: *'Oh?'*
> M: *'Well, when I was a teenager I was in love with my older brother Andrew.'*
> C: *'You were intimate with him?'*
> M: *'We had a sexual relationship for about two years until he left to join the Navy. I really missed him for months. Then Gary took his place.'*
> C: *'Your younger brother?'*
> M: *'Yes. And over the next few years I was also with Danny as well. I thought that if they came to me they would leave Sally alone.'*

It was obvious that all the brothers felt that they had 'rights' and even approached Mary when she was living on her own. I did not dwell on this issue for more than a few minutes. There were other family problems and I wanted to get an overview of her family-of-origin. Sibling incest rarely happens in a family where there is adequate parenting.[15] Since Mary was not clear about the abusive nature of what had happened, it was quite a few sessions before she realized that she was the victim of incest.

Mary was far more concerned about the turmoil in her adult relationships. The following part of the genogram shows her adult history with sexual partners:

Mary had a variety of relationships with single men before her early twenties. Since then her partners have tended to be married. It was a concern to her that she tended to end such affairs by getting involved in another affair. There were unresolved feelings about giving up Kylie for adoption. She also had two abortions and there was some regret over not having Kylie with her - even if it meant caring for her as a single mother.

I encouraged Mary to read *Women Who Love Too Much*[16] by Robin Norwood. A week later she began to think about the implications:

Mary: *'I always went along. I would do whatever he wanted.'*
Counsellor: *'It was hard to stand up for yourself?'*
M: *'No, I wasn't a wimp. I just used to think that whatever he wanted was most important.'*
C: *'Can you give me a specific example?'*
M: *'Well, with Craig. He didn't want the baby. Though I knew it was wrong - and I wanted the baby - I still went through with the abortion. The bastard didn't even come with me.'*
C: *'You had to face it all alone?'*

M: 'Sally drove me, but she couldn't come into the clinic. (tears) But it is so typical. I did it for Craig, but I don't think he gave a damn.'

C: 'So you gave and gave. It is disappointing that it made no difference.'

M: 'Yes, it has always been that way.'

This was progress. Mary was beginning to recognize the pattern of her relationships.

M: 'I get tired of the quick sex with Sam. Whenever he's in the mood he wants to jump into bed with me.'

C: 'And you never refuse?'

M: 'Well, no. Sometimes I manage to distract him, but – no.'

C: 'Were you ever able to refuse sex with your brothers?'

M: 'I was glad to be with Andrew. He loved me. But it wasn't the same with Gary and Danny. Even when I was on my own in the flat in Melbourne, Danny would come around half-drunk. Eventually he lost interest.'

C: 'So saying no has been hard, even when you really wanted to refuse.'

M: 'Yes. (hesitantly) I suppose it hasn't helped how I feel about myself?'

C: 'Yes, that is a good connection. There doesn't seem to have been any boundaries in your home. Did anyone knock before entering your room?'

M: 'Are you kidding me? Some of the houses were so broken down that Sally and I didn't even have a door to our room. No one knocked. Not ever.'

C: 'That is just an example of an attitude that dominated your home. No one had any rights. When the boys wanted something – that was all that mattered. They could intrude and get their desires met at your expense. Do you suppose that your father set the pattern?'

M: 'Like when he raped Mum?'

C: 'Yes.'

M: *'I think that it was on the night that she was trying to break up with him. I suppose it was funny that she had Andrew through that night?'*
C: *'I can't think of any more terrible circumstances in which to begin a marriage - or a family.'*
M: *'And I think of what I have taken for granted growing up! It is no wonder I go along with men, even when I think better of it.'*

Over the Christmas break Mary confronted her mother about the violence she experienced while growing up. It was surprising that her mother did not react in a sharp and hostile way. Mary reported, 'I feel stronger. More in control of my life.' She realized that when she was growing up there was so little emotional responsiveness from her mother that she sought emotional closeness with her brother. Perhaps even the shared secret had some appeal. But as Bank and Khan conclude, 'If the love becomes eroticized over a long period of time, the bonding of the siblings becomes more intense, the struggle for separate identities more difficult, the contempt for the parents more profound.'[17]

Another area of change for Mary was in her relationship with Sam. She could tolerate more conflict. 'I can see now that an argument is not the end of the world. It is not even the end of the relationship. I never saw any problems worked out in my family, but now I can see how it is possible.' This was associated with another point of growth. Mary was able to acknowledge her anger. 'Sometimes I feel like punching him in the face.' But paradoxically in recognizing it and feeling it, she was better able to control her reactions. Nor was it such a large step to be able to feel anger at the abusive circumstances of her childhood.

In the final session we discussed her dreams for the future. She wanted to train for a career in alternative medicine. I realized how far Mary had come when she made a passing comment that she was able to refuse when Sam wanted sex. She observed, 'I am not compelled to meet his needs.' And eventually she broke off the relationship without the need to get into another affair.

About a year later Mary was engaged to a man three years younger than herself and married him a few months later. She rang me again when she found out that she was pregnant and asked if I would baptize the baby later that year. I naturally agreed and I had the joy of baptizing young Matthew.

There is also a spiritual dimension to the healing process. Some survivors will feel damaged at the core of self, or so polluted as to be beyond either forgiveness or cleansing. The message of grace in Christ has an obvious relevance. There may also be an opportunity for some creative use of liturgy to facilitate the healing process, perhaps to express anger and hurt and eventually to arrive at a place of giving forgiveness. This must not be hurried. *I recently saw a young man who was becoming more aware that he had been abused as a child. The brother who had abused him was entering a religious order and was asking for forgiveness. I encouraged the survivor to move slowly and said to him, 'For the moment begin to feel the pain. Perhaps later you will be able to give the forgiveness that he seeks.'*

The pastoral care and counselling of survivors is a major need in the Church.[18] Nor should we neglect the care of the perpetrators. For them there is both forgiveness and the hope of change. In this difficult task there are many resources for the Christian counsellor, not least of which are those provided by God through his grace. The Holy Spirit is 'alongside' and 'within' birthing the New Creation: 'So if anyone is in Christ, there is a new creation: everything old has passed away; see, everything has become new!' (2 Corinthians 5:17). The counsellor may be the 'midwife', but it is God alone who gives the miracle of birth and new growth.

Exercise

Reflect on the problem St Paul addressed in his first letter to the Corinthians in which a man was living with his father's wife (1 Corinthians 5:1-2). Do you consider his action was justified? Was it wise pastorally? The apostle wrote about the problem of immorality in the Church, but this incident was particularly scandalous. 'This is not found even among the pagans.' What would it mean for the Church to 'mourn' in our day?

To read further

Judith Herman, *Father-Daughter Incest,* Harvard University Press, Cambridge MA, 1981. This is a classic and comprehensive treatment of this topic.

Wendy Maltz, *The Sexual Healing Journey: A Guide for Survivors of Sexual Abuse,* HarperCollins*Publishers,* 1991. This recent book is very useful in the area of treatment of the psychological wounds of adults who were abused as children.

David Sakheim and Susan Devine, *Out of Darkness: Exploring Satanism and Ritual Abuse,* Lexington Books, New York, 1992. A very ugly topic. Christians have an opportunity to help such survivors with spiritual resources.

INTRODUCTION TO THE DYNAMICS OF MARRIAGE COUNSELLING

The need for marriage counselling is growing in our society. Relationships appear to be under greater pressure and the statistics of divorce are alarming. In this situation there can be no simplistic answers, but Christian counsellors with skills in this area are increasingly needed by the Church.

Early practitioners of marriage counselling were medical doctors such as physician-sexologists, gynaecologists and psychiatrists, as well as educators, lawyers, social workers and clergy. The rise of the profession began with counselling centres such as Abraham and Hangnail Stone's New York City clinic (1929) and Paul Popenoe's American Institute of Family Relations in Los Angeles (1930).[1] The American Association for Marriage Counsellors was formed in 1942. The British Association for counselling is based in Rugby.

Some psychoanalysts and other counsellors who worked with individuals in troubled relationships became frustrated with the lack of change in marriage and family patterns. This led to an interest in General Systems Theory.[2] Significant advances came in the 1950s. Psychiatrist Murray Bowen's study in schizophrenia was very influential. He understood the family unit as the focus of the problem.[3] Also Gregory Bateson, a social scientist, was interested in schizophrenia and proposed the 'double bind' theory. Nathan Ackerman published *Family Psychiatry* in 1958.[4] Other leaders have included: Virginia Satir, Carl Whittaker, Sal Minuchin and pioneers of the Milan school. In the past decade Australian social worker

Michael White has developed an original and effective style of therapy which is now recognized internationally.[5]

All the schools of marriage counselling use the concepts of how systems function as a whole. This describes what happens in marital or family interaction in terms of the larger picture and not the various parts. It is difficult to grasp the principles because we tend to think in terms of linear causation: A leads to B to C etc. Systems theory is more dynamic and interactional. Imagine five marbles in the lid of a coffee jar. On one level the marbles interact in linear terms but if the lid is moved then there is an effect on all the marbles at the same time. In systems thought, components are seen as behaving in terms of their position in the network, rather than according to their nature. There is the recognition that each component may well function in a different way outside the system.

Systems theory better describes the dynamic quality of marriages and families. This theory has led to a therapeutic approach which has a focus on systemic forces rather than the specific content of symptoms such as school behaviour, eating disorders, obesity, alcoholism, adultery, or lower-back pain. One systems concept is triangles, which has a broader relevance than the 'eternal triangle' of the marital affair. For example, one therapist explained the bad behaviour of a teenager as an attempt to hold the parents' marriage together. 'After all, the only time that I have ever seen you two agree is when you condemn what Bobby has done!'

I have found a thorough understanding of one approach to marital therapy is helpful in counselling couples. It brings depth and coherence to counselling practice. Techniques can then be drawn from various other approaches and integrated without therapeutic confusion. I have no particular ideological commitment to any of the schools of thought: it is more a question of style. Any of the main theorists in marital counselling can provide a comprehensive map for working with couples.[6]

An introduction to Murray Bowen

In counselling I draw on the theory and practice of Murray Bowen who trained as a psychiatrist and had a position on the staff of the Menninger Clinic from 1946 to 1954. He noticed at one point that he could think more objectively about the patients on the ward when he was away from the clinic. This insight led to conceptualizing groups of people as an emotional field and the family as an 'emotional unit'. The field regulates the attitudes and behaviour of the members to varying degrees. He also began to appreciate that the functioning of a family was more understandable when considered in the context of the multi-generational past. After a particularly tense time with his own family he applied his theory to his own struggles and shared the results at a national meeting of family therapists in 1967.[7]

According to Bowen, every person has some degree of unresolved emotional attachment to his family. This relates to Bowen's concept of differentiation of self. The level of differentiation can be equated to the capacity to say 'I' when others are demanding 'you' or 'we'. Differentiation also describes the ability of an individual to maintain emotional autonomy in a relationship system. But autonomy is not synonymous with isolation. Bowen understood that the higher the level of self, the greater the ability not only to maintain a self in relationship to others, but also to permit others to be themselves. The lower the differentiation of self, the more intense a person's emotional need for others to think, feel and behave in certain ways. The lower the level of basic differentiation, the more tendency there is to 'borrow' self from others to shore up the level of functioning.[8]

Undifferentiation leads to relationships characterized by emotional intensity and reactivity. The family of origin is relevant because the adult's level of self-differentiation largely depends on the degree of differentiation attained while growing up in the family system.

The character of unresolved emotional attachment takes many forms. It can range from an intense, conflictual relationship to an overly idealized, harmonious bond. The critical issue is not the mood of the relationship, but how much the feelings, thinking, and behaviour of each person is regulated by emotional forces in the relationship.[9] One of the therapeutic goals of this approach is to work on change in the self while maintaining contact with the family of origin. Unresolved tension in a family can lead to the development of symptoms. As Michael Kerr explained, 'It is easier for the family members to make accommodations that make it possible to live with the symptom than it is to address the underlying relationship process that fosters the symptom in the first place.'[10]

Another important concept is emotional distance. This kind of distance is emotional. The two extremes are 'fused' relationships and 'emotional cut-offs'. Both are motivated by a lack of differentiation. Distancing may be the result of a lack of emotional space in the relationship. Friedman observed that partners may separate because they have grown distant, but most couples probably separate because they are not able to achieve any separation at all.[11] A more well-defined self is able to balance these emotional forces.

Emotional cut-offs can be seen in terms of physical distance. For example, *I recently had a funeral service for a man who died in a local nursing home. He left his wife and three young children when he was in his thirties. He lived with a de facto and had two children by her. He only saw his original family once in the next ten years, though some of his children regained contact when he was placed in a nursing home after a severe accident. There was some discomfort at the funeral with the two families which the father had kept separate with his emotional cut-off.*

It can also be an internal state when an individual withdraws into television, books, fantasy, alcohol, drugs, or depression. In fact such cut-offs raise anxiety and shift problems onto other people in the family system. This emotional dynamic adds to many of the difficulties that occur with second marriages.

The model of Bowen provides a way of looking at family dynamics in the Bible. One example is the family intrigues of Abraham's descendants in the Book of Genesis. There are powerful triangles with mothers and favourite sons, intergenerational family patterns such as the wives of both Abraham and Isaac are said to be 'sisters' instead of 'wives', an emotional cut-off when Jacob fled from Esau (Genesis 27: 41-45) and the trickery of Jacob comes full circle in his being married to Leah instead of Rachel. There are wonderful themes of encounter with God, as if each generation can go astray and then 'wrestle with God' and return (Genesis 32: 24-32). There is a sense of redemption with scenes of reconciliation between brothers, for example, Joseph after being sold into slavery uses his position in Egypt to help his father and to bless his brothers (Genesis 45: 1-24). It is all very human and yet caught up in the larger plan of God.

Romantic love: A case study in idolatry

Romantic love has been likened to the seraphim in the Book of Isaiah, 'Each had six wings, with two he covered his face, and with two he covered his feet, and with two he flew' (Isaiah 6:2). You don't know where you are going, and you can't see clearly who you are with, but, oh my heavens, you do fly![12]

Although systemic factors are very important in relationships, there are also unconscious dynamics that influence marriages. A case in point is the modern concept of romantic love. Since it is so basic to the way most modern couples tend to understand their relationships, this will be explored here in some detail.

Sexual attraction has been celebrated throughout recorded history. The Song of Solomon in the Old Testament is an ancient example. 'O fairest among women' (Song of Solomon 1:8). Before the Middle Ages the dominant form of love was 'heroic love' with the central theme of the pursuit and capture of the woman. Perhaps as early as the twelfth century a mythology of courtly love began to develop and has had an enormous impact on Western culture.

Our modern concept originated in 'courtly love'. There was time for leisure, the arts, musical appreciation, companionship and refined manners in the courts of royalty. In this environment an idealized notion of love evolved.[13] 'True love' was equated with the ecstatic adoration of the female who was the embodiment of all perfection. This love was chaste - though with some erotic overtones. It remained beyond any hope of physical satisfaction. The ideal was a spiritual love that could not mix with the clay of married life.

The helpless man in love would pledge absolute obedience to the woman. Even the somewhat silly stereotype of the knight who sets off to slay dragons was not so far from the ideal! As Jungian analyst Robert Johnson observed, 'He sees a special reality revealed in her, he feels completed, ennobled, refined, spiritualized, uplifted, transformed into a new, better, whole man.[14] Troubadours were inspired to sing romantic ballads and to tell long stories such as that of Tristan and Iseult.

In the late twentieth century the ideal lives on. Romantic love is a kind of spell (that 'old black magic'). The lover is out of control. The signs are obvious: the stricken couple move towards each other at the speed of light, talk endlessly on the phone, have secret gestures, pet names and indulge in long, breathless gazing into each other's eyes. Communication is spontaneous and open, trust is high and each shows remarkable sensitivity to the partner's feelings. Harville Hendrix has noted four aspects of this experience:

1. Recognition, 'It is as if I have known you before.'

2. Timelessness, 'I feel as if there never has been a time that we haven't known each other.'

3. Reunification, 'When I am with you I feel whole.'

4. Necessity, 'Without your love I would kill myself.'[15]

Romantic love is notoriously blind. It involves an initial pretence: both lovers try to appear more mature and less needy. Negative traits in the partner are either ignored or denied. There is little that could be labelled logical.

As Shakespeare wrote, 'Reason and love keep little company

together nowadays: the more the pity, that some honest neighbours will not make them friends.' (*A Midsummer Night's Dream*, Act III, Scene I). It is a natural high. Some people get addicted to the 'rush' of this drug and have serial affairs with little commitment. There is an almost conscious demand that the lover or spouse will always provide such ecstasy or spiritual intensity. Our Western culture is the first to make such love the basis for marriage. Perhaps the one lesson we can learn from the divorce statistics is that it is not an adequate foundation for a long-term relationship.[16]

The expectation of 'being in love' is pushed by the mass media. But it is not all glamorous. There is also a dark reality. Many people spend their lives with a deep sense of loneliness and frustration; love affairs end in tragic disappointment and bitterness. Sometimes the only joy is vicarious through the romances of Mills and Boon. Rarely do people think that the problem lies in the illusion of romantic love. Johnson has underlined the reason for this: 'Romance must, by its very nature, deteriorate into egotism. For romance is not a love that is directed at another human being; the passion of romance is always directed at our own projections, our own expectations, our own fantasies. In a very real sense, it is a love not of another person, but of ourselves.'[17]

When we examine the reasons that one person is attracted to another, it becomes clear that largely unconscious forces are at work. This is most obvious in those puzzling cases of seemingly foolish marital choices. Anna lamented, 'How could I have been so blind? My father was violent, and now I find that my husband hits me as well.' Sometimes, but not often, there is more insight. Bill mused: 'In relationships I always end up in the role of the rescuer.' Perhaps this makes some sense in the context of what Freud wrote about as patterns of repetition-compulsion. He described the tendency of adults to repeat traumatic situations of childhood in order to gain some mastery later in life. Thus a young girl hurt by repeated disappointments and shameful incidents from an alcoholic father may choose a high-risk spouse to replay the old dramas.[18] She is easily 'hooked', such are the mysteries of attraction! This kind of destructive pattern is familiar to every counsellor.[19]

But even individuals from less disturbed childhoods can make perplexing choices. There is an exercise that I find valuable with couples preparing for marriage. Each is asked to draw a large square and then to divide it into four smaller squares. In the squares they list on one side the strengths and on the other the weaknesses of each parent. After this has been done, with a few attributes in each box, I ask each of them to tick any attribute that belongs to the other. The result is often quite a surprise since the couple will recognize an overlap on negative traits. This would support the observation of Hendrix that: 'No matter what their conscious intentions, most people are attracted to mates who have their caretakers' positive and negative traits and typically the negative traits are more influential.'[20] The closer the 'fit' the more passionate and compelling the attraction.

I can illustrate the levels of awareness from my own marriage. Jennie and I have worked at our marital relationship for the last twenty years. It has been a satisfying union and a source of genuine growth for both of us. During our engagement I remember thinking that Jennie would be presentable in any group in which we were likely to mix. At a semiconscious level there was a limited understanding that I repressed most of my emotions and so needed a partner who would provide some fire in our relationship – or it would have died of boredom. At a completely unconscious level I needed to work on some issues relating to my mother's perfectionism. Such insights may take years. Sometimes it is very painful to admit 'home truths'.[21]

Romantic love has a hidden agenda. What is highest on the list is the healing of childhood wounds. The unrealistic expectation is outlined by Hendrix, 'The lovers believe they are going to be healed – not by hard work or painful self-realization – but by the simple act of merging with someone.'[22] There are other dynamics as well. Jung saw a shadow side to the personality, where aspects of the self are repressed or denied. Take, for example, the young child who was not allowed to be angry. He may force these forbidden feelings behind a screen of repression and grow up with hardly any awareness of an angry impulse. When it comes to choosing a wife, he will come to a fork in the road. He may find himself very much at ease with a woman who also represses anger, 'She is my kind of person, I feel comfortable with her.' On the other hand he may unconsciously desire wholeness and marry a woman who is easily enraged. This will certainly be the more interesting marriage! It is my impression that adults from healthier and happier homes will tend to make more realistic choices in their marriage partners because such choices are informed by more conscious factors.

There is a down side to romantic love. The spell can quickly wear off. The irony is that the 'wearing off' frequently happens when commitment begins. This is the reason why many couples have a difficult time in the engagement period and some end their marriage in fireworks in the first year. The key to understanding this is that the feeling of safety leads to permission to relax and be oneself. Infantile needs come to the surface: expectations of endless attention, sacrificial gifts and continual praise. When gratification is not instant the power struggle begins. Emotional reactivity rises and the 'other-centred' ideal of romantic love seems a distant memory.

One example of an infantile expectation is the belief that the lover can read minds, 'If she really loves me she will know all my needs without me saying anything'. This leads to ridiculous scenes. For example, *Sue has had a difficult day caring for toddlers at home. She thinks to herself, 'Wouldn't it be nice if John bought some flowers on the way home from work.' John has been preoccupied with problems in keeping an advertising account and a gift for his wife is the last thing on his mind. When he comes through the front door, Sue is in a rage. 'Why didn't you bring me some flowers? You never think about me.'* As silly as this may sound, it is a central dynamic in many relationships.

In the above example, Sue has an unconscious belief that John has the capacity to meet her every need. He 'has it all'. When her needs are not met there must be a malevolent reason for his withholding. This adds to the frustration, resentment and bitterness. Sadly, this logic leads to tantrums, financial and sexual blackmail, bullying, even violence. This negative behaviour comes from desperation and the infantile tactic, 'If only I can cause him enough pain, he will return to his loving ways.' Gradually it may dawn on her that her husband has neither the skills nor the motivation to meet her deepest needs. Of course, an even deeper realization is possible: the spouse has attributes of the wounding parent and is a most unlikely ·candidate to be able to meet such needs.

And yet it is only at this point that the relationship has a chance to be based on something other than the illusions of romantic love.

There are no short cuts. In a healthy relationship, one relates to the partner on the basis of inner wholeness, not need. An enduring and satisfying relationship is the result of two people who see each other as ordinary, imperfect and human, and yet can still manage to love each other without illusion and inflated expectations.

In theological terms romantic love is idolatrous. An idol is regarded as a source of salvation. The prophet saw the deluded pagan saying to what he had made, 'Save me, for you are my god!' (Isaiah 44:17). Many people speak of human love in a similar way, 'I will be happy when I find a wife.' The popular film *Pretty Woman* illustrates the secular theme of salvation, the corporate raider becomes more humane in his business dealings and is even cured of his fear of heights on the balcony. The prostitute has her sexuality redeemed and she finds her integrity in settling for nothing less than marriage. Love conquers all!

The answer to idolatry is truth. We can affirm what is part of the divine generosity of creation. God has given to us the gift of erotic love, the joy of attraction, the delight of sensual touch and sexual play. The Christian tradition has been guilty of exalting spiritual realities at the cost of the physical dimension. However, the two belong together. The challenge of 'agape' love is to transcend our self-focus and find spiritual wholeness. Morton and Barbara Kelsey have written, 'Loving is demanding. We cannot love consistently and fully, nor can we bear the tensions in which love and sexuality involve us, unless we experience the persistent, tender, loving mercy of the dying and rising God. And yet without human love our spiritual love seems likely to dry up and disappear. These two movements to full human and divine intimacy seem to be strangely intertwined.'[23]

Towards a conscious marriage

In the early years of marriage counselling it was common for counsellors to try to help the couple to do better what they were already doing. They were taught how to negotiate contracts and resolve conflict. But this approach did not address the surrender of illusions. It easily becomes a more refined version of a power struggle. I am convinced that we need to be more conscious about what motivates us in relationships, more accepting of personal desires and realistic about what needs can be met within the marriage.

Harville Hendrix has listed ten characteristics of a conscious marriage:

1. The realization that love relationships have a hidden purpose, namely the healing of childhood wounds. There is in time a shift of perspective from surface needs and desires to an understanding of the unresolved childhood issues. What is puzzling in the relationship becomes a stimulus for insight.

2. A more accurate image of the partner is formed. Romantic love confuses the lover with childhood caretakers including both their positive and negative features. Such illusions are let go. The partner is increasingly seen as another wounded human being struggling to be healed.

3. Each person takes responsibility for communicating needs to the partner. In an unconscious marriage the couple will tend to cling to the childhood belief that the partner will intuitively know all their needs. In a conscious marriage the importance of open channels of communication is recognized.

4. Interactions become more intentional. Instead of the usual emotional reactivity a couple will learn to behave in a more constructive way. This may include setting goals for spending time together.

5. The needs of both are valued. The magical view of the other as fulfilling every need gives way to a mutual responsibility to care for the other. There is a more realistic balance of giving and receiving.

6. Negative aspects of the personality are acknowledged by both partners. (Unfortunately most couples deny faults and project their own negative traits, thus adding to hostility in the relationship.)

7. Non-power tactics are used to meet personal needs. A partner is a potential resource for meeting needs; but the usual power play with cajoling, haranguing and blaming is doomed to failure.

8. Both search within themselves for unacknowledged strengths and abilities. The more common pattern is that individuals will look to their partner for attributes that are thought to be missing. A common example of this is the lament, 'John always pays the bills. I am so hopeless with money.' This attitude contributes to an illusionary sense of wholeness, not as an individual but as a couple.

9. A spiritual dimension is nurtured in both the self and in the marriage. Hendrix speaks of being 'united with the universe'.[24] However, there are many resources within the Christian tradition.

10. The real difficulty of creating a good marriage is acknowledged. An unconscious marriage is based on the belief that everything rests on the choice of the right partner; a conscious marriage is based on the commitment to be the right partner.

There are no fully conscious or completely unconscious marriages. There is always a mixture. However, Hendrix has identified important aspects of a marital relationship.

St Paul wrote to the believers at Ephesus about the Christian ideal of marriage. 'Be subject to one another out of reverence for Christ.

Wives, be subject to your husbands as you are to the Lord. . . Husbands, love your wives, just as Christ loved the church and gave himself up for her' (Ephesians 5: 21-22, 25). I suspect that his teaching is completely misunderstood as being about power, when the real emphasis is on the quality of love. I see a parallel in the first letter to the Corinthians where the apostle wrote about sexual relations: 'The husband should give to his wife her conjugal rights, and likewise the wife to her husband. For the wife does not have authority over her body, but the husband does; likewise the husband does not have authority over his own body, but the wife does' (1 Corinthians 7:3-4). The basis for abstinence is only 'by agreement for a set time' (1 Corinthians 7:5). St Paul clearly emphasized the mutuality of the relationship. This is implied in his understanding of love. There is also a healthy appreciation of conscious choice in a mature relationship. It is a vision of a conscious relationship in Christ.

I would summarize the basic essentials of a growing relationship as:

- A willingness, both with oneself and with the partner, to be honest and vulnerable.

- A commitment to grapple and struggle deeply for a better relationship, and not to accept pseudo-solutions.

- A resolve to clarify and communicate a real self to the partner and to encounter the deeper self of the lover. This is a freedom to be fully who we are in the relationship and allow the other person the same expression of the self.

There is, of course, nothing new here. It was said long ago by St Paul:

> Love is patient; love is kind; love is not envious or boastful or arrogant or rude. It does not insist on its own way; it is not irritable or resentful; it does not rejoice in wrongdoing, but rejoices in the truth. It bears all things, believes all things,

hopes all things, endures all things. Love never ends. . . And now faith, hope, and love abide, these three; and the greatest of these is love.' (1 Corinthians 13: 4-8, 13)

Exercise

Write in your journal the story of your most significant relationship. What did you expect in the early stages? Did this prove to be realistic? To what extent have your attitudes to marriage been shaped by attitudes in your family? society? or the Bible.

Can you think of any other illusions that dominate the expectations of relationships in our society? How would you think that St Paul would address such themes? Do you think that the concept of idolatry is still as relevant in theological analysis?

Further Reading

C. B. Broderick and S. S. Schrader, 'The History of Professional Marriage and Family Therapy', pp. 5-32, in *Handbook of Family Therapy*, eds. A. S. Gurman and D. P. Kniskern, Brunner and Mazel, New York, 1981. An excellent review of the history of marriage counselling.

Harville Hendrix, *Keeping the Love You Find*, Pocket Books, New York, 1992. This is written for singles with superb exercises to help self-discovery. He develops some concepts introduced in his earlier book and it is most helpful for understanding the dynamics of relationships.

R. A. Johnson, *The Psychology of Romantic Love*, Arkana, London, 1983. Johnson is a Jungian analyst and he explores the concepts of romantic love as embedded in myths and modern attitudes.

M. E. Kerr and M. Bowen, *Family Evaluation: An Approach Based on Bowen Theory*, W. W. Norton and Company, New York, 1988. This is a comprehensive treatment of Bowen's theory. It is difficult reading but valuable for understanding the key concepts.

MARITAL CONFLICT

I once heard a somewhat simplistic formula about marriage: Conflict + Love = Growth. There is an element of truth in this, especially if love includes a degree of commitment and self-sacrifice that is conveyed in the New Testament idea of agape love. I have seen countless couples survive various crises and grow in their joy and satisfaction in the marriage. In this chapter I will outline some of the practical aspects of counselling couples with relationship difficulties. This will include assessing and working towards a better resolution of marital conflict.

The first interview

The first interview really begins at the point of first contact. The more motivated spouse will usually ring and arrange an interview. One possible exception is when the partner has decided to leave the marriage and wants to leave the abandoned spouse with a caretaker (i.e. the counsellor). Such agendas are not always obvious.

The first meeting with the couple will give a number of clues that can be meaningful. How do they greet you? Christian name? A title such as Mr, Dr, Rev., Pastor? Each indicates something of the relationship expected. Where do they choose to sit? In my office there are a sofa and two additional chairs. Couples who come for premarital guidance inevitably sit together; those in marital distress sit as far apart as the room allows! Generally I find that the more motivated partner will sit closer to me.

One person is usually reluctant to enter into counselling or has already made up his or her mind to leave the marriage. But it is a matter of the highest priority to engage that distancing spouse in the work to be done. This will help to build a 'working alliance'. I usually give that spouse considerable attention, affirm their perspectives and try to be empathic to the pain they have experienced. Unless that spouse is 'hooked' there will be no second interview. Sometimes both partners will want to work on the presenting problem and when this occurs it is a good prognostic sign. Occasionally both want the relationship to end and they can be helped to part with a minimum of hurt to themselves and their children.

I generally schedule ninety minutes for the first appointment. This gives me time to make a preliminary assessment (described later) and to give both partners an opportunity to speak privately with me later in the interview. When the spouse is alone I begin with, 'Is there anything that you can only say to me without Bill/Mary being here?' I may then be told about violence or alcohol abuse or some 'dark secret'. I always ask a specific question about whether there is or has been an affair. It is a powerful secret which has an influence on the progress of therapy. Usually this will be answered truthfully. Only once have I discovered later that a person lied to me at this point.

In the first session a couple will usually demonstrate their fighting style. This is a source of valuable information. Are they out of control, sarcastic, mutual in their blame, verging on violence, passive or silent? Sometimes there are clear roles: one may be submissive while the other is aggressive and overbearing. Any expression of conflict may be taboo, with the result that there is great reluctance to address any issue directly. It is informative to see what attempts are made to get out of the rut. This will usually reveal a limited range of coping styles and a restricted capacity to adapt.

Another question to keep in mind is, 'Why now?' Usually something has led to the decision to seek help. Has it been a severe fight, an affair, a decision to leave or suicidal thoughts? There may also be a need to consider referral if there is a risk of suicide or a psychotic breakdown. There are some cases in which I would prefer to work in tandem with a specialist counsellor or agency. These include alcohol abuse, drug addiction, eating disorders and chronic violence.

It is helpful to give some indication of how long counselling might take: 'I would like to see you both for six sessions. You may well see some improvement by then and we can reassess the situation.' Sometimes it is a good idea to give an impression of how you see the problem and the way forward. *One couple were worried about violence in their relationship. They understood their Christian faith as being incompatible with any conflict. Any disagreement was against God's will. However every eighteen months or so they had a fight which got out of control. The last one ended up with more than bruises. I normalized conflict with the comment, 'If you fight that rarely, then it is amazing that you haven't killed each other!' and explained that they would need to learn to fight more often and with more purpose – then there would be no need for the Mount Vesuvius explosions.*

The act of coming to see a counsellor can be reassuring and a source of hope. But progress needs to be made quickly if both partners are to remain engaged in the work of therapy.

In previous chapters I have described the main skill of counselling as reflective listening. This is still important, but working with couples tends to be more active: clarifying, refereeing, asking questions, teaching communication skills and assigning homework tasks. I encourage the couple to take increasing responsibility for their progress and affirm useful initiatives they undertake. I model careful listening and this is one way of demonstrating communication skills.

The genogram

For every counselling case, I routinely do a genogram in the first or second session.

Eugene O'Neill, the great playwright, once observed, 'There is

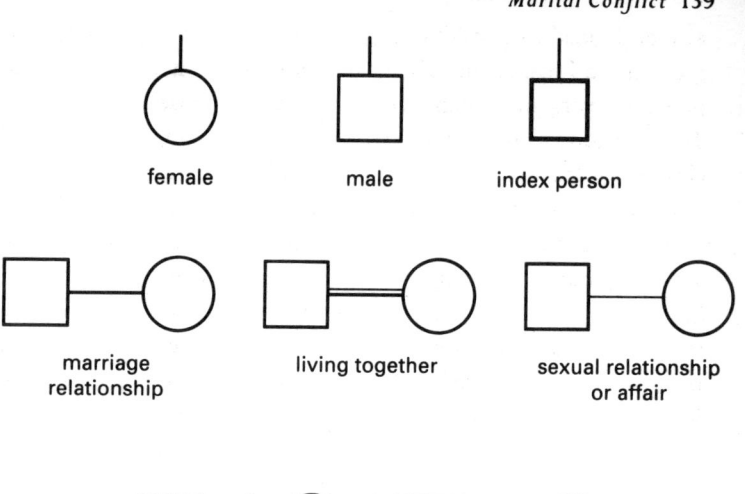

female   male   index person

marriage   living together   sexual relationship
relationship   or affair

separation   divorce

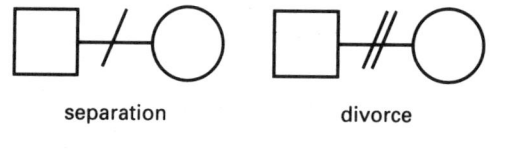

death   adoption or   twins
               fostering

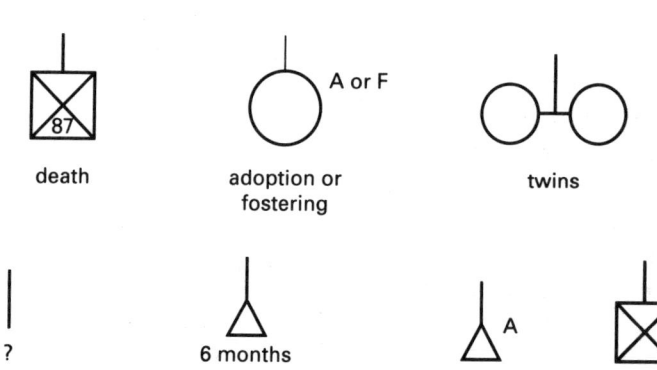

?   6 months

pregnant   miscarriage or   abortion   stillbirth
                  death in the womb

migration

no present or future, only the past happening over and over again.' This is certainly true of family themes and the genogram is a simple way of organizing information about families over three generations.

Some counsellors use it to keep track of who is who in the wider family; others use the genogram as a rich source of hypotheses relating to family emotional patterns. It shows the strengths and vulnerabilities of a relationship in the larger context. The following symbols are commonly used:

This scheme is flexible enough to incorporate additional symbols which can be devised by the counsellor. The following is an example from 'Tom' and 'Nancy'.

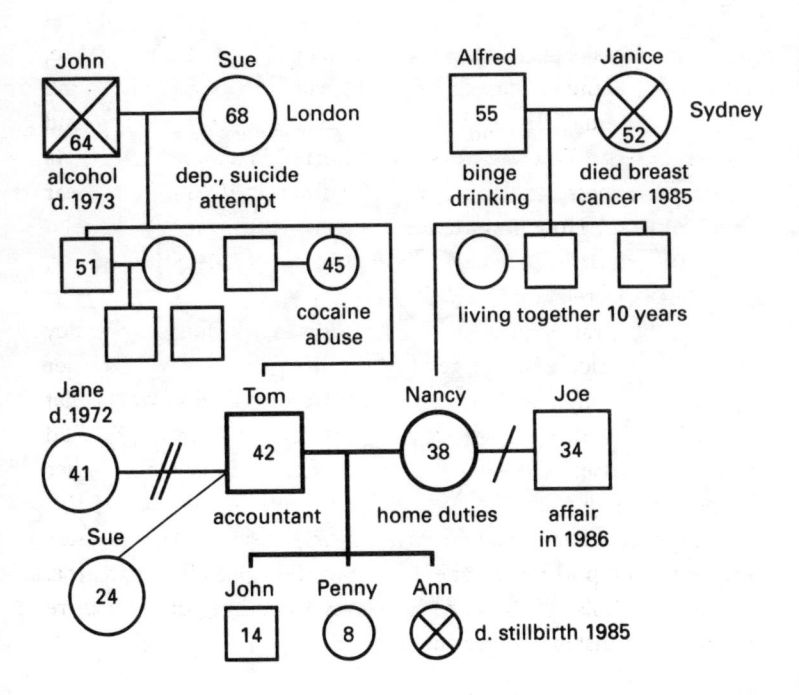

The following are usually on the diagram:

1. Names, age, highest level of education, occupation, and significant problems;

2. Dates of birth,[1] death, marriages, divorces, separations (anniversaries tend to raise anxiety or cause sadness), any other significant stressors or transitions: accidents, illness, change of job, moving house, etc; especially note these if any have occurred just before an escalation in marital conflict;

3. Geographical locations of parents and other family members;

4. Ethnic and religious affiliations.

This provides the bones of the genogram. The flesh is the emotional patterns. This can include such themes as: alcohol abuse, addictions, genetic defects, suicide, violence,[2] accidents, job instability, sexual abuse, criminal behaviour, occult activity, and mental illness.[3] Who are the success stories? What are the criteria (business success, academic, sport, or financial)? Are there clear gender roles?[4] How important are sibling positions? Who are the 'black sheep' or 'scapegoats'?[5] What are the family rules, taboos, hot issues, secrets and family scripts?

In the illustrating genogram we see that both Tom and Nancy grew up in alcoholic homes. Nancy lives much closer to her immediate family and tends to get involved in the dramas on that stage. In 1986, the year after the stillbirth of her daughter, she had multiple stresses following the death of her mother: her father increased his drinking and her younger brother was admitted to hospital because of schizophrenia. This might explain her need for additional support which she sought in the brief affair with Joe.

Other symbols can be used to convey something of the nature of the relationships. These include:

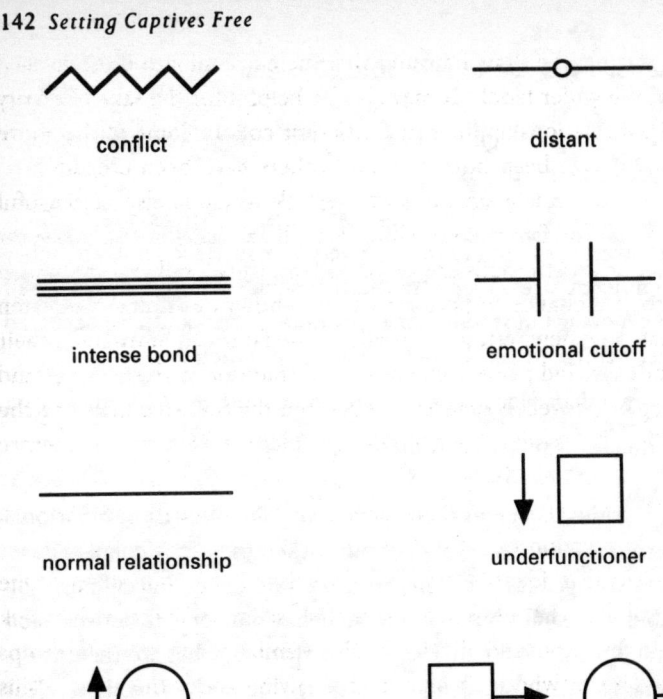

conflict

distant

intense bond

emotional cutoff

normal relationship

underfunctioner

overfunctioner

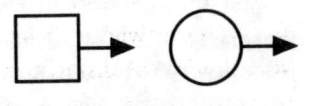

pursuing husband
distancing wife

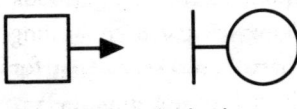

pursuit and rejection

fixed distance and tension

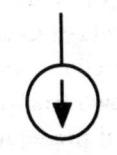

symptomatic child

A line can be drawn around the nuclear family to distinguish it from the wider family. It may also be helpful for the sake of clarity to draw relationship lines in a different colour. Some of the above symbols have been borrowed and others have been created.[6]

A genogram is a simple concrete task which is also very useful in marital and family counselling. Stagoll and Lang noted, 'No great verbal or artistic skills are required, and thus family members can be given a chance to perform competently in a strange and often threatening new setting . . . It allows the family to 'normalize' their experience and place it in a historical tradition with successes and struggles, as well as failures.'[7] It is often the first step in seeing the problem in a systems perspective. Couples can become more aware of the 'emotional baggage' that was brought into the marriage. It is more objective and enhances self-focus, rather than the more usual projection of: 'It's all your fault!'

Genograms identify issues to work on in counselling. One example is the presence of family secrets. These will block communication and divide family members into various camps according to who is in or out of knowing about the secret. This also leads to distortions of perception, raises anxiety and perpetuates triangles. When such themes are allowed to continue they will cause difficulties in current relationships and affect succeeding generations.[8]

There is an interesting spiritual approach to dealing with past family themes advocated by surgeon Dr Kenneth McAll in his book *Healing the Family Tree.*[9] He has had experience with healing present problems by using a special Eucharistic service to 'pray for the dead'. It is an unusual approach which I do not find entirely convincing. However I have been recently asked to preside at such a service and I will trust that God can use it as a means of healing. I do think that there is a great deal of value in thinking about spiritual problems in the widest possible context.

I recommend that a counsellor-in-training learn the genogram by beginning with his or her own family. It is helpful in clarifying the issues, which is an essential prerequisite to working with others. It is to the degree that the counsellor is able to be clear with his or her first family about self, values, and commitments that will determine the level of maturity that is brought to other relationships - including the therapeutic one.

The assessment of marital conflict

In the first session the counsellor considers, 'What is wrong? Why is this relationship not working? Where is the pain?' Such questions are basic to assessment. Although it is part of the process throughout the counselling period, it is important at the beginning when an initial sense of direction is needed.

Each counsellor will have various criteria for assessment. One obvious indicator is the developmental stage of the marriage: engaged, newlywed, first baby, young children, adolescent children, 'empty nest', retirement, frail aged or dependent care. Other criteria may include: presenting symptoms, degree of cohesion, communication, sense of reality, affect, boundaries, attitudes, etc. Clifford Sager outlined a system of assessment based on contracts. He specified the following determinants: dependence, passivity, distance, abuse of power, dominance or submission, fear of abandonment, need to possess or control, level of anxiety, mechanisms of defence, understanding of love, gender identity, sexual expectations, cognitive style, and self acceptance.[10] These are all useful and at some level are taken into account by most counsellors.   I have found the most practical approach is to assess the level of conflict. Phillip Guerin jnr has suggested a model for evaluating and treating marital conflict which works with a range of couples and presenting difficulties.[11] The four-stage approach includes:

Stage I
This stage is usually found in couples during courtship, or who have entered a recent de facto relationship, or in the first years of marriage. There is a low level of marital conflict. All the signs of a healthy relationship are present: communication is open,

polarization of power is minimal, the individuals are generally self-focused (with only occasional bursts of projection), the level of reactivity and criticism is low, and trust is still secure. It is the 'cocoon' stage and normally will not last for ever!

Tom is a fifty-year-old divorcee who is planning to get married. Maggie is thirty-seven and has not been married before. They have known each other for five years, but only in the last few months has the relationship become intimate. The date for marriage has been set. They came into counselling because of conflict between Maggie and Tom's two teenage children. The couple are beginning to see that a blended family is more complicated than they had thought.

Stage II
There is more turbulence in this stage. Conflict can be intense. The picture is mixed: communication is reasonably open but criticism and reactivity have increased, there is a more restricted expression of personal thought and feelings, projection is more prevalent and the couple will experience conflict as less safe. However, credibility is still high. It is clearer that there is a power struggle in the relationship. This is marked by a 'win or lose' mentality, but it is more playful than desperate. The progression from expectation to alienation has now reached hurt and anger with a residue of resentment. One indication of this stage is longitudinal – unresolved conflict has lasted less than six months.

Claire and Bill have been married for four years. They came to see a counsellor because of a crisis. Both had been reasonably happy in the marriage. The problem was that Bill had too many drinks at the office Christmas party and he slept with one of the secretaries. Claire has been obsessed about the incident. Bill can't understand what happened and was quick to assure Claire that it will not be repeated.

Stage III
The stress in the relationship is now very high. The emotional climate may be marked by extremes of 'hot and cold'. Reactivity

may be sudden and sharp. The power struggle is now deadly – as if personal survival depends upon winning. There may be a limited capacity even to exchange information, either personal or general. What may be labelled 'self-disclosure' is often no more than a dumping of accumulated emotions and is inevitably heard as criticism or complaint. Credibility is now fading. Self-focus is fleeting and projection is the usual means of interaction. Bitterness has accumulated. It is usual for at least one of the couple to have withdrawn into numbness and detachment.

The conflict in this stage is characterized by high emotional arousal, polarized positions of fixed distance, and rigid blame of the other spouse. The relationship is stuck in mutual pain. A sense of despair may be felt acutely by one of the partners. The possibility of divorce is now an open issue. The marriage is clearly in trouble.

Don and Barbie have been married fifteen years. Over this period there has been occasional violence and a number of affairs by Barbie. Money has been a topic of dispute for nearly all of the marriage. Their children tend to take sides and join in the family 'uproar'. Don has recently become a counsellor at Lifeline and wants to work on improving the marriage.

Stage IV

The end of the marriage is now in sight. This stage is marked by the decision of one or both to engage the services of a lawyer. This is not always the 'point of no return' but it usually places the couple in an adversarial context. There is usually a mood of resignation in the individual who has sought legal advice.

Angus and Sue have been separated for eight months. They are having intense conflict about the property settlement and visitation arrangements. David's lawyer suggested that they see a counsellor to try to work out current problems.

It is not always easy for the counsellor to know whether the relationship is beyond reconciliation. Some couples enter counselling with a surface willingness to work on issues but one partner may have a hidden agenda of divorce. Sometimes self-justification is the reason, 'I did everything I could.' Sometimes a husband or wife will want to leave a dependent, poorly functioning spouse in the care of the counsellor. Since it takes two to make a marriage work, the couple both need to be willing to participate in the counselling process. The reality is that either can 'pull the plug' and then the counselling enters the separation mode.

Appropriate interventions

I will now outline how the assessment of the stage of conflict relates to appropriate interventions.

Stage I

This is the 'honeymoon' period of the relationship. The couple have accumulated little emotional baggage and there is an abundance of motivation, open communication, trust, and low anxiety. Difficulties can usually be met with an educational approach. This is because they can generally use information in a functional way, rather than getting caught up in dysfunctional patterns.

Most marriage preparation courses are based on such an educational approach, which seems appropriate to the developmental stage of the couple. At one church I was involved in such a course which 'graduated' over a hundred couples per year. The topics included marital expectations, values, fears, conflict resolution, legal and financial matters, sexuality and birth control, and a rehearsal of the wedding ceremony. Although there is a lot of value in these courses, there is an inherent dilemma that the couples most motivated to come will need it less than the more passive and withdrawn couples. The latter are harder to reach through adult education courses and are less likely to seek help when the relationship is in trouble. I also think that a greater emphasis on family of origin issues might be beneficial.

An example of what might be taught are the 'fair fight rules' of David Mace:

1. Know what you are fighting about.

2. Stick to the topic.

3. Don't attack the other person (e.g. call names).

4. Time your fight as carefully as possible.

5. Keep quarrels private.

It sometimes helps couples to realize that conflict is natural and can potentially contribute to the growth of a relationship. The analogy of 'weeding a garden' is often appropriate.

In this stage a straightforward educational and problem-solving approach works.[12] This appears to be a natural approach for clergy and it can be very helpful when the contact is part of marital preparation. Teaching about principles of responsible relationships from the Bible and practical advice based on experience in marriage can be quite helpful. The major drawback is that this approach is useless with more intense conflicts.

Stage II

A couple will usually wait until they feel stuck and out of control before seeking help from a counsellor. This is true for Stage II as well as the later stages. It is important to begin by affirming the pain that both are feeling. Yes, there may be problems that require help from a counsellor, but this does not mean that the marriage is on the verge of divorce. Such a reassurance based on an accurate assessment can be a source of relief!

In this stage the issue of conflict can be directly addressed. Since the problems are not so chronic or complex, progress can be made by focusing on the presenting issue.

Dan and Joan sought help because an emotional pattern of pursuit and distance was causing frustrating difficulties. Dan worked long hours as a junior partner in an accountancy firm. Joan understood the need for establishing his role in the company but complained when he took on the voluntary job of treasurer at a local football club. The counsellor coached Joan to experiment with being more distant and paying attention to her feelings. After a few weeks Joan discovered that she pursued as a means of soothing inner anxiety. Dan was initially delighted with the extra space but then found that he was getting angry. He used his time alone as a way to calm down, but found to his surprise that he needed Joan to take the initiative for emotional contact, even in the form of 'nagging'.

It is important to help the couple change their perspective. When a marriage is in difficulties each person tends to become an expert on the behaviour of the other partner and project blame in the process. The therapeutic process tries to reverse this and to enhance self-focus.

Joan soon began to find other ways to meet her needs. She joined a Chinese cooking class and saw some high school friends for coffee. She reasoned that she was a social person and needed more emotional support than was available in the marriage. Joan also pointed out that she was acting for herself and not against Dan. Gradually they realized that they had a common problem in both wanting and fearing intimacy. The way was clear to explore ways to find a better balance.

Couples also tend to confuse closeness with sameness. However, it is almost axiomatic that 'opposites attract'. Such initial differences can add spice to the relationship, but later may become irritating. Couples will tend to invest enormous energy in the 'blaming game'. This involves both in looking for 'who started it'. The search for the beginning of the sequence is futile, since it is usually more of a circular dance; 'the behaviour of one partner maintains and provokes the other.'[13] *In the previous example, Joan used her pain as a stimulus for personal change, which soon led to changes in the relationship.*

The counsellor can help the couple to see the cost of unresolved conflict: emotional distancing, numbness and the possible death of feelings, destructive triangles, game playing, bitterness, self-fulfilling prophesies, and employing the children in family warfare. Couples in difficulties will usually have poor conflict resolution strategies which provide an important target for intervention.

Or again the genogram can lead to insight. *Dan admitted problems with trusting Joan. This was connected with his father's addiction to gambling. He grew up with the unspoken rule 'Don't trust', which was part of survival in an environment of broken promises. All along Joan had been blaming herself. 'What have I done wrong?' It suddenly made a lot of sense!* Couples in this stage can benefit from insight. It helps to see what they have experienced as frustrating in a larger context and to use their mutual regard in productive ways.

A good indicator of the severity of problems in a relationship is the level of 'good will'. To what degree is there respect and expressions of care for the other person? A husband in Stage II said of his wife, 'I really love Anne and I want our marriage to work, but . . .' Both are more willing to work on the problem once it is clearly identified. Another strength of couples in this stage is that they can still say, 'I am sorry.' This helps in lowering emotional reactivity and changing dysfunctional patterns.

Stage III

It is essential to distinguish this stage of conflict from the previous two stages. If the counsellor moves too quickly to focus on the couple's interactional style the result will be to create further confusion.[14] More groundwork is necessary.

It is hard to predict exactly how the couple will present in the sessions. There may be so much emotional reactivity that roles such as pursuer and distancer are anything but clear. This is characteristic of intense fusion, with the reaction of 'distance, the two ping-pong back and forth between fusion and distance. Over time, the emotional climate tends to deteriorate.'[15] The couple may appear to have lost control over the cycles of conflict. This is, of course, highly damaging to the relationship: it erodes caring, rubs salt in emotional wounds and diminishes self-esteem.

It is usual for the emotional distancer to repress feelings. This is a system of containment, a kind of 'filing' of emotions away and the result is the loss of awareness that the pain ever existed. 'This phenomenon contributes to the myth that emotional distancers don't have feelings, they are cold and emotionless.'[16] Under pressure, this defence can break down and feelings flow in every direction. This can be very frightening because of the perceived loss of control. I have also found that there may be a risk that the distancer, usually the male, could become suicidal for a short period.

The initial task for the counsellor is to restore order. Structure reduces anxiety. It is best not to allow the couple to interrupt each other or make personal attacks. If this is impossible then it may be wise to see them separately for a few sessions. It is important to become more issue-oriented. For example:

Husband: *'She thinks I lie!'*
Counsellor: *'You have a credibility problem with your wife.'*

Process is more important than specific content.

Counsellor: *'So you believe John when he tells you that he has paid the bills, but not when he tells you who he has had lunch with. What criteria do you use for when to believe what he has said?'*

This also helps the couple to begin to think rather than simply react. It is too simplistic to assume that venting feelings will clear the air – it may further confuse matters. More often than not explosive displays of anger are part of the relationship dance. In fact, the ventilating of anger can give a false feeling of being in charge.[17] Alternatively, if the other partner has had trouble expressing anger then it may be helpful to empower that individual which may heighten conflict. This will help to end the myth that one spouse has a monopoly on any one emotion in the relationship.

It is natural under stress to focus on faults of the other, but this is not likely to lead to significant change. The counsellor has the goal of enhancing self-focus which reduces the natural tendency to blame the partner and introduces healthy change into the relationship. The basic rule is that self-focus reduces reactivity.

A review of current stresses has the effect of broadening what may be a limited perspective.

Jack and Carrie were aware of difficulties in their capacity to resolve arguments, but they did not appreciate the effect of accumulated pressure from the loss of Jack's job, the deteriorating health of Carrie's mother, their youngest child's falling grades, and financial problems.

The larger context also helps to address what might be a secret fear that they are failing in their marriage because they are bad people.[18]

Bitterness is usually an important dynamic. Guerin used the metaphor of making deposits in a 'bitter bank' and collecting interest. This metaphor is self-focusing and may help an individual gain awareness of the real cost of making such investments. The counsellor can help to trace bitterness back to early expectations in the relationship. This may provide opportunities for comparison with prior family experiences.

> Counsellor: *'You were disappointed when Jack didn't notice your extra efforts in cooking. Were those feelings familiar?'*
> Carrie: *'Yes, once I brought home a report card. Every grade was improved, but Dad only grunted.'*

This links present feelings to past experiences. It also helps to contradict such myths as: 'I was happy until I met Jack.' The genogram may reveal bitterness as a family pattern. Jack can see that men in his family typically have negative images of women; Carrie can see a long history of women as passive martyrs.

The genogram can also be used to identify family-of-origin triggers for conflict, conscious and unconscious contracts, role expectations, family rules, classic double binds, jealousy (usually linked to excessive dependency), and 'crazy-making situations'.

Although I have described this stage in terms of turbulent emotions, this is not always the case. There may be icy hostility with almost nothing said. The mood may be quiet and despairing – like being at a funeral when death was unexpected. But whatever the mood, progress in this stage is usually very slow.

A final thought about Stage III. One partner may have a fantasy solution. This is an idealized answer to the problems. Such a 'solution' may be divorce, living alone, an affair, or death of the spouse. This may provide the content of daydreams. Unfortunately this person will move away from working on the relationship towards the dream. If this is a problem – which may be sensed in lack of commitment to the counselling process – it may be necessary to have this possibility brought into the open and 'reality tested'. The counsellor can then more realistically point out that divorce is an option but hardly a solution.

Some marriages are remarkably stable in spite of intense and turbulent conflict. It is one way of binding anxiety and there are some positive aspects:

1. Conflict can provide a sense of emotional contact with the other person.

2. The tension and arguments justify both partners maintaining a comfortable emotional distance without feeling guilty.

3. It is easy to project blame onto the other and then feel in control as well as self-justified.

4. Since it absorbs anxiety, Kerr pointed out: 'So spouses in a conflictual marriage are less vulnerable to physical, emotional, or social symptoms. In addition, children of conflictual marriages are less vulnerable to symptoms.'[19]

This stage is quite a challenge to the counsellor. Progress is one step at a time. I find it helpful to think in terms of what Michael White calls 'unique outcomes'. From session to session we can notice progress by underlining the differences in the evolving relationship. Often the couple hardly seems to notice, but identifying the change is very encouraging.

It is commitment that makes all the difference. Not a commitment to romantic bliss, but to the partner in a realistic sense, 'Commitment means that one will not make a silent judgment and withdraw, wishing the "loved" person dead, but that one will risk conflict, again and again, to achieve the pleasure of mutual attentiveness . . . the acceptance of the ordeal by conflict is caring'.[20]

In addition to commitment, the most important factor is self-focus. I am reminded of the words of Jesus: 'Why do you see the speck in your brother's eye, but do not notice the log in your own eye . . . first take the log out of your own eye, and then you will see clearly to take the speck out of your brother's eye.' (Matthew 7:3,5) In this stage it is easy to despair in the face of difficulties, but I have also seen miraculous changes.

Just this last weekend I thought a relationship between close friends of ours was 'beyond hope', but my wife fasted and prayed for a change in heart. It now seems that her prayers have been answered and I am again working in a productive way with the couple.

Stage IV

Theologian Paul Tillich once described reality as that which we have to adapt to since it will not adjust to us. This is certainly true in the breakdown of a marriage. It is not any particular emotion that dominates, though anger and bitterness are certainly common. The sad reality is that, 'Marriages, like people, most often die as they have lived.'[21] Pain is the only constant. As Virginia Satir once observed about the hurt of rejection, there are two messages heard by the individual: 'No!' and 'You're no damn good!'

The end is usually resisted by one partner, but even that person's motivation to change will not be enough to save the marriage. The only glimmer of hope is when the partner who has initiated legal action has some ambivalence. In this case the counsellor can:

- Help each spouse to determine his or her 'bottom line'.
- Define what options remain other than divorce.
- Encourage both partners to understand more fully in what ways they contributed to the failure of the marriage.[22]

The importance of drawing a bottom line is obvious. Usually it is psychologically necessary for the reluctant partner to be able to let the relationship go, *for a wife to say to herself, 'I can live without being married to him.'* Only then can she say, 'These are the things I cannot *or will not tolerate in the marriage.'* Ideally it is not a reactive position. It is then possible to assure the spouse that this position is acting for the self and not against the partner. A bottom-line position evolves naturally from self-focus. What is my attitude on my spouse's drinking? Toleration of affairs? Verbal violence? It is also necessary in the process of separation. What access do I want? What property settlement? Will I take this to court? There is no right solution for all people. Rather, the bottom-line position should derive from an individual's self-respect, values, integrity, and dignity.

Another approach to counselling at this stage is to help draw up a contract of 'structured separation' as recommended by Donald Granvold. The couple negotiate a written contract specifying expected behaviour in the following areas: commitment to ongoing counselling, duration of separation, frequency of contact between partners, sexual intimacy between them, dating, sexual contact with others, privacy and access to children.[23] This structure is helpful in such an uncertain time because it is so objective and concrete. Granvold later added the following items to a separation contract: no final decision until the end of the agreed period, financial support, homework during counselling, and renegotiation.[24] This has the intention of allowing decisions to be made about the future of the relationship in an ordered and, hopefully, more secure way.

When is it time to tell the children about a separation? Perhaps it is best done when the parents have made concrete plans. They should not try to 'tell it all'. Glenda Banks gave as a general rule: 'Don't bite off more than your child can swallow.'[25] It is helpful to stress that the children were not responsible for the divorce, and that both parents will continue to love and care for them. Unfortunately, in this tense time it is easy for the children to become victims of displaced rage. Other inappropriate behaviours include attempts to win children as allies, quizzing for information about the ex-partner and asking them to be 'adult' confidants. Sometimes it is important to help the separating couple to distinguish marital problems from parental responsibilities.

It is generally acknowledged that children adjust better with both parents having free access. However, there may be factors which affect the welfare of the children, such as mental illness, alcoholism, violence and sexual abuse. In addition, court custody battles exact an emotional cost from all involved. In this difficult period one role of the counsellor is to help with 'damage control'.

In spite of all the difficulties, the extended family should not be neglected. The counsellor should encourage children to visit grandparents (who may worry about ever seeing them again!), aunts, uncles, cousins, and family friends. This may also open up other avenues of support. If the church fellowship is not too judgmental about the separation, this may be an important source of acceptance and concrete acts which can do much to convey the love of God.

The reluctant spouse may feel considerable anxiety about the future. Reassuring messages can help: 'What you are going through is normal'; I have every confidence that you will survive and make another life for yourself'; 'You are not going crazy' and, for Christians, biblical promises such as 'God is faithful, and he will not let you be tempted beyond your strength.' (I Corinthians 10:13) If distress is very high, it may be necessary to assist him or her to sort out priorities, list daily responsibilities, verbalize fears and rehearse new behaviours. If the person remains unrealistic in still chasing the spouse, then some form of confrontation about 'letting go' will be necessary.

The emotional distancer will generally present as more calm. There is a risk, however, that this person will move too fast out of the relationship. This can mean going to live with the 'other person' or moving out of town. Sometimes this is an attempt to cover feelings of loss. It is also possible that 'they are running faster in response to their spouse's desperate behaviour, afraid that they might look back at their own ambivalence and change their minds.'[26]

The legal system is best left to the guidance of lawyers specializing in Family Law. There are, however, difficulties that can spill over into counselling because the relationship has been placed in this adversarial context. Lawyers may well have goals such as getting the best deal for their client or winning sole custody. These goals may be counter to therapeutic aims and a wise balance is needed. In the past I have advised couples to look at services of mediation which attempt to help people work out their own settlement, with the proviso that legal representatives of both parties should check over any written agreement. [27]

Counselling in this stage is often with only one spouse, the other having left or having no desire to work on the relationship. The Bowen style of therapy is not limited by access to only one partner. Introducing change through the more motivated person can reverberate throughout the family system. The focus usually begins to shift from the partner to the self and then taking responsibility which is essential for the future. It is fundamentally a focus on increasing strengths rather than shoring up weaknesses.

The present high divorce rate is not because marriage is less important, but because marriage has become all important. Expectations are so high that individuals have no tolerance for the imperfect marital partner or a less than ideal life style. It is sad that couples ask so much from each other and appear so unwilling to give in return. [28]

Is divorce a failure? Sometimes yes and sometimes no. It is a therapeutic success when a person can take responsibility for past actions, learn from experience, have insights into what went wrong, gain some awareness of emotional patterns from the original family and be willing to trust their real self in a new relationship. The process of recovery and changing the 'stumbling blocks into building blocks' is well described by Bruce Fisher in *Rebuilding: When Your Relationship Ends.* [29]

It is my hope that the Church can respond with compassion and sensitivity to couples in marital crisis. Sometimes the people will find a better future together; sometimes separation and divorce appears to be the only course of action. Then we can discover whether the Church is indeed the 'second chance' community.

Exercises

Interview a number of couples who have gone through a period of crisis in their marriages. Include a few who have separated and divorced. Can you identify the stages they passed through? What did they find helpful? What advice and response were regrettable? Assess the role of clergy and church members in their experience.

Also look at your own genogram. What themes will help or hinder your work in developing as a marriage counsellor? Can you identify possible countertransference issues you will face?

To read further

P. Guerin, Jnr, L. F. Fay, S. L. Burden, and J. G. Kautto, *The Evaluation and Treatment of Marital Conflict: A Four-stage Approach*, Basic Books, New York, 1987. I have depended on this book for much of this chapter. It is the most helpful guide to working with couples in marital distress that I have found.

TECHNIQUES IN MARRIAGE COUNSELLING

In this chapter I will outline some practical exercises which will enable a couple to better communicate and defuse anger in the relationship.

When a couple has indicated a willingness to work on their relationship, we usually contract to meet together for a number of sessions. This may be quite informal, but nevertheless I would consider it morally binding. When the problems appear to be less serious it may be for as few as six sessions; more if the difficulties are more entrenched. Stage II conflict would generally fit into this time scale, but if it was complicated by a major problem such as alcoholism then counselling might need to be open-ended. In marriage counselling the counsellor will usually teach the couple more effective ways of communication.

Harville Hendrix has suggested a number of helpful exercises.[1] I will outline a few of these: mirroring; caring behaviours; behaviour change requests; container transaction.

Mirroring Exercise

The purpose of this exercise is to train the couple to send clear, simple messages and to learn to listen carefully to what has been said. The sender has the initial task of expressing a thought or feeling. He or she begins with the word 'I'. For example, 'I woke up this morning and felt anxious about going to work.' The receiver listens carefully (without interruptions!) and then paraphrases the message, 'This morning you woke up feeling that you would rather stay at home than go to work. Did I understand what you said and felt?' The asking for clarification is important because it shows a willingness to try to understand.

The sender then affirms the feedback, 'Yes, that's it,' or clarifies, 'Not exactly. I woke up wanting to go to work but dreading what was going to happen.' The process continues until the sender is satisfied that the full message has been heard. I would usually allow about ten minutes. Then the couple swap roles. This should be practised until it is quite natural for both partners. [2]

This exercise is central to the work of improving communication. But it is not as easy to carry out as it may appear. In the beginning it may be necessary for the counsellor continually to enforce the 'rules', especially when emotions are hot and reactivity is high. Most couples tend to lose control and go into 'automatic pilot'. There is a great temptation to interrupt, become defensive, justify oneself, interrogate, anything but listen carefully and clarify! Listening is a skill which can be taught and learnt reasonably quickly although some caution needs to be exercised in setting this as a homework exercise. If the couple have difficulties in keeping to their roles then it should first be more thoroughly practised in sessions with the counsellor.

In my experience, couples usually find this exercise very affirming. It is a rare experience in some marriages for anyone to feel 'heard'. Individuals are often amazed at how valued they feel. It is something of a luxury to have their partner's full attention, and there is the additional benefit of a rise in self-esteem resulting from being taken seriously.

Claire Bickmore, a local psychiatric nurse, has suggested a written version of this exercise. The couple write a page or so in their mutual journal either to initiate a topic or to respond. Then after the writing and response, a time is set aside to talk about what is in the journal. This method also has the advantage of providing a record of their improving communication.

Caring behaviours

It is not unusual for a couple to gradually 'take each other for granted'. With unresolved conflict; the relationship deteriorates to a point where there is more mutual pain than benefit. In the power struggle the couple stop giving to each other. The atmosphere may be icy or turbulent with hot exchanges but the effect is that two people feel alone and totally unloved. The purpose of this next exercise is to reintroduce positive experiences into the relationship.

The counsellor asks each partner to make a list of ten examples of past behaviours by the spouse that have communicated love and caring. For example, the husband may begin his list:

1. Kisses me as I leave for work.

2. Cooks a special meal.

3. Spontaneously cuddles me, etc.

The wife may list:

1. Phones me at home.

2. Writes me a love letter when away on a trip.

3. Notices how I dress, etc.

It is important not to list unrealistic expectations such as: 'Buys me a new car.' What is listed are simple affectionate gestures that mean a great deal. This exercise changes spontaneous behaviours - sometimes forgotten since the courtship period - into target behaviours designed to please the partner.

Sometimes a person will do things that are intended to communicate caring but which the spouse does not in fact appreciate. Therefore the person making each list must be the authority on what was or is experienced as 'caring'. This helps the couple to see that what pleases one may not be the same for the other and is a step towards better differentiation of self.

It is sometimes hard for individuals to remember any caring behaviours at all. I then ask them to recall the courtship period, 'How did you treat each other when you were first in love?' Another difficulty can be the negative request to refrain from hurtful behaviour: 'Please stop putting me down in front of your friends.' It has to be a list of positive caring acts not a request to stop wounding behaviours. The list might also include some items of a wish list with suggestions of what might be pleasing. Again, it must be emphasized, that it is each person's responsibility to write a personal list of gestures that are to be caring without either partner judging what should be appreciated by the other.

Then I ask the couple to exchange their lists and each to attempt one behaviour from the other's list each day. There is no score card. They are both given the task of focusing on the behaviour 'with no strings attached'. It may seem artificial at first, but this exercise almost inevitably changes the mood of the relationship and raises the level of goodwill. The exercise also helps to counter the tit-for-tat mentality of the power struggle. There is also a need for each partner to experience being loved if they are both to face the painful issues that have accumulated in the relationship.

After a while these behaviours may need to be 'spiced up'. Hendrix recommends that each partner make a list of surprises to delight the other. This list is not shared. Each partner then takes the initiative and selects from their list an item pleasantly to surprise their partner. This might include arranging tickets for a concert or making a picnic lunch. The surprises might be encouraged on a monthly or even weekly basis.

Behaviour change requests

The negotiation of change is an obvious part of the counselling process. Irritating behaviours can aggravate and be upsetting in the healthiest of relationships, so the next exercise involves each partner making a list of specific requests for change. The other partner can choose to comply or not. This is similar to the caring behaviour exercise in that the emphasis is on the giving rather than a contractual obligation.

In specific terms each partner makes a list of the spouse's irritating behaviours. This is commonly in the form of 'I don't like it when . . .' Each of these items is then recast in the form of a desire that underlies the frustration. For example, 'I don't like it when you drive too fast,' becomes 'I would like to feel safe and relaxed when you drive.' Then it is changed into a request to meet that desire such as: 'When you are driving, I would like you to observe the speed limit. If the road conditions are bad, then I would like you to drive even more slowly.' These items can be rated in order of importance. The list is then given to the partner.

This exercise has the potential benefit of changing frequent criticisms into a more positive plan of action. It is also important to allow time in sessions for the couple to work on resolving 'hot issues'. Sometimes the presence of the counsellor helps the couple to feel safe enough to address the difficulties and gradually either to tolerate expressions of conflict or keep them within workable limits.

Container transaction

Anger is a problem that must be addressed. Like Hydra, the nine-headed serpent, it has many forms. Some people explode in bouts of rage. Others try to throttle their rage but let it seep out as corrosive criticism, or may even further repress it until it becomes severe depression.

This 'container' exercise allows the couple to express anger and resentment in a safe environment. It is similar to the mirroring exercise in allowing expression without the partner invalidating, countering or denying the anger. This is especially important in resolving the resentment and bitterness inherent in Stage III. When one person has an intense frustration or angry reaction, he or she says, 'I am angry. Are you willing to listen?' If the other person is too busy, then a time is arranged as soon as possible. The containing partner then takes a few deep breaths, tries to visualize the other as a hurting child and then indicates a willingness to listen. It may also be helpful for the container to put on some imaginary protective armour (Christians might consider Ephesians 6: 10-17).

The angry person has some rules to follow: Describe behaviour that is upsetting, but do not call the spouse abusive names. Express anger with words, but do not touch the other in a hostile manner or damage property. For example, an angry wife might say, 'I am angry that you forgot to pay the bill,' but not 'You are so irresponsible!' The receiver reflects back the feelings and content, in the same way as the mirroring exercise. Perhaps the listener can also say, 'I want to hear more about your anger.' In this way the containing partner is affirming the other's right to be angry, but not necessarily agreeing with every part of the point of view. Once this has been done the angry partner can convert the frustration into a behaviour change request.

In the counselling sessions both partners need to get a chance to work on their anger. It is quite common for a person to be seen as the angry one in the relationship. But it is unlikely that either one will have a monopoly on angry feelings. The more silent partner may be repressing even more unresolved anger, but has not taken an opportunity to express it. With this sort of attention the anger can begin to dissipate. The container exercise can potentially lead to quite a lot of reactivity, so it is wise to keep practising it in the presence of the counsellor until the level of tension is reduced.

I have seen many couples in which unresolved anger has blocked their capacity to love. All too often this will include Christian couples. St Paul wrote about the value of dealing with anger, 'Be angry but do not sin; do not let the sun go down on your anger.' (Ephesians 4:26) Clearly it is to be accepted, but not to be allowed to fester into resentment and bitterness. I am certain that something in us 'dies' if we stop feeling any of our natural emotions. God created us to be 'fully alive' (St Irenaeus).

There is a tendency in the power struggle for the couple to be too serious and too rigid. This can make it difficult to try anything different. I find it best to introduce these exercises with a sense of gentle playfulness and humour. Harville Hendrix has a total of sixteen different exercises. I have not tried them all in counselling but those I have used have proved most beneficial.

Triangles

Occasionally you can still find a three-legged stool in an antique store. Such primitive furniture has limited appeal but provides an example of the stability of the triangular base. Triangles are stable in relationships as well. This is such an important concept for clinical intervention that I will now look at the theory of triangles in some detail. Murray Bowen has added a great deal to the way we understand triangles. He saw dyadic relationships (between two people) as less stable because of competing needs for autonomy and connectedness. Therefore the triangle is the basic molecule of emotional systems. It is the smallest stable unit.

Triangles provide a paradigm for the way people manage the intensity of emotional attachments. In any three-person system there will be significant differences in the way individuals relate to each other, such as two tending to be closer to each other with the third as an outsider. The bond between the closer two may be warm and intimate or highly conflictual. The distance to the third person can also vary. It may not be initially obvious, but according to Bowen's theory each of the three people plays an equal part in contributing to the stability of the system. The comfort of the positions will vary: if the couple are close and happy then the third person may feel painfully excluded; if the couple are always fighting then it may either be cosy or embarrassing to be the outsider.

Bowen observed that three interconnected relationships can absorb more anxiety because the pathways are in place that allow tension to be shifted around the system.[3] The lower the level of differentiation in the marriage or family, the more important the role of triangles becomes for preserving emotional stability.[4]

This seems very abstract until expressed in concrete terms. *Arthur and Maggie have been married just three weeks and they have their first fight. Maggie rings her mother and Arthur goes to the pub to be with his mates.* This illustrates two triangles which are activated by the rise in tension. The respective allies help to soothe the sudden pain and indirectly calm the marital relationship so things can return to normal.

Triangles are natural. Such patterns of relationships are as ubiquitous as the air we breathe. However, it is easy to see that triangles can be harmful. They can lead to secrets and private lines of communication. Triangles can also heighten conflict. This is seen in the classic mother-in-law triangle. If the counsellor is to assess the potential destructiveness of a triangle then there is a need to pay attention to the unresolved and avoided issues in the primary relationship. If these issues are resolved it will soon take intensity out of the other relationship.

Bowen also saw that a lack of differentiation in the family raises anxiety; and intensifies triangles. Problems tend to occur when the triangles become rigid or entrenched. The most obvious indicator is when people 'always' take sides. Triangles can interlock and the intensity spills over. But when anxiety is low the patterns may be hardly visible.[5]

Triangles endure through the generations. Once the emotional pattern is in place, it may well outlive the people who participate in it. Children may act out a conflict that was never resolved between great-grandparents. We can see that a triangle is not necessarily created by the individuals presently involved. Anxiety tends to activate, not create, triangles. The genogram can be a helpful tool to identify such patterns through the family. It is an objectifying process and the recognition of a triangle is often the first step in making changes.

One of the most common problems in a troubled marriage is the extramarital affair.[6] This has been called the 'eternal triangle'. Affairs are inevitably destructive. 'By far the largest part of extramarital activity is secret and furtive, violate of the emotional entente existing between the spouses, productive of internal conflict and guilt feelings on the part of the one engaging in such acts, and anywhere from infuriating to shattering to the other if he or she discovers the truth.'[7]

Another example: *Will and Marg have been married eight years. There has not been much 'sparkle' in their relationship for quite a while. Will became attracted to a colleague and what began as a few drinks after work ended up with sexual involvement. Will is now less troubled by Marg's emotional coldness, the affair has drained away some of the tension from the marriage. This is a false calm before the emotional storm when Marg finds out about the relationship.* The affair illustrates the principle that powerful triangles that involve another person outside the immediate family almost always represent an externalization of the dysfunctional process going on in the family.[8] Thus it helps to keep the real issues, such as unresolved conflict in the primary relationship, 'safely' underground.

News of the affair may lead the couple to seek counselling. Sometimes it is revealed in the first weeks. My first response is to balance the 'blame'. The 'innocent' spouse has been equally involved in an 'affair' through overinvolvement in work, relatives, church, club or in parenting children. This counteraffair has also been at the expense of the marriage. *How long has it been since Marg has been spontaneous and affectionate? Will may also have to face how he has used his affair as a refuge from pain in the marriage.*

In these rocky waters, progress is usually very difficult. It is natural that bitterness and resentment will escalate. The betrayed spouse may become obsessed with details: Who? When? How many times? Is the other person a better lover? Intense jealousy is the norm. *It may also be difficult to get Will to make up his mind about the future. If he has difficulty choosing, then it may be advisable to encourage him to take time out to think about the issues. This might mean that Will is encouraged to take a room on his own for a few days or a week, not see either his wife or his lover, and then try to come to a decision.*

If he decides to end the affair, there should be some evidence of the loss and the grief can be addressed. If there is no sign of loss, then it may well be continuing in a covert manner. Until a decision is made one way or the other it is difficult, perhaps impossible, to make any progress in therapy. It should also be noted that some people will want to keep both the affair and the marriage. Generally this is unacceptable to the spouse.

Usually there is intense reactivity. It is difficult for each person to examine the distance in the marital relationship that preceded the affair. Once the husband and wife can begin to understand the meaning of the affair in the wider context of their relationship, then they can make moves to shift their positions in the triangle. Reestablishing trust is a slow process. Sometimes it is necessary to slow the people down since some couples will want to embark immediately on a second honeymoon. It is better to go back to courtship and rebuild the relationship with companionship and mutually enjoyable activities. I have also found that a renewal of marriage vows near the end of therapy is a wonderful ritual of new beginnings.

An affair sometimes means the end of a marriage, but this is by no means certain. Many relationships deepen through the crisis and both partners come to appreciate more fully the love that they have for each other.

There are, of course, other potent triangles. One source is the in-laws. In the Bible, a shift of primary attachment was described, 'Therefore a man leaves his father and his mother and clings to his wife, and they become one flesh.' (Genesis 2.24) This separation is not easily attained. It is painful to watch some of the dramas that can surround the marriage ceremony. When one side pays for the reception, cars, flowers, and photos, the question then becomes, 'Who controls the event?' Money does not even have to be a factor, emotional ties and family loyalties can strangle a couple in the formative years of their marriage. Initial disapproval may lead to attempts to undermine and destroy the relationship. *I once encountered a mother-in-law who offered a holiday house to her daughter and a potential lover to 'get away from the pressures at home'.* Sometimes the couple unite in the face of such interference. This may lead to an emotional cut-off to ease tension, but this is a tactic that does little to reduce the destructiveness of the triangle.

It is often possible to encourage the spouse least caught up in the triangle to experiment with different moves. *One example of this was a 'disapproved of' husband who invited the in-laws over to watch a video of the wedding while his wife was away visiting friends. This was detriangling because he took the initiative to move closer to the distancing in-laws and did this in the absence of his wife.*

Another intervention is to locate conflict in the troubled relationship. *A case in point was a couple who had a very calm marital relationship, but terrible difficulties with both sets of parents.* The conflict in the 'calm' marriage had to be faced in order to clarify the real dynamics in the marital relationship and to lessen the spillover of emotional reactivity onto other relationships. As a general principle, a spouse who fails to address issues in his or her own family of origin will import such issues into the present relationship and one symptom of this will be a tendency to overreact to in-laws.

Children are inevitably triangled. For example: *Maddie shares deeply in long conversations with her eldest daughter Angela. Her husband Thomas is emotionally distant and justifies this as concern about work. Maddie often confides to Angela her dissatisfaction in the marriage and recently let slip that Thomas had had an affair the year before.* [This triangle has become rigid and it will not be easy to initiate changes.] *If Thomas makes a move towards Angela, perhaps to help her with homework, he may find resistance from Maddie criticizing his parenting. Her real message is in effect saying, 'Keep away! I have exclusive parenting rights.' Maddie is in a position to most easily introduce change, perhaps encouraging Thomas to help with homework or go out bowling with Angela.* In healthy families the focus of conflict varies. Systems with more fluid triangles can tolerate more conflict because of that capacity for distribution around the various relationships.

A more subtle triangle is that of the 'acting out' adolescent. *Johnny has been missing school and was caught shoplifting last week. The parents drag their sullen youth into their pastor's study in the hope that he will be straightened out. Johnny is in the role of the 'identified patient'. However, the unconscious dynamic is that Johnny has noticed that the only time his parents ever agree is to condemn him. Johnny is acting in a way to take the heat out of his parents' relationship and this is his best chance of maintaining family stability.* This illustrates the principle that children can become symptomatic when caught in a destructive triangle. The symptoms vary and may include anorexia, depression, criminal behaviour, and attempts at suicide.

Blended families are fertile ground for difficult triangles. These include: the 'wicked stepmother' triangle, left out grandparents, replacement mother role, 'my dad' versus 'your mum', etc. The mixture of family loyalties and new demands makes the situation difficult indeed.

One advantage of recognizing triangles is that the pattern, not the person, becomes the problem. Couples can be helped to deal with rigid triangles by:

1. Keeping conflict focused on the issue. It helps to deal directly with the conflict in the relationship where it belongs and not to displace anger onto someone else.

2. Avoiding using a child, even a grown-up one, as a 'marital therapist' or go-between.

3. Distinguishing between respect for privacy and 'playing secrets'. Gossip and secrets encourage triangles because such behaviour requires that two or more persons conspire to exclude another or others.

4. Keeping lines of communication open without inviting others to blame or take sides in battles.

The rules of 'defusing' a triangle are: stay calm (anxiety and intense emotions drive triangles), stay out (leave the other two to manage their own relationship: no advising, helping, criticizing, blaming, fixing, lecturing, analysing, etc.), and keep in emotional contact with the other two people. This neutrality is calming. It is an indication of a higher level of self-differentiation when an individual is able to keep the problem in the relationship from which it is trying to escape.

One advantage of working with the Bowen model of family

therapy is that it enables the counsellor to see the person who is willing to make changes. This can be a non-symptomatic member of the system. Self-focus can be encouraged and small changes can be made that can have quite profound effects in the family system. It should not be forgotten that the counsellor in marital therapy is quickly triangled into the marital relationship. This is natural and gives the opportunity to model effective detriangling moves by maintaining both neutrality and emotional connectedness.

Marriage counselling can be very satisfying. I often find myself feeling stimulated and full of energy at the end of a session. Sometimes after the most acute crisis a couple can use what appears to be very little given by the counsellor, and then build on this foundation a stable and satisfying marriage, even after the disclosure of an affair. But it can also be the most perplexing and frustrating form of counselling. You can work with a couple and find all that you thought had been gained 'falling down like a house of cards' and the relationship breaking up. Perhaps this kind of work is inherently unpredictable. It is counselling 'on the edge'.

Exercises

Practise in your training group the reflecting and container exercises by role playing marital couples in distress. The most important skill is the counsellor learning to guide the couple in performing the exercises.

If you have a spouse or very close friend try writing the journal exercise. This may be a way of exploring spiritual themes in your relationship.

MARITAL CASE STUDIES

A few years ago a recently married couple in the church came to see me. They were in a crisis. The husband, Tim, was making out a will and he proposed to leave a business he was starting up to his daughter who was a recent graduate in business studies. His wife, Elaine, who also had children from a previous marriage, reacted sharply because she felt her children were being left out of family property. I soon realized that the issue was loaded by experiences in previous relationships. Tim had lost nearly everything in the property settlement from his divorce two years before. Elaine's previous marriage had ended when her husband of twenty years went to live with a male lover. I explained the concept of 'ghosts' from previous relationships and soon they were able to focus on the immediate issue of conflict without opening previous wounds.

This was a simple intervention to a distressing problem. It is not often that such dramatic results occur in the first session. At the time I felt like something of a 'miracle worker', but later realized that the conflict was basically at Stage I and therefore easy to resolve.

Couples who seek counselling generally have poor styles of communication. This is not always the case, some couples can communicate but are not able to resolve conflict. This leads to difficulties in meeting legitimate needs in the relationship. There may also be dysfunctional patterns of behaviour. It can be puzzling that couples are so often stuck in destructive patterns, but partly this can be explained by Harriet Lerner's observation that 'repeating the same old fights protects us from the anxieties we are bound to experience when we make a change.'[1] These can then become the target of counsellor intervention.

The following dysfunctional patterns of behaviour are common: *pursuer and distancer; underfunctioner and overfunctioner; deselfing for the relationship.*

Pursuer and distancer

Marital therapist, Tom Fogarty, has described the nature of much couple interaction in terms of an emotional pattern of pursuing and distancing. It is common for the husband to present in the interview as reserved, calm and logical whereas the wife appears more spontaneous and emotionally responsive. This is not a rule because couples and circumstances vary, but it seems to me that in our culture females tend to be more emotionally pursuing and males more distancing.

Pursuers may have grown up feeling somewhat emotionally deprived. In the extreme these are people who have an insatiable need for closeness, crave physical closeness and constant reassurance. In general pursuers are characterized by:

1. Affinity for time together.

2. Ready expression of feelings.

3. Allow access to personal space, e.g. 'I don't mind if you just drop by.'

4. Go through life at extremes of 'full speed ahead' or 'dead stop'.

5. May easily feel rejected or label themselves as too dependent.

6. Place a high value on talking things out.

7. Make demands explicit.

8. Have difficulty saying goodbye.

Distancers may have had problems establishing independence in childhood and had to strive to be a distinct self. They tend to keep their distance and typically:

1. Have an affinity for time alone.
2. Avoid expressions of feelings, especially on the needy or vulnerable side.
3. Guard personal space, consider themselves private people and self-reliant.
4. A deliberate and steady rhythm of action.
5. Object-centred: the object may be a book, TV or computer screen.
6. Expectations left implicit.
7. Have less apparent pain with endings.

These differences may be complementary during the courtship period. It is easy to see that two isolators will hardly meet – let alone get on – and two fusers will quickly drive each other crazy. There is a comfortable balance which can lead to marriage. However, with the stress of married life these styles of managing intimacy may become unbalanced. The perception of the distancing partner will be that of being crowded, trapped, controlled, smothered and absorbed. The pursuer is also in distress because he or she will feel isolated, unsupported, unloved, or rejected.[2]

An example of this is Bill and Libby who came into counselling with conflict over how much time they spent together. Bill told the therapist how he had recently gone into a retail business and this required long hours of work. Libby had just given birth to a second child and she had to work part-time to make ends meet. Both were feeling overwhelmed by the extra demands. In this stressful situation Libby would challenge

Bill, 'Late again! Why aren't you home more often?' Predictably, this raised Bill's anxiety level and he would escape to read the paper. The last thing he wanted to do was listen while Libby spilt her emotional overload. Both were seeking a means to release inner tension but ended up reacting to each other. The next scene began with Libby maintaining a reactive distance. Bill realized that there was a change in the atmosphere and asked, 'What's wrong, dear?' She answered glumly, 'Nothing.'

This may lead to peaks in the conflict and then periods of relative calm. But it will happen again and again. Guerin noted: 'If the stress and anxiety remain high, and this pattern recycles more and more rapidly, the disappointments, anger, and hurt begin to accumulate.'[3] Libby may tire of her attempts to move towards Bill and retreat to an 'island of invulnerability'. Sometimes this is characterized by a state of numbness common in Stage III conflict.

The solution to a problem like Bill and Libby's is not to be found in simplistic answers. The advice of friends and well-meaning professionals is often to push one side of the 'see-saw'. Some marriage enrichment programmes emphasize intimate conversations and self-disclosure – the pursuing dimension. On the other hand Dr Glenn Wilson of the Institute of Psychiatry in London expressed doubts about the ascendancy of female values in Marriage Guidance Councils, 'If the councils were dominated by men, they'd probably be advising women to let their men retire to their dens in peace to play with their model planes; and that might create less strain on the marriage.'[4] Neither approach is satisfactory.

The problem is due to a dysfunctional pattern in the relationship, an imbalance of intimacy and solitude. Distancing is a normal way of managing intensity or emotional reactivity in a relationship; it can help an individual to become calm enough to reflect, plan and generate new options for the future. It is not the result of a lack of feeling, but is more likely a response to an overflow of emotionality. However, too much distancing can be intensely frustrating to a spouse and escalate conflict.

When a couple are in such intense conflict, the pursuer tends to believe that all that is needed is more togetherness; the distancer is equally convinced that the only need is for more space in the relationship. An initial approach then is to ask the couple to begin to observe how they regulate their relationship. Some objectivity may help each of them to realize that the problem is not completely the fault of the other person. The couple may begin to sense some ambivalence in themselves. This awareness may help them to be more willing to try different behaviours.

For instance the counsellor may coach the pursuer to be more distancing and then to notice the results. Some couples retain a sense of playfulness and homework assignments like changing roles on alternate days can enhance self-focus and change ingrained patterns. Gradually both can begin to solve problems and find ways to meet needs for both space and emotional connectedness. It is important to find a satisfying balance that works for them. *One couple I saw a few years ago started lessons in ballroom dancing, which I thought was a wonderful metaphor of the rhythm they sought in their marriage.* Once a level of self-focus has been achieved, and some objectivity, it is possible to work towards a more satisfying balance of emotional pursuit and distance. The most important variable is the degree of self-differentiation of the marital partners, since well-differentiated people are not easily threatened by each other, their relationships are more flexible.[5]

As a postscript, some recent research in human biology suggests that these patterns of pursuit and distance are located in biological differences between the sexes. For example, the male brain appears to be more compartmentalized. This results in being more object-centred and the emotions tend to be cut off from the capacity to verbalize.

Anne Moir and David Jessel concluded, 'A woman brings to the relationship emotional sensitivity, a capacity for interdependence, a yearning for companionship and for sex to reflect that emotional intimacy. A man, if not totally blind to the importance of emotions, has a less demanding emotional nature. He has the capacity for independence and sees his duties in the marital contract in terms of providing financial security. He wants a 'good' sex life, as a result of which his wife will people the small state with the family he needs . . . and make solid his own foundations in life.'[6]

Underfunctioners and overfunctioners

In a tense family system there may be extremes of underfunctioning and overfunctioning. Underfunctioners tend to be labelled as 'the sick one', 'the spoilt brat', 'the irresponsible son', 'the black sheep', or the 'troublemaker'. Sometimes the labels are psychiatric: depressed, schizophrenic, agoraphobic or anorexic. Addictions also fall into this category: 'Mum, do you have any money? Dad spends all his on beer and the races.'

Overfunctioners tend to get the praise from family and friends. Some of their characteristics include:

1. Know what is best not only for themselves but for others as well.

2. Move in quickly to advise, fix, rescue, and take over when stress rises.

3. Have difficulty staying out of the problems of others and allowing them to struggle with their own issues.

4. Avoid worrying about their own personal goals and problems by focusing on others.

5. Have difficulty sharing their own vulnerable underfunctioning side.

6. May be seen as people who are 'always reliable' or 'always together'.[7]

Overfunctioning is a form of pursuing because the focus is on the other person. What is not so obvious lies beneath the surface of the overfunctioner's competence. There may be such unwelcome feelings such as anger, sadness, anxiety and the emptiness of unfulfilled needs. Unfortunately, if some of the overfunctioner's needs were to be met in the relationship, it would mean being 'one down'. And this might be a blow to pride.

This unhealthy balance is often seen in relationships. An overfunctioning 'rescuer' can have a stable relationship with an underfunctioning alcoholic spouse. This pattern, though obviously dysfunctional and limiting, may be a good neurotic compromise. If there is little motivation for change, it may be advisable to try to introduce therapeutic movement elsewhere.

According to Bowen's theory of family systems, anxiety may be tied up in various symptoms. Alcoholism is one example of dealing with anxiety, but there are many other ways: drugs, overeating, chronic mental illness and addictions. Sometimes physical symptoms such as cancer, heart disease, ulcers, and asthma may also be seen in this light. In another sphere social dysfunction might include criminal behaviour. This pattern provides yet another way of understanding why families can be stuck.

If the balance in the relationship is to improve then there will have to be some changes. This is difficult because the over-functioner tends to feel self-righteous, the insider in most of the family triangles, and the one the family always speaks *to* rather than *about*. It is generally hard for overfunctioners to admit that they also have a problem. However the overfunctioner is usually the key to change. If there is a husband with a chronically depressed wife, the counsellor might encourage the overfunctioner to stop giving advice and begin to be more vulnerable and to share personal needs with the underfunctioning partner. This helps him to relate to her areas of competence. If this does not happen, 'it is far less likely that the other person will put energy into their own recovery and they will have to work twice as hard even to be in touch with their own competence.'[8] Nor is there motivation to assume responsibility when a spouse appears willing to 'do everything' in the relationship. The challenge for the overfunctioner is to shift focus from taking responsibility for the partner, to playing a responsible role in the relationship.

When such patterns have been established in a relationship for many years, change tends to be slow and painful. It may be helpful to say to the couple trying to adjust that occasional failures are a normal part of recovery. These barriers are not overcome without the seeming defeat of returning time and time again to old ways of relating. But growth is its own reward. A more balanced relationship becomes possible. It is more satisfying and reflects an authentic self.

Deselfing for the relationship

What do these imbalanced relationships have in common? A young woman has put up with her husband's repeated affairs for many years, an older man has been dominated by every whim of his wife, a newly married woman is under intense pressure to play fantasy roles after her husband has watched porno movies. Harriet Lerner observed a common pattern of deselfing in marriages 'when too much of the self becomes negotiable under relationship pressures.'[9] When a person has substance in his self, it is seen in the way he relates to his spouse. He can be more true to himself rather than being coerced into fulfilling what others need, wish, and expect. Obviously there is give and take in most relationships, but a deselfed position is a one-way street – the partner always takes. This can result in: chronic anger, bitterness, feelings of depression, anxiety, low self-esteem and even self-hatred.

When an individual overfocuses on the marriage relationship at the expense of life goals and personal development, the result is deselfing. There is a cultural dimension in this, women have been conditioned historically to sacrifice the 'I' for the 'we', just as men have been encouraged to bolster the 'I' at the expense of reasonable connectedness to others.[10] It may appear that males have more self but it is often a pseudo-self which is acquired at the expense of others and this pattern requires the relationship to be imbalanced. It is, in this sense, a 'borrowed self'. The inequality may be most obvious with issues such as power, sex, money, and children. Sometimes the man is in a deselfed position. The stereotyped image of the 'henpecked' husband would be an example. Another dimension for many Christians is the traditional teaching of 'death to self' in the Church. But I think that this teaching is confused with the way conversion changes the 'old life', as the apostle said, 'We know that our old self was crucified with him so that the body of sin might be destroyed, and we might no longer be enslaved to sin.' (Romans 6:6) Christ came to give us life and wholeness – not to diminish us through pseudo-piety.

There are harmful results from deselfing. There may be a tendency for marriages to become polarized. This can accentuate open and hidden conflict. It is also possible for two people both to deself, seeking greater harmony for the relationship, but this can be at the expense of children who become dysfunctional because such a family has little capacity for an individual to function with autonomy.

In spite of such costs, many marriages acquire stability through deselfing. Thus, when a counsellor helps a deselfed person to grow, this can lead to the break-up of a marriage. When he or she begins to be more assertive or reclaim more of the self this introduces change into the relationship – and all change is risky. For example: *Beth was married to George who served as a major in the army. She returned to college and had an ideological conversion to feminism. This led to her rejection of what she saw as Christian 'baggage' and she refused to attend church with her husband. A 'women's group supported Beth in her progress towards independence. This resulted in a rapid shift in roles in the marriage and George threatened to leave. At this point they sought counselling: George wanted his 'old' wife back, Beth wanted George to assume more responsibility at home.*

Such couples usually need to slow down and regain their balance. It is not possible for Beth to deny her own growth towards wholeness, but it is her responsibility to pace changes to what it is possible for George and the family to manage. Even small steps are sometimes met with frustrations and derailments – 'change back' moves which are to be expected in the process of change. The temptation is for one partner to begin with a 'big bang' and then to become discouraged when results are minimal. There is some virtue in thinking small and taking time for the rest of the family to adjust. There is often a need for counselling when making such changes.

I should also add that seeing only one partner for marital issues is a risk for the stability of the marriage. If the counselling is 'successful' that person will change and may grow out of the relationship. If possible, the counsellor should see both partners and encourage both to change 'in step' with each other.

Lerner lists the characteristics of a person higher on the selfhood scale. He or she can:

1. Present a balanced picture of both strengths and vulnerabilities.

2. Make clear statements about beliefs, values, and priorities (behaviour is congruent).

3. Stay emotionally connected to other significant people (even under stress and emotional pressure).

4. Address difficult and painful issues and take a position on important issues.

5. State differences and allow others to do the same.[11]

A conscious marital relationship is possible only to the extent that both partners are able to be adult and relate to each other from wholeness of self.

Progress is possible only by self-focus. What usually happens in a relationship under stress is that each partner will project blame onto the other. This is perfectly natural, but when the expected responses aren't forthcoming, the result is a feeling of powerlessness which leads to an inevitable 'stuckness'. Yet when an individual begins to define himself there will be an initial rise in anxiety, which can lead to considerable turbulence in the relationship, but in the long run, to a more satisfying marriage. A more clearly defined self is potentially very attractive. I have often heard it said by a person who has been divorced for a year or so that their previous partner is now more attractive. I think this is due to the new level of independence which reflects a higher level of self. An important therapeutic goal is to introduce this 'attractive element' into the relationship while there is still time to save the marriage.

It is also important not to neglect the wider family. The genogram can be used to plan moves to bridge the emotional cutoffs. This not only helps to lower anxiety in the family, but also enables an individual to restore communication contact with other family members. The most effective way of self-defining is *in* the relationship.

A case study

A couple who attended a Seventh Day Adventist Church came to see me just six months after their marriage. They were in their mid-thirties and neither had been previously married. I found them somewhat intense and very devout in their religious commitment. They were attractive, very much in love and had a healthy capacity to laugh at themselves. There were problems in the relationship but goodwill was high. It was a case of Stage II conflict.

The main difficulty was the intensity of conflict when it erupted at home. Betty came from a family in which her father was violent both to her mother and less frequently to all the children. Mark never saw his parents fight but had found that he has a 'fiery temper'. He had not been violent with Betty but she was very frightened.

I heard the following in our first session:

Betty: *'I want us to be able to talk openly about our problems. But then you shout at me.'* (sobs for a moment)
Mark: *'I just get angry . . . maybe frustrated because I can't say what I want.'*
Counsellor: *'There are two areas for work that I can see. One relates to your childhood experiences, but perhaps more important for now is to improve your style of communication when tension is rising. I would like you to learn the mirroring exercise . . .'*

The rest of the session was spent on trying out this exercise and addressing a 'hot issue' relating to credit card expenses. In later sessions the couple practised this skill. I also helped them both to be more self-focused by thinking about their respective family-of-origins. Both were able to talk freely about experiences in childhood. Mark was able to see that he lacked a good model of conflict resolution. He thought of himself as naturally somewhat aggressive, but he could learn to become appropriately assertive. Betty was fearful because of suffering violence as a child. She tended to interpret any anger as a threat of physical danger, but now she was an adult and had choices such as phoning the police if she was concerned for her safety. It was understandable that any expression of anger led to feelings of being without power but the reality of the present situation was different. We also discussed some theological issues such as 'Does God allow anger?'

We were able to explore some stresses on the relationship. Mark had a demanding job as a foreman at a factory. Betty was worried about whether she would be able to have any children. There were also pressures from both families – his mother had had a stroke recently and her brother was now separated from his wife and young children. There was a discussion about possible ways of reducing stress and finding new ways to be together. These ideas were suggested:

- A weekend away from home.
- Betty wanted to join a health club and exercise more regularly.
- Go to a concert together.
- Talk with one of the church elders about having children.
- Also talk to their GP about possible tests.

They both thought that these were good options and they arranged to have more time for joint activities. At one point it was necessary to discuss the validity of 'being good to yourself' and how this reduced pressure on the relationship. Betty found this a challenging thought since she had been convinced that God was more 'honoured by self-sacrifice'.

Not everything went smoothly in counselling. A couple of months later, Mark pushed Betty across the room in a fight that got out of control. This was labelled as violence. It was necessary for Betty to learn to recognize the indicators when there was a possibility of a loss of control. A strategy was developed in which she would recognize early-warning signs and leave the house for a ten-minute walk. It was also important to rebuild trust as her 'worst fears had come true'. I also had a few sessions with Mark to help him to find words for his anger. Gradually there was more satisfaction in the 'together time' and a more realistic appreciation of what needs could be met in the relationship. I was able to be quite direct in dealing with the conflict since the goodwill and greater stability characteristic of Stage II were present.

Hard cases

Therapeutic success does not necessarily rest solely on 'keeping the marriage intact'. If the couple has been helped to work through their grief, let go the dream of their marriage, gain insight into causes of the breakdown of their relationship, resolve property and custody disputes, work towards clearer parenting roles and take personal responsibility for the future – then much has been achieved.

However, many unanswered questions remain. I recently began to review past cases and tried to identify the dynamics that were sometimes present in marriages that failed. Two general categories stood out: violence and destructive intergenerational themes and midlife issues.

Difficult cases can prove to be most instructive. Our failures can lead to a dissatisfaction with the way we work. This in turn can lead to looking at the cases from different perspectives and eventually trying different techniques. For example, Freud developed his understanding of transference through the abruptly terminated case of Dora.[12] I hope that there will eventually be better ways to handle the cases marriage counsellors find more difficult.

Violence and other themes

There are some intergenerational behavioural patterns that can dominate families. These include chronic violence, child sexual abuse, alcoholism, addictions, debilitating mental illness, suicide or self-destructive behaviour, and criminal activity. The therapeutic interventions outlined in this book may be of some help but the destructive power of such themes is not easily limited.

One example was a policeman who could not forgive his wife for a single incident of marital infidelity. There was a history of violence and alcohol abuse in his family. He was emotionally cut off from his father and had refused to see him for over fifteen years. He could never forgive his father for incidents in his childhood. There was good initial progress and after about ten sessions the couple thought that they could continue on their own. I was pleased that the issues appeared to be resolved. A few months later the wife called about her husband's abusive behaviour. He was frequently shouting at her in a humiliating way in front of the children. One day he came into her place of work and caused a scene. He was unable to calm his overpowering jealousy. It was sad, but this behaviour finished what remained of his wife's goodwill. They separated a month later. He was living in a small boarding house and drinking heavily. There were fears that the husband might now be homicidal.

This case illustrates the counsellor's experience of working with a motivated couple, seeing progress in small areas such as communication and patterns of caring behaviours, but then seeing that the marriage is lost. It is hard to identify exactly what went wrong. It 'feels' as if there is an overall momentum towards destruction. This may sound pessimistic, but I think it accurately portrays a common experience in counselling.

I have tried to conceptualize this in terms of Chaos Theory, which is a recent advance in the physical sciences and focuses on the 'messy' aspects of nature. I have written elsewhere on the potential contribution of this theory to marital therapy.[13] In some systems an increase in intensity leads to completely unpredictable behaviour. This is seen in some mathematical equations when there is an increase in parameter values. I find it significant that a complex system can contain both stable and chaotic behaviour. This certainly illustrates what is often seen in families with themes such as violence. There may be periods of quite normal behaviour followed by destructive outbreaks. It is as if the family is out of control in trying to avoid cycles of blame and heated conflict. Then they enter a chaotic region with abusive and violent behaviour.

The chaos model is sensitive to whatever causes an increase in the pressure on the system. One or more of the variables will tune the system and these may be as concrete as a husband losing his job, an eviction from an apartment or a teenager running away from home. It may be possible to be alert to such factors and intervene to help the stability of the family. We can also help the couple recognize cues that point to an escalation in the conflict, as if this indicates a 'pathway into chaos', and then try new behaviour. Even such a simple guideline as 'Go for a ten-minute walk' breaks the pattern with a cooling-off period.

It is difficult to make progress with very destructive family situations.[14] It is almost useless to advise guidelines when the power of destructive family dynamics is likely to overwhelm any interventions. I have drawn attention to the possible contribution of Chaos Theory, but I think there is a need for further research and therapeutic advance.

One thing I can advise is to keep trying different tactics. Sometimes I alternate between seeing the couple, an individual or the wider family. It is also important to work in cooperation with specialist or support groups where possible. This includes Alcoholics Anonymous, women's refuges, Gamblers Anonymous, adult children of alcoholics groups and parole officers. And when you are 'going backwards' in treatment, consult with other colleagues or arrange to have supervision with a specialist in that area. The question of referral should also be considered. It is also a good time to pray and ask for a 'miracle'.

A possible parallel is that in the Old Testament, the Lord is,

A God merciful and gracious,
slow to anger,
and abounding in steadfast love and faithfulness,
keeping steadfast love for the thousandth generation,
forgiving iniquity and transgression and sin,
yet by no means clearing the guilty,
but visiting the iniquity of the parents,
upon the children
and the children's children,
to the third and fourth generation. (Exodus 34: 6-7)

Perhaps it is encouraging that God's judgement only lasts a few generations, but his grace extends to the 'thousandth generation'.

Midlife issues

The 'midlife crisis' is a cliché of modern life. It is hard to define the term but it is easy to observe that many people in their middle years will question their values and style of life. [15] Perhaps it is disillusionment with such goals as power, money, status and occupational success. This appears to be most common with men who have devoted themselves wholeheartedly to their work. For women it is often a refusal to continue with a family focus in life. This crisis appears to change the meaning of what time remains in life. It is recognized as finite and more dense with significance.

Couples frequently come into counselling with a crisis over life orientation. The surface issues vary and can include such things as a younger woman, a gay lover, a conversion to feminism, a change in career, or a desire to sail around the world. [16] If there is a common thread it is possibly the need to redefine identity.

A couple who had been married more than ten years came to my office

in a state of confusion. The husband was unsure whether he wanted to remain married. He was an elder in the Uniting Church and successful in his employment. His wife couldn't understand the problem. She was doing her part in what she considered reasonable for a marriage. She devoted herself to caring for their children and providing the best possible home life. But something was very wrong. It wasn't even as simple as wanting another woman. The husband felt that married life was now quite alien and he wanted to try being single again.

The impression I have is that an individual can inhabit the roles of marriage but have a growing dissatisfaction. There is a gap between the 'false self' of marriage and the experience of a 'true self' imprisoned in the relationship. The pressure builds until there is a crisis. This may be a surprise to everyone because it is so sudden, but it is generally a problem that has been long in the making. When such people present in counselling there is usually an intense crisis.

If possible, try to slow everything down. Structure helps to reduce anxiety. It may be helpful to make a strict agreement to work on problems for a set number of sessions and to put off irreversible decisions for as long as possible. There is often an air of unreality and it takes time to get a sense of perspective. Sometimes it is valuable to do a crossroads exercise. This involves listing all sides of the dilemma and the potential options. All the practical details are considered. Are they ready for such change? Look at the consequences from the perspective of other family members: how will the children feel? parents? friends?

Malise Arnstein once asked a superb question of a man thinking about leaving a marriage, 'What is this woman going to want from you that is similar to what your wife wanted?' He stayed in the marriage! I call these 'reality choices' and it is my view that reality needs to be highlighted in such situations. I sometimes offer individual sessions to the partner least motivated to work on the relationship. The old roles will no longer work in what is hopefully the beginning of a new chapter in the marriage. But there is a high mortality rate from such crises in marriage.

I would also like to mention that counsellors should not neglect the important healing dynamic of forgiveness. This is a natural element in Christian counselling because we believe in a God of grace who has forgiven us in Christ. It should not be hurried and in my experience tends to begin to emerge at the right time. David Stoop and James Masteller have identified six steps of forgiveness:

1. Recognize the injury. The extent of the injury is acknowledged. I was hurt by . . . It may be helpful to prepare a list of what was done.

2. Identify the emotions involved. This will include: fear, anger, guilt and shame.

3. Express the hurt and anger. It is natural to do this in counselling or with close friends. Many people find it helpful to write letters expressing the hurt – but *not* to be sent!

4. Set boundaries for self-protection. One example of this is a court order to limit a violent spouse. But emotional boundaries are equally important such as trying not to blame oneself for the failure of a relationship.

5. Cancel the debt. This may be something of an act of faith. It may be helpful to write cancelled across the letters or to burn them in a private ceremony.

6. Consider the possibility of reconciliation. Both must be involved in this process. However, it is not always possible.[17]

I think it is easier to raise this possibility with Christians, but it should not be neglected with others in counselling.

The opportunity for clergy

A member of the clergy can take the initiative. Sometimes he or she will be alerted to marital difficulties by people in the congregation. It is an easy matter to arrange to visit, see the wife briefly after a Bible study or ask the husband to go to lunch. These and other natural means are available to the clergy in the normal course of ministry. This gives an entrance to the problem before 'things explode' and a more proactive rather than reactive stance can be adopted.

The traditional role of clergy also has a lot of advantages over the normal practice of today's helping professions. A pastor, for example, is welcome to visit the home. In this case a picture may be worth a thousand words. The home is the locus of family life. How people act in this setting is often very different to their behaviour in the office of the counsellor. Some themes might be obvious, such as an impoverished environment, inadequate or rigid boundaries, role distinctions. It is worth observing how children interact at home rather than in the more formal office setting.

Clergy are part of a community of faith. It is possible to ask for the support of other members in a crisis. *I recall this happening when Dr Don Lawrence, a local psychiatrist, was working with a suicidal woman. I saw her as a parish priest and had a lay assistant regularly see her for lunch. The relationship with this woman became quite significant because the suicidal patient's only other support was a very shaky relationship with a married man.*

There are a lot of potential advantages to getting involved in a local church. There may be groups such as Bible studies, social events, prayer groups and informal gatherings such as coffee after worship services. The opportunity to give to others can be healing. It may be something as simple as joining the organizing committee for the next fete. All this can be very important because such involvement is in a nonclinical environment, which removes the person from the stigma of the mental health scene. It may be less of a threat to see a pastor than a psychiatrist or clinical psychologist.

In a local church there are usually individuals who have suffered a similar crisis. If the pastor is called in to help a couple who have lost a child to cot death, then a follow-up visit can be arranged with an another couple who have lost a child in the same way. This may also be possible with other difficulties: a grandparent suicides, an alcoholic spouse, learning difficulties in school, a youth who runs away from home.

Another example of the opportunities that ministers have in their normal course of duties are the rites of passage: baptisms, confirmations, marriage ceremonies and funeral services. Such rites can be seen as the way our society attempts to deal with areas of concern in families, such as change and separation. The access that officiating clergy have to the family is unique at such times. Often conflicts emerge at these points in the life cycle: 'You won't baptize him Roman Catholic!'; 'I want my stepfather to give me away'; and 'That picture was promised to me by Aunty Margaret.' The family may go through more changes than the recipients of the rite (usually with a lead time of about six months). Typically at such times all relationships 'unhinge'. This is important in therapeutic terms because change is easier in a state of flux.

A marriage is like an iceberg with the visible part being only about an eighth of the moving mass. Intergenerational themes may be very obvious in premarriage preparation interviews. The alert pastor can focus on emotional cut-offs, non-acceptance by in-laws, patterns of poor conflict resolution, alcoholism, childhood sexual abuse and issues with previous marital partners. I have found that a genogram is always helpful. Young couples are usually quite defensive about their own relationship, but may be more open to discuss their families-of-origin. I have also found that building a relationship with them may help a couple to return later if their marriage strikes trouble.

Baptisms do more than sanctify birth. My oldest daughter was born a week after my father died. A few relatives articulated the folk theology: 'One goes; one comes.' The birth of a child can place considerable pressure on a marriage, with the reinvestment of emotional energies and incessant distractions. A baby also offers a new source of triangles.

There are other changes in family life in which a pastor can become involved. People who are going through a divorce often seek support and sometimes a ceremony of letting go can be a great help. After separation, one of the partners will often seek out a new church. Retirement, remarriage, serious sickness and other changes can lead to a reappraisal of one's life.

Death is possibly the most important event in the life of a family. The prelude can be an opportunity for profound change such as deathbed reconciliations. After a death, individuals will try to work out unresolved issues, 'from a family systems point of view, grief and its components and aftershocks, sadness, and pain and loss, differences in functioning and the urge for replacement, all are the residue of the unworked out part of the relationship.'[18]

One advantage of the Bowen therapy that has been referred to in this book is that it provides an approach which can be used for all these transitions. Fundamentally it is a focus on the dynamics of the larger system and especially the family of origin. The practice of strategies such as working on triangles and emotional cut-offs enables people to function better. Another advantage is that the pastor can work with a single motivated member of the family. The cooperation of other family members is not essential.

Marriage counselling is similar to other forms of counselling in the need to face reality. So often it is the emotional reality of pain. Chaperon expressed it in these words, 'So, respect for pain, as simple as that may sound, is fundamental to the whole structure of human reality. Life lived on the basis of denying pain is life spent in the illusion of invulnerability; it is actually life unloved, unfelt, like a story that is merely skimmed.'[19] Self-respect is often the reward of such a struggle regardless of whether or not the marriage survives.

Exercises

Have any of your friends' marriages broken up? What can you identify as the most important factors? Perhaps you could ask what they saw as the central issues?

Think about your ministry in the church. Are there any unique opportunities for counselling with families in times of transition? Any suggestions could be discussed with clergy and lay leaders.

To read further

E. Friedman, *Generation to Generation*, Guilford Press, New York, 1985. This book written by a rabbi is sensitive to the dynamics of religious communities. It is also an easy to understand introduction to Bowen's concepts.

Daniel Levinson, *The Seasons of a Man's Life*, Ballantine Books, New York, 1978. This was the research basis for later books on the mid-life crisis.

Stephen Shapiro, *Manhood: A New Definition*, G. P. Putnam's Sons, New York, 1984. This book has surprisingly conservative conclusions about what role men are to fill after the feminist movement has changed our society.

THE COUNSELLOR
LEADING A GROUP

We live our lives in various groups: the nuclear family, extended family, single parent families, colleagues at work, neighbourhood, clubs, church, ethnic association and nation. To be human is to be in group relationships.

It is surprising that counselling groups are not more popular. I think that it should be the 'treatment of choice' in more cases. Many people seek counselling because of relationship difficulties. This may be felt as loneliness, conflict, frustration of needs or regret. Some clients are aware of patterns of serial relationships which seem to get nowhere. Sometimes it is a problem of social skills, but more frequently there are residual hurts from experiences in the family-of-origin. The natural place for this work is in a group setting. Encounter groups were part of the human potential movement and this kind of counselling has remained popular in the USA. [1]

One of the great appeals of joining a church is the potential to join various groups such as Bible studies, guilds, parish council, working bees, and committees of all kinds. I have often noticed that once the 'meeting' has finished, the socializing continues with coffee and talking. There is a natural hunger for relationships. It is the need to belong. In some church groups a deeper sense of sharing can lead to healing experiences - perhaps through a study group - and a deep sense of community develops. In group counselling these natural dynamics are present and with expert leadership there is opportunity for personal growth. It is also my conviction that being a member of such a group is the best way for the trainee counsellor to learn interpersonal skills and to develop self-insight which is so essential in becoming an effective pastoral counsellor.

A number of years ago I led a group in an Anglican parish. There were about eight members in what was labelled a Growth Group and the ninety-minute sessions were held weekly. The group continued for two years with some changes in membership. The following extracts from group sessions are used with their permission and details have been altered to preserve anonymity. I should also add that normal social rules tend to be suspended in such groups. Individuals will speak frankly about matters not usually discussed in general conversation. There are some crude interchanges in the examples from this group. It is typical of what often happens (but if the reader feels that they may be offended then it may be advisable to go on to the next chapter). Some of the principles in this chapter can be used by clergy and lay leaders to deepen the experience of participants in church groups.

What heals in group counselling?

The group is a powerful means of giving hope. It is natural to share in the struggles of others, to 'cheer from the sidelines' and then to rejoice in the victories that come. When change is obvious in some members it reinforces in others the possibility that they might also be able to change. This is not based solely on a group camaraderie, but on the much more realistic basis of genuine growth. In this sense growth is contagious.

There is often a useful flow of information in groups. This may be as mundane as the name of a reliable electrician or where to get a low-interest loan. In the early stages of the life of a group such advice is common and, although it is not always highly productive in terms of group processes, it can convey some mutual interest and caring.[2]

A lot of learning in groups is imitative. The group leader or leaders can provide models of assertiveness, self-disclosure, accurate listening, and sensitivity. But more important are the points of identification with other group members, similar feelings, common situations and useful ways to approach problems. Often people say, 'You too!' and then find a similar way to cope with a difficulty.

A woman who had been divorced a few years before modelled the way out of a poor relationship for a younger group member. Eventually Annette was able to say, 'There was not much for me at home – then or now – not much at all from George.' This was the first time she was able to say even a little about how she felt. It was a turning point in her becoming more of a person in her own right.

Mature group members will exhibit tolerance of feelings, an introspective stance, an effort to understand rather than to react emotionally, and eventually a greater understanding of the group process.

There is an opportunity to universalize difficulties. The intensity of some negative emotions can be frightening. *One man, Albert, shared a deep hatred for a former high school principal who had humiliated him in his first years at grammar school. The intense desire for revenge returned when he saw him at a ten-year reunion. Although the principal was now an old man in a wheelchair, Albert said, 'I just wanted to kick him in the balls a few times – about half-an-hour would have done.'*

In normal conversation it is hard to admit to such feelings. Yet people may carry for years intense rage, bitterness, resentment, and guilt. Some problems are seen as frightening, shameful or socially unacceptable. A young woman might admit that she experienced feelings of sexual attraction to a female friend at work. This might encourage a middle-aged man to speak about his homosexual experiences as a teenager. Almost every dark secret has some echo with other group members.

The setting of the group allows members to experiment with new social behaviours. *A young man, Daniel, had been very repressed and somewhat confused about sexual matters. He found it hard to approach a woman that he found attractive. In group, he blurted out to one of the women, 'You are sexy, you make me feel horny . . . I would like to take you to the Lakeside Hotel.' This was quite a step. Needless to say the young woman did not take offence, but was affirmed in her sexual attractiveness. It was an area in which her self-esteem was particularly low.*

In this and similar cases of experimenting with different behaviour, the group functioned as a 'halfway house' in which the different ways of relating could be practised and then later generalized into daily experience. Needless to say it is to be hoped that Daniel later found a more subtle approach!

In a similar way groups function as a 'hall of mirrors'. In groups individuals are soon confronted with aspects of their own behaviour. And often the way of acting was completely hidden to them. Being part of a group may be the first opportunity for a person to get accurate and honest feedback. Such comments are all the more convincing when all or most members of the group agree. This includes critical assessments, 'Why were you so insensitive to Sue's crying a moment ago?'[3] Perhaps even more significant is positive feedback, 'I thought that you were strong in standing up for yourself when Mark swore at you.' Sometimes the positive is harder to believe and again group consensus is important. Yalom underlined the importance of such insight, 'Self knowledge permits us to integrate all parts of ourselves, decreases ambiguity, permits a sense of mastery, and allows us to act in concert with our own best interests.'[4]

Group members will frequently speak of the group as a 'family' or being 'like a family'. In fact groups recreate the experience of the original family. Characteristic tensions can be understood as sibling rivalry, sexual tensions, competition for parental or family attention, struggle for status and dominance. Distinctive family roles such as scapegoat, lost child, parentified child, family mascot and clown may be replayed. It is an opportunity to challenge fixed roles inherited from the family-of-origin. Memories may be stimulated and regressive fantasies can take an individual back to early feelings. When negative experiences are brought back to be relived in the 'here and now' of group there is an opportunity to change the meaning of the experience.

The experience of group can be instructive at a number of levels. Information and mutual support are available through self-help groups. Some groups can help form better social skills such as assertiveness and lead to greater self-awareness through interpersonal feedback. In a therapy group the leader will have some awareness of childhood dynamics through understanding developmental theory, and then there is the potential for bringing to light more unconscious determinants of behaviour. Group counselling also tends to change symptoms into interpersonal issues. For example, the counsellor might translate depression into passive-dependency, obsequiousness, inability to express anger, hypersensitivity to separation[5] and then it is addressed in the 'present tense' of group.

Forming a group

There are certain predictable stages in the life of a group. I will outline these and explore some of the issues that are commonly raised. But I should say something about forming a group. My first group began with a few parishioners who approached me to begin a group. It included four reasonably close friends and a married couple. With such a mix there were a lot of risks in the group being too ingrown and potentially messy. I can say, from more experience, that a group is not easy to form and that initial compromises are usually made. However, in this instance, I soon added a few other members from my private practice and the group quickly settled down.

After admitting that there is no ideal selection of people for a group there are some guidelines that are helpful:

- Mix the members for age and gender.

- Avoid suicidal patients because such a person can consume the energy of a group especially in the formative stage.

- Avoid individuals who are isolated and have no history of relationships (in psychiatric terms such people might be labelled schizoid).

- Exclude anyone with a history of dropping out of groups.

- Alcoholics generally make poor members of general-issues groups.

- Also avoid anyone with a history of psychotic breakdowns.

There are specialized groups for people with eating disorders or with chronic pain, but these will tend to have an educational component and will not necessarily work on the same principles as given here. More poorly functioning individuals such as psychiatric patients should be kept to a hospital setting. This is also a specialized group and needs a high level of professional supervision.

In an average group I would expect a few people with depression or tension problems, perhaps one or two with instability in relationships, a person suffering grief from a loss of a family member or divorce, and some with work-related problems. There may also be a psychologist or cleric in training participating in the group as a member. There should be something of a healthy mix. I will always meet the potential members before the first session group for screening purposes. This can usually be done in an individual session of about thirty minutes. It is important to be satisfied that each candidate for group falls within the scope of whatever guidelines are set.

The setting is also important. In one group we had about ten members and we met in very attractive church premises: good wall-to-wall carpet, easy chairs that seat all at the same level, electric wall heating, curtains for privacy, easy parking and reasonably close to the centre of the city. It was an ideal setting. Participants chose where to sit. After a few had sat down the cotherapist and I would sit with some chairs between us. In this way seating tended to change from week to week. Since this group was a professional group, we paid normal commercial rates for the room.

About ten to twelve members is about right. Six is the absolute minimum; but in practical terms you need about eight to average this in weekly sessions.

I will now describe some of the important dynamics of groups. Although few church groups will be of such an intensity - either in interaction or awareness - it is helpful even in leading a Bible study group to understand such elements of group process.

Developmental stages of group

Groups tend to take on a life of their own. But there are some predictable stages in which the issues tend to be similar. It is helpful for the leader to have a framework in knowing what to expect. The stages will include: *formation, transition, cohesion,* and *termination.*

1 Formation

In the first meeting of the group there is a lack of shared history. Members will have little idea of what to expect and this will raise anxiety. I usually state my rules which include:

- Not to identify other members of the group in conversations with others or relate incidents in group that might betray confidentiality.

- The leaders are prepared to see a group member for an individual session and the contents of such sessions will not be raised by the leader in group. If two members have a conversation outside group, either member may refer to it in group and work through any issues.

- Participants are encouraged to put their feelings into words not actions.

- If a member cannot make it to a group then it is their responsibility to leave a message with the leader's secretary. A latecomer should knock then enter.

- There is a 'pass rule' which allows some security, because a member can choose not to speak. (I repeat the rules whenever a new member joins the group.)

Such rules are kept to a minimum. However, norms will quickly develop in the average group. Some of these are not helpful and may be challenged by the leaders; other norms are helpful or quite harmless and tend to be accepted without question. After this I am silent and wait for someone else to begin speaking.

Anxiety is usually the first shared group experience. The lack of guidelines about what is expected creates an ambiguous situation and this can be very uncomfortable. Participants usually proceed on a 'trial and error' basis. They will search for commonality, similar feelings, past experiences and current concerns. In this awkward time norms for group behaviour are being established. How does each individual structure the situation? How is anxiety handled? Small talk, humour or appeals for help? The alert group leader will notice that people will act in ways that have drawn approval from authority figures in the past.

The members will all be asking themselves, 'Do I belong in this group?' This is a normal part of group formation. It is a resurgence of the childhood issue of belonging, to the group initially but ultimately within the family-of-origin. Some members may find the beginning of group very threatening and encounter infantile fears of being engulfed or controlled by others.

The group leader is initially seen in 'glowing' terms. It is an idealizing transference which has something to do with the need for an omniscient, all-caring parent. The ambiguity tends to stir up childhood longings. This is a form of regression and it can include feelings of helplessness, dependency and confusion. There may be resentment of anyone in authority. This is sometimes called 'counterdependence' which stems from a fear of dependence.

In the first session of one group it was immediately asked whether we would open with prayer. I thought for a moment. Although most of the members were committed Christians, others who came later might not have such an allegiance. So I allowed it for the first session. This was challenged as being authoritarian. One male member was quick to address the issue, another fumed throughout the session, and another was completely unconcerned. He wanted to know how he had performed at the end of the session and I was seen as a teacher handing out grades. The next week I reflected on the different reactions to me as a leader. How short was the fuse? For Albert it was five seconds, Donna was ninety minutes and for Mark it was indefinite. I also decided on the issue. Members could begin group in any manner they wished, but it became part of the group process and others could choose to comment on any aspect of what was said. No one ever chose to pray in the subsequent sessions.

Each stage of group development has unique learning opportunities. Some members will gain the most in working on issues of forming trust and belonging to the group.

One middle-aged woman was on the fringe of the group for months after she joined. Although she was regular in attendance, she was not able fully to join in the process. She eventually linked this to her recent divorce and a fear of close relationships. Once she was able to identify her reluctance, she 'fully joined' the group.

A group largely composed of psychiatric patients is likely to stay in the stage of formation for a long time. Such people have profound difficulties with trust in relationships.

A lot of nonverbal cues are obvious in this stage of group. Who sits near the leader for extra support? Who sits near the door for 'a quick escape'? Who addresses whom? Some will use furtive glances to try to gain conspiratorial eye contact. Who avoids eye contact? Who sits with crossed arms and legs? Any seductive gestures?

I remember a group member who sat through his first group session in a heavy overcoat and dark sunglasses. He hardly said a word, but the nonverbal 'keep away' was eloquent.

The central issues are trust and belonging. Am I part of this group? In what way am I similar to the others? How fully am I committed to work on my issues? These are the real questions beneath the sharing and occasional clashes of this period.

2 Transition

This stage of group is characterized by the struggle for power and dominance. More 'negative' emotions are shared: outbursts of anger, resentment, envy, disappointment and intense sadness. One sign of a group moving to this stage is open criticism of the behaviour of other group members. Gradually social conventions are abandoned. *One male member said to another who was more hesitant, 'Are you sitting on the fence because you are shit scared of sharing?'* Although not all members compete for group influence there is an underlying theme of power struggle.

There is a variety of reactions in this stage. Not everyone will demonstrate overt anger or aggression. A few will not be assertive in group, instead they may exhibit withdrawal, passivity, and compliance. The occasional member will be more passive-aggressive with sabotaging manoeuvres such as appearing to be compliant, but breaking the rules of group. In the words of Scott Rutan, all members need to 'learn to balance anger and withdrawal with assertiveness and compromise.'[6]

Members begin to ask themselves, 'How am I different from others in this group?' This is part of becoming a distinct self in relation to others in the group. *One group member felt a call to join a monastic order. This was very different from the experiences of other group members and a very different expression of faith.* The genuine community of a group begins when people can be themselves but remain in relationship to others in the group.

If there ever was a honeymoon period for the leader, it is over by now! Group members will begin to test the group contract in different ways. Some members will begin to express disappointment in the leadership and express the wish for a 'real leader'. This may include some realistic perceptions of the limitations of the counsellor. But some expectations will be the result of initial idealizations. Almost everyone will have some measure of disappointment in not turning out to be the 'favourite child'.

Some members will look for every opportunity to challenge the leader. This may be expressed in rejecting statements, complaining, and even questioning professional competence. *One older woman made a 'slip of the tongue' and called the group 'class'. I asked whether I was the 'teacher'. This was too much of a challenge to self-examination, and she made the devaluing comment that 'You don't have much life experience, not enough to be a teacher.'* So there are usually leadership challenges. In this case a member will want to order the group in a different way or take on the role of therapist. Some members will express a fantasy such as that of unseating and replacing the group leader. This may be a facade for covering conflicts about dependency. Other members will defend the leader at all costs, perhaps even seeing the leader as frail and threatened by such a challenge. This may be a feeling of transference from past experiences with weak or unreliable parents. It is up to the leader to recognize and address such issues.

I have a style of leadership in groups that invites reactions to me as a leader. This is a result of provocative interventions and members sometimes complain that I 'stir things up'. Sometimes transference themes are addressed as part of this: *A middle-aged divorced woman said to a younger member, 'You never know, you could wake up one morning in bed with a psychologist who would solve all your problems.' I thought that it was an obvious reference to her relationship with me. So I gently tried to raise the issue. I first of all mused about her 'philosophic detour', then the implicit belief that she could only achieve wholeness through a relationship with a man and finally that it was a psychologist that was necessary. I could have gone even further with a question such as: 'How many male psychologists do you know?' However she was showing signs of defensiveness and I held back*. The transference dimension emerges in a very natural way in group. In this process the leader might highlight an interactional process or an attitude that is expressed about leadership so that the extra dimension becomes grasped as a group or personal insight. [7]

The simplest illustration of this stage is that of the pecking order of free-range chickens. A hierarchy is soon formed in the farmyard. So too in group!

3 Cohesion

Intimacy is an issue in the mature group. It is essentially a question of 'near or far'? Will I trust myself to this process? How much am I prepared to risk? Some members will finally admit the real reason that brought them to group: 'I think that I might be gay', or 'I am frightened that I might hurt my child when I get angry.' Group cohesion is facilitated by an increase in morale, mutual trust, tolerance of difference and a willingness to work through issues. A pseudo-intimacy may have developed earlier but this could have been the result of repressing negative affect. In time this will seem artificial; as Yalom noted, 'only when all affects can be expressed, and constructively worked through in a cohesive group, does the group become a mature group – a state lasting for the remainder of the group's life, with periodic recrudescences of each earlier stage.' [8]

In the mature group, members will emphasize interactions and responses in the group as the primary source of learning. Outside events will be used to illustrate group issues. Members can tolerate anxiety and examine problems in a more realistic manner. The distinction between expressing feelings and destructive personal attacks is easily made. Individuals will more easily recognize that abrasive behaviour serves more as a defence of the vulnerable self than malice towards others. There is a greater awareness of the intrapsychic and interpersonal elements in group interactions, with members learning to respond from both perspectives. It is clearly a working group.

A good example of the depth of insight was when a middle-aged man Anthony grew critical of a young man in the group. The young man's voice was said to be 'flat' and without modulation, in short he was 'boring'. In the next session Anthony missed a lot of the emotion expressed by the young man. I raised this with him because he was usually so sensitive to the shades of emotional expression. He then became more hostile and rejecting of the young man. By the end of the session, he had said, 'I know that I have been angry with you, Bill, but it is really my own children that are upsetting me. Every time I ring them they are dismissive and spend as little time on the phone as possible. I need to learn to sort out my feelings more accurately.'

Such an understanding of transference is typical of more insightful members and their awareness of the dynamics of a mature group. I have also found that the issue of sexual attraction is more openly discussed. When I was in training as a psychologist in Boston, I was a member of a therapy group. As the group progressed there were open admissions of sexual attraction between members. At one point a member expressed the fantasy of the female group leader being like a 'sex goddess'. There are usually also many veiled allusions to sexual themes. *In one group a recently divorced woman reported a dream about a snake coming at her through the grass. Her associations were poison, danger, and death. I asked, 'What gender was the snake?' 'MALE!'*

Deeper insights may be offered by the group leader. *In one session an older woman was exploring her placator role at work and how the men there tended to take advantage of her good nature. When asked for group feedback a few responded with empathy and shared similar experiences. One other member expressed some annoyance. I said that I felt a pull on my mean side, I felt sadistic towards her. This was a powerful intervention based on my attending accurately to my own feelings. It was immediately confirmed when the woman said, 'You know it is strange but even my cat is nasty towards me at home . . . maybe that explains the behaviour of my ex-husband as well.'*

Yalom expressed the role of insights based on such self-awareness, 'the therapist . . . may feel angry towards a group member, or exploited, or sucked dry, or steamrolled, or intimidated, or bored, or tearful, or any of the intimate ways a person can feel toward another. These feelings represent data - a bit of truth about the other person - and should be taken seriously.'[9]

The mature group is a strange mix of interactions. It has a kind of corporate life and the momentum can be quite surprising. It is important to be able to observe the process as objectively as possible and use therapeutic judgment to highlight what is most significant. It is also helpful to have thought about goals for each member. For example: Mary is a chronic pain patient and is struggling to express anger, Will has problems with authority figures and this will erupt in his relationship with me, Annie lacks confidence and needs to hear from the men in group how attractive she is, Marcus is painfully shy and sometimes has slightly bizarre gestures when he is nervous and Nancy needs to grieve the loss of her marriage. Naturally such goals are revised and changed through the process of group.

4 Termination

There was an established group at the institute where I trained in Boston. Each year a couple of the incoming trainees would become leaders of the group. In this way leadership changed each year but the group continued with quite stable membership. However, most groups eventually come to an end. I have led a couple of groups that met for over two years. Some groups are planned for a limited time, say twelve weeks or six months. When a group approaches the end of the life span there is a phase called termination.

It is a time of mixed feelings which include separation anxiety, fear of abandonment, frustration over unresolved conflicts, an awareness of mortality or death, anger and sadness. There can also be joy and celebration. *One group member left at the end of the first year. She had made excellent progress on a number of issues. She was moving house and she brought a bottle of champagne to end the last session. I thought it was appropriate.*

Sometimes it is daunting to explore the complexity of the emotions raised by ending the group. We live much of our lives in a fantasy of timelessness and endings shatter the illusion. If emotions are facilitated, then sadness and grief are usually expressed. But this may be only the tip of the iceberg. It is sometimes necessary for the leader to confront the group about the depth of what is felt – it is a loss that cannot be recovered. In the words of one therapist it is important 'not to bury the group too early'. I would estimate that in a group that has lasted a year, termination should be the dominant focus for at least the last four weeks.

At times the prospect of termination can lead to a crisis. *Three months before the proposed end of group a few of the members realized that the group was in a 'death phase'. One member left the group and others began to discuss whether it was worth continuing. We discussed ending the group early. A turning point was reached when a number of members realized that the way they had left various groups in their past was important. They identified various losses such as a job, place of living, family or marriage. This was recognized as important to their psychological wellbeing. It became a priority to stay and use the time remaining to address such issues.*

There is a unique opportunity in this phase. It is similar to that offered in the termination of individual counselling. James Mann worked out a time-limited style of therapy with individuals that uses the impending end of treatment to bring issues to the surface.[10] The principles can be easily adapted to group counselling.

The transference dynamic can be very intense in termination. In effect it is another severance from mother. This is one explanation of why the group will seem to regress at this time, primitive fantasies may emerge, magical expectations and a desire for an omnipotent leader. It is helpful for the leader to be strong in focusing the group on the task at hand but also to be human in countering such transference distortions. Yalom noted, 'many patients develop conflicted and often distorted feelings towards the therapist, the transparency of the therapist plays a crucial role in working through the transference.'[11] I found that I had a powerful countertransference reaction to ending the group referred to in this chapter. In my family, sadness and grief were always avoided. I had a powerful urge to end the group early. When I realized that my urgency was related to attitudes inherited from my family-of-origin, I had the insight to slow it down so that therapeutic work could be done.

Leading groups is one of the most exciting and challenging forms of counselling. It is exciting because almost anything can happen. It is challenging because more of me is on the line, to be confronted and questioned to a degree unusual in individual or family counselling. It can be quite exhilarating.

Members of groups have a unique opportunity for growth. It is a 'hothouse' for learning social skills. There is a constant challenge to be more assertive and less avoidant in interpersonal relationships. Important family-of-origin issues will be raised through the re-creation of 'family'.

I have described themes that arise in therapy and encounter groups. Some of these dynamics will occur in the very deep sharing of intimate Bible study groups or task groups in the local church. *One Baptist church sponsored a coffee shop in the local shopping centre. It was an outreach to unemployed youth in the area. A great sense of fellowship developed among the team. A new youth leader came and made some significant changes in the operation. There was considerable conflict and the team agreed to meet for extended periods to sort out the issues. The pastor, a Clinical Pastoral Education supervisor, was asked to lead this group.*

Exercises

Observe the working of a group that you are part of in the church. Can you identify any of the stages or themes discussed in this chapter? For example, think about how a group such as parish council operates. In what way is the role of the chairperson similar or different to the role of group leader in this chapter?

To read further:

Howard Clinebell, *Growth Groups*, Abingdon, Nashville, 1972. Somewhat dated but written by a leader in the field of pastoral care for the last three decades.

J. Scott Rutan, *Psychodynamic Group Psychotherapy*, Macmillan, New York, 1984. Very helpful book with both theory and practice nicely balanced. I was once part of a group led by Scott Rutan and he is a master clinician.

Irvin D. Yalom, *The Theory and Practice of Group Psychotherapy*, 3rd edn, Basic Books, New York, 1985. The classic book in this field. Essential reading!

GROUP COUNSELLING
AND SELF-ESTEEM

Self-esteem is a concept which may appear somewhat intangible. However, there is nothing more important to psychological wellbeing than the value a person places on himself or herself.[1] The nature of this self-evaluation has a profound influence on one's thoughts, emotions, desires, values, and goals. There is a unique opportunity in the experience of group counselling for a person to raise their self-esteem.

Nathaniel Branden has identified two basic components of a healthy self-esteem:

1. *A sense of self-efficacy.* This is similar to self-confidence. *It is illustrated by a young academic who is working at a research institute that is on the edge of scientific advance. He contributes fully to the team effort and pushes his thinking into unexplored areas, rejecting the routine and pedestrian in his quest for better theoretical models.*

2. *A sense of personal worth.* This is a realistic valuing of the self. *In the words of a middle-aged woman helping in a church soup kitchen, 'I am not perfect, but I can serve Christ and my gifts reflect my uniqueness.'* Self-esteem is not pride. Pride is a self-congratulation on 'what I have', whereas self-esteem is more about recognizing 'who I am'. *A young woman applied for a job*

with Community Aid Abroad. She interviewed well and she believed that she had answered the questions to the best of her ability. She missed out on the job. It was a blow to her pride, but not to her self-esteem.

Josh McDowell has written that self-esteem is a 'new name for a biblical concept'. He observed that St Paul related to Timothy and Titus in different ways, Timothy needed far more encouragement, 'Let no one despise your youth' (I Timothy 4:12) and 'God did not give us a spirit of cowardice, but rather of a spirit of power' (2 Timothy 1:7). Clearly the apostle accepted himself, 'But by the grace of God I am what I am.' (1 Corinthians 15:10) Thus McDowell concluded, that a healthy self-image is 'seeing yourself as God sees you no more and no less.'[2]

Low self-esteem can be a prison of sorts. Branden noted that people can become 'the psychological prisoners of their own negative self-esteem. They define themselves as weak or mediocre or unmasculine or cowardly or ineffectual and their subsequent performance is affected.'[3] Such a self-estimate can be intensely uncomfortable and lead an individual to resort to psychological defences. The result may be pretence, self-deception, denial, and role-playing. Self-esteem bought at this cost is empty. It leads to an impaired sense of reality, with evasion, entrenched areas of blindness, and self-censorship of unpleasant thoughts. In contrast, the psychologically more healthy person is both aware of and welcomes reality.

How does self-esteem develop? Psychologists have theorized that an infant's first look at the self is through the parents' eyes. It is very important to 'ooh' and 'ah' with the newborn baby, to cuddle, surround with love and to admire the inherent beauty of that miraculous gift. The experience of being loved, cherished and nurtured is the origin of a positive self-esteem. H. S. Sullivan called this the formation of a 'looking-glass self'.

It can, of course, also be negative, as in this case from my practice (with details altered for confidentiality): *A thirty-year-old woman came to see me. She was so thin and frail I thought she looked like a refugee from Somalia. She had been anorexic for the past five years. When she was twenty she married a somewhat reckless young man with a 'drinking problem'. The marriage broke up two years later, when she was five months' pregnant and had a fourteen-month-old daughter. When asked about her childhood, she said, 'It was a disaster'. Her father owned a hardware store and was reasonably well off but he was very stingy with money. He was also violent and verbally abusive. Mother was no help. She was an alcoholic and gambled every cent not spent on the booze. The children were often hungry. Clothes were bought three sizes too big 'so they would last'. The deprivation was symbolized by the absence of any birthday celebrations. Nor were there any Christmas presents. The children were so embarrassed that they lied about what they 'got' to their friends. Although there was no incest in the family, her first sexual experience had been date rape when she was thirteen.*

If you grew up in such a home, what kind of image would you have of yourself? *Is it any wonder when she said, 'I feel like dog shit, completely worthless.'*

Alice Miller made the observation that is almost axiomatic: the way I am treated as a child is how I will end up treating myself for the rest of my life. The child who is being abused can only endure, hopefully choosing how best to defend the self and survive in such circumstances. And yet as adults we have some capacity to choose. There is always the potential to rewrite destructive life scripts.

Research in self-esteem

We have no difficulty in explaining why a person who grew up in an impoverished or abusive environment has low self-esteem; or the reverse, about how an individual from a healthy family will appear to have a robust sense of self-worth. The real test for understanding self-esteem is the outwardly successful person who is widely admired and yet has chronically low self-esteem. This is illustrated by the high achiever who feels like an 'impostor' and worries about being 'found out' (see P. R. Clance, *The Impostor*

Phenomenon, Bantam Books, New York, 1985).

Here is an exercise:

1. Recall a specific recurring situation which you tend to avoid facing. Recreate it as vividly as possible in your imagination. Think about the people, feelings expressed, arguments that take place and all the unexpressed feelings. How do you avoid dealing with the problem?

2. Select three adjectives that describe how you feel about yourself in the situation, then write them on a sheet of paper.

3. Re-create the same scene in your imagination but now respond as if you were the kind of person you would like to be. Imagine yourself acting differently and courageously meeting the difficulty.

4. Again think of three adjectives to describe how you feel about yourself and write them down.

5. Compare the two lists of adjectives.

The first list is usually very negative with words such as: failure, defeated, loser, wimp and gutless. The second list is more positive: confident, calm, successful, in control and powerful.

Bednar has identified avoidance as the most important dynamic in low self-esteem. When we avoid an unpleasant emotion, overlook an unacceptable impulse or try to escape a situation of conflict, the result is a negative self-evaluation. This endures in the lower value placed upon ourselves. However, when a challenge is met it leads to a positive self-evaluation. It is the 'internal critic' that has the last word!

Such self-evaluations are the primary source of feelings for self-approval or disapproval and these inevitably reflect the degree to which a person has developed a response style that exhibits coping or avoidance.

The experience of a group is so rich in relationships that there are plenty of opportunities for members to consider their own styles of avoidance or coping.

There are frequent situations of conflict and challenges to acknowledge unwelcome emotions. There is also feedback from others. Bednar listed four assumptions related to self-esteem:

1. Virtually everyone gets regular doses of negative feedback and in general it is valid.

2. We receive and enjoy positive feedback, but tend not to believe it.

3. Self-evaluations are normal.

4. Understanding this self-evaluative process gives an opportunity to manage our self-esteem.

Now to consider this in more detail.

Negative feedback

Virtually everyone will get critical comments from family, work and the social environment. In general this feedback is perfectly valid. This is also true in working groups. Once trust develops, the members will begin to risk giving critical comments. This is typical of the second stage of group development. For example, *a teenager is overly passive in an adolescent group. A more active young girl challenges him, 'Why do you expect us to do all the talking?'* A powerful aspect of groups is when this is reinforced by other group members. If everyone in the group thought that this teenager was passive, it would be hard for him to continue to believe that he was seen as active.

Sometimes other group members will confront a member about sending double messages: *'Annie, you say you are happy and you are smiling, but your hands are clenched and your jaw is tight. It seems to me that you are angry over what Andrew said.'* It is natural for the other members to confirm or to disagree with what has been said. There is then an opportunity to face the emotion, in this case anger, and then integrate it into a more accurate picture of the self. With a more accurate self-appraisal, she becomes more 'in touch' with reality and this is essential to coping well with life. And coping is reinforcing to self-esteem.

Positive feedback

People receive affirmation and enjoy it, but tend not to believe it. Since flattery is soon challenged in most groups this positive feedback is usually perfectly valid. But why isn't a compliment actually believed? The problem is one of impression management. It is natural to try to present the best side of ourselves, but this leads to the self-reproach that others 'only like me because of my mask'.

This helps us to understand why successful people often have negative self-evaluations. Bednar explained that there was a flaw in the process of image management:

> The more persons act in ways dictated by external sources, the more alienated they become from themselves . . . If people continually present themselves to others in ways that are artificially designed to be pleasing, then any inter-personal feedback about their pleasing qualities will be a reflection of the facade they have presented rather than the enduring qualities of personality. [4]

Thus in response to praise the person concludes that he or she has conned the other person. It is flattery because of acting ability.

There is a natural group process that helps to counter this. As trust grows, individuals will share previously hidden parts of themselves, experience empathy and find deep intimacy. This helps feedback to become more believable since the mask has been dropped and the 'real self' seen.

Self-evaluation

Self-evaluations are normal for most people. There is also a stimulus for such self-evaluations by participating in groups: *Do I like the way I cowered before Alice's rage? No, but I feel good about disagreeing with Mark. I can take conflict after all. I didn't collapse!* There is the inevitable difficulty of dealing with aggressive or bullying individuals at close range.

George joined the group. He was a smooth-talking real estate salesman, but with an edge of hostility beneath his constructed persona. Sally and Jan were quickly intimidated and before the end of the first session both wished that he would leave the group. In the weeks that followed George became willing to accept feedback. He saw that his aggression related to his defensive interpersonal style. This encouraged Sally to acknowledge openly her private feelings. In this way Sally was able to confront a type of person that caused her difficulties in her normal life, to gain in confidence and boost her self-esteem.

Group interaction also raises the individual's awareness of such self-evaluations. This may happen through direct questions, 'How do you feel about what this member was saying? Is there something that you do not want to hear?' Persistent styles of interaction are soon obvious to others in the group and this forms the basis of initially mild and then usually more direct confrontations. There is also plenty of opportunity to take risks and try out new behaviours, often to experience both the positive self-evaluations and praise of group members. This is very reinforcing.

I should also add that self-evaluations are based on a process of avoidance or coping, not on outcomes. I have often seen people go back to their family and confront a difficult situation only to get more garbage dumped on them. *A young woman was encouraged by a group to check with her mother about an abusive uncle. The question was whether he had sexually molested any other children in the family. This was a reasonable question. However it violated the secrecy code in that family and the response was, 'And how do you know that you are my daughter?' This was a very hostile retort but nevertheless the daughter felt good about herself!*

Sometimes individuals will have so deeply repressed the link between patterns of self-evaluation and low self-esteem that their self-hate seems to have no cause. The chronic malaise is free-floating. When things are so vague it is hard to understand feelings of self-depreciation and despair.[5] Groups help to sharpen up such awareness. Accurate feedback helps to establish the links between what is happening in the group and how an individual feels. It is the 'here and now' quality that is most helpful and gives the group experience such intensity.

It is so immediate. For example, *a group leader can say to a member, 'Yes, I know that you are feeling embarrassed at being caught out in approval seeking again, but I notice that you are more willing to stay with that unpleasant emotion. In facing that reality you are coping and that is foundational to feeling better about yourself.'* Groups readily applaud honesty, courage, openness, and willingness to face personal problems. Bednar concluded, 'When clients are actually experiencing stress or engaged in avoidant behaviour is the most opportune time to have them try to identify and describe their patterns of behaviour and self-evaluations that accompany them.'[6]

Managing self-esteem

Understanding this self-evaluative process provides an opportunity for better managing self-esteem. An individual can choose to confront difficult issues, clarify uncertain interpersonal situations, experience uncomfortable emotions and integrate past experiences. Groups are often used to try out being more assertive, express a wider range of emotions or adopt a different role. *One member experienced a breakthrough when he was able to cry in the group and not be intimidated by his 'macho' self-image.* Groups offer an opportunity to make such changes. The common experience is accessible to all present. There is time to work through the issues raised. Here the process of group is the agenda.

Feelings of personal worth can be changed, first of all by becoming aware of patterns of self-evaluation, then changing behaviour and, finally, by noticing different evaluations. This is the central dynamic of managing self-esteem. When an individual understands this process there is far more freedom to take responsibility for feelings of self-worth. Since affirmations from others are so intermittent, it is best to focus on internal assessment which is largely under our own control.

This should not be confused with positive thinking or self-flattery. Genuine self-esteem management is based on an accurate understanding of the self - especially coping with responses to challenges such as heightened stress, interpersonal conflict, negative emotions and daunting situations. Groups provide an opportunity to take risks and receive the dividends in better self-esteem.

A case study in self-esteem

Nancy joined the group a few weeks after it started. She was initially quite timid. She offered very little in terms of participation; more or less what was asked of her without being mute. In the next session she said that she was having difficulty at work when she would freeze up in committees and feel like she was choking with anxiety.

A group member asked her how she felt about talking now? She said she was very nervous. I asked how she would rate her level of anxiety on a ten point scale. She said, 'About a score of nine.' Bob replied, 'But to me you hardly look nervous at all. I am surprised that you see yourself as more than a five!' Others in the group confirmed this observation. Also Nancy was surprised that she was not as transparent as she felt.

In the weeks that followed Nancy gradually became more active in the group. She was a member of a local Wesleyan church and had been elected onto the governing council. This caused her considerable anxiety, but she felt that God had led her to serve in this way. The group heard about her various traumas on the committee and supported Nancy in overcoming her anxiety. But the main change was in her participation in the group.

At one meeting, after a tense encounter in which Sally confronted Alfred on his intimidating interpersonal style, various other members of the group offered their impressions. Sally had just received a promotion and was leaving the area. I said, 'I wonder who will take Sally's role of "taking on the giants"?' There was a moment of silence. Then I took a risk, 'I think Nancy is tough enough to handle Alfred.' To my astonishment, Nancy immediately said, 'Now that you mention it, I have some reactions to Alfred's way of speaking to the women in the group. Alfred, you speak in a patronizing way and I find it offensive . . .' This was a step of courage and the change in her way of interacting in the group was dramatic.

At the end of the year she summarized her progress in the group, 'When I first joined the group, I wasn't sure what to expect. I knew I was fearful of speaking in front of others, and gradually I have become more comfortable . . . When I was able to face Alfred, and later my boss at work, I found an inner strength I did not know I had. I feel good about myself for the first time that I can remember.'

Trish Nove summarized from her experience of self-esteem groups:

An effective group is a self-esteem building process in itself: group members no longer feel alone in the shared responsibility of the task; they add their sense of identity in belonging to the group; they gain confidence in being able to practise new skills in a supportive environment; and in the process of inter-acting in the group they are actually practising new self-esteem and self-assertiveness skills.'[7]

The benefits of self-esteem are obvious. As self-approval increases, the frequency and threat of adverse situations decreases. In the old patterns of avoidance, an individual is very vulnerable to anxiety, fear and internal conflict; instead the experience of coping raises the threshold of what is threatening. This may happen very quickly in the 'hothouse' of a group. As individuals face difficult aspects of group experience then more confidence is gained, the group is less threatening and social situations seem easier to manage. In this way, the new patterns of behaviour are transferable into the 'real world', perhaps even more so than in individual counselling.

Perhaps the most important dynamic in both conversion and spiritual growth is the encounter with God. This will inevitably involve turning from patterns of avoidance. As St Paul wrote long ago about God the Father, 'He has rescued us from the power of darkness, and transferred us into the kingdom of his beloved Son.' (Colossians 1:13) This new way of living is a better foundation for self-esteem which must always include the spiritual dimension.

Exercise

In Genesis 1 God makes humanity in his own image (Genesis 1:26-27). After the disobedience of the first couple they hide from the Lord (3:8). What significance do you see in this avoidance upon self-esteem? Are there any indications about how they feel about themselves?

To read further

R. L. Bednar, M. G. Wells, S. R. Peterson, *Self-Esteem: Paradoxes and Innovations in Clinical Theory and Practice*, American Psychological Association, Washington, DC, 1989/1991. This is a brilliant psychological study of self-esteem. It integrates sound research with innovative clinical practice.

Mary Cutts Blowes, *Self-image God-image*, self-published in Australia 1993 (order copies from Tamar, PO Box 613, Civic Square, ACT, 2608). This small book addresses self-esteem from a theological perspective and is sensitive to women's issues in the Church. Very valuable.

A PERSPECTIVE ON THE
SPIRITUAL DIMENSION

The story is told about two brothers. The older one stayed on the family farm whereas the younger followed his sense of vocation and joined a silent order in a monastery far from home. After fifteen years the monk returned to his family and the older brother asked, 'What have you achieved by your years of prayer?' The monk said nothing but went to the nearby river and walked across *on* the water. The older brother hailed a ferry and joined the younger brother on the other side of the river. He was unimpressed. 'Why should I spend fifteen years to accomplish what I can obtain with the payment of a penny?'

Somehow this story captures some of the uncertainties about what is worthwhile about the spiritual life. Is it the capacity to perform a miracle? I would think not. Is it a sense of depth – of no longer skimming the surface of life? This would be closer. But I think the essence would be in exploring a relationship with a personal God. The 'penny' is trivial, the miracle is crass, but the reality of knowing God – that is everything. And counselling that is in any way Christian will give a 'sacred space' for such encounter.

In this final chapter I will first give a case study. This will be followed by a suggested theoretical perspective on the spiritual dimension in the counselling process.

A case study of a depressed Christian

A few years ago a middle-aged woman called Sandra came to see me. The referral had been made by the pastor of a Pentecostal church where she was a member. She was well-dressed and attractive. I heard that she worked full time as a computer consultant. She was married to a GP and described her relationship with him as 'never better'. But it was soon obvious that she was quite depressed, with the following symptoms: one to four hours sleep each night with early wakening; feeling lethargic; loss of five kilos in the previous four months; and self-esteem at rock bottom. She had recently been to a funeral and 'wished it was me'. She had gone to her pastor with problems with guilt. He had tried to assure her of forgiveness through biblical promises, but she did not feel forgiven and it was then suggested that she make an appointment with me.

Sandra was desperate enough to come, even though seeing a psychologist was quite alien to her way of thinking. Why wasn't God sufficient to meet all her problems? However she trusted her pastor's advice. I diagnosed her depression as serious, but without an immediate risk of suicide. It was recommended that she immediately see her doctor for a medical assessment and discuss with her the possibility of antidepressant medication. I also lent her a copy of *Beating the Blues* which she began to read and to work on the exercises.

There was little for concern in her family history. Sandra reported that her mother loved her but in a non-expressive way. I was more worried about what I heard about her husband's family. There was evidence of alcoholism and other addictions such as gambling. George, her husband, was not an alcoholic but had been addicted to tranquillizers. He had low tolerance to stress and tension. Although Sandra minimized it, he could be verbally abusive. About five years earlier he had gone into a residential programme and had recovered from the addiction. This was an enormous relief to Sandra and dramatically changed the quality of her family life. But she could not understand her present depression, 'It was a terrible period of my life, but now everything is fine. Why do I feel so awful?'

It was difficult for her to acknowledge just how bad she felt. She kept expecting Jesus to remove all the negative feelings. When her mood did not lift through prayer, it was a sign that she lacked faith. I explained that she needed to face her emotional pain and I encouraged her to begin a journal to record her reactions to events in her life. In the following sessions Sandra began to be more frank about her childhood. Her mother had been very domineering and ruled the home. When she was nine years old she committed the 'unforgivable sin' in her parents' eyes. She stole ten dollars from her mother's purse. When her parents discovered that she had taken the money, there was a severe beating. But even more distressing was the emotional withdrawal from her as a 'bad girl'. She also endured censure from the teacher at her small country school. Things never seemed the same after that incident.

I asked Sandra to write about her childhood memories in the journal. It was an important opportunity to work through her mixed feelings. She was worried about her sadness. Would she go crazy if she wallowed in it? She was also frightened of her anger.

It was quite a step in her progress when a few weeks later she said that she had felt some 'fleeting anger'. Significantly it was the day of her wedding anniversary. She then told me of her husband's affair with a friend of hers. I was surprised to hear that she had not felt any anger about it – just disappointment. In fact the mistress remained a friend.

In that session Sandra also told me about a frightening dream: '*I am in a room with no windows. There are two blank walls. On one is a plaque with a picture of a bunny on it and an inscription. I turned around and I saw a real rabbit sitting there. The rabbit said, "Go on, do it." "What?" "Pick up the knife." I turned in horror and the rabbit on the plaque said, "Go on, commit suicide." Then I ran out the door into a beautiful green field. There was a freshly dug grave with a plaque soon to be put on the tombstone, "Here lies a holy sister."* '

I explained the Jungian method of understanding dreams by association from the symbols.[1] She came to realize that it was her 'niceness', symbolized by the soft rabbit that would end up killing her. It was clear to both of us that she would have to face her anger.

Another breakthrough came a few weeks later. She was able to speak with her daughter about how terrible her marriage had been when George was addicted to drugs. This led to her feeling disloyal but also relieved. She also remembered aspects of her childhood and she began to recall happier times when she felt that her parents did love her. Somehow such incidents had been forgotten in her pain. It was comforting to be able to hold on to some positive memories. It is a common experience in counselling that remembering more about the past - not just the horror of past wounds, but thoughts of better times - introduces more texture to other memories.

Sandra also found that a number of people in the church had begun to seek her out and to speak more intimately with her. They looked to her for pastoral care and wanted her help in solving their problems. I asked for her thoughts about why this might be happening? She realized that it was because she was working on her own issues and she was no longer willing to brush off people with a quick, 'I'll pray with you about that.' She was facing her own difficulties and could now help others to face theirs. This was encouraging because she could see that because she had more empathy through being aware of her painful experiences, God was now using her in a new area of ministry.

The time came when Sandra felt strong enough to consider how she felt about her marriage. She was more in touch with her anger and she asked me, 'But if I feel the anger, how do I know that I will still love George?' I said, 'There are no guarantees. I don't have a crystal ball, so I do not know where you will come out. However, you have begun to be honest with yourself. Can you stop now?' In the next two sessions she was able to express the depth of her anger, 'I think that I hate him.' This was a breakthrough and, as I explained later, she no longer needed to convert her anger into self-hate. As the 'knotted string unwound' she found that she remembered affectionate moments they shared together, 'The years were not all hell.' She became softer towards him. She found herself being affectionate and spontaneous. This was because she wanted to be loving - not because it was her duty as a wife.

There was a religious journey as well. Sandra went on a trip to the coast to be on her own for three days. When she prayed about forgiving people who had injured her, she felt God say, 'Don't forgive people, forgive instances.' She then wrote pages and pages in her journal. In a vision she saw Jesus on the cross and he spoke to her: 'This has made you worthy.' It was a time of deep spiritual insight. She also fell into an acute depression for a night and she couldn't sleep. Satan was accusing her of betraying her Lord. But after this 'crucifixion', she experienced Jesus in the garden after his resurrection. He came to her and put his hands on her face, 'Do you love me?' Three times he called her name, Sandra. Then Jesus asked, 'Do you love my Father? If you know and love me, you know and love my Father, because he and I are one.' Then Jesus went on, 'Do you love yourself?' She couldn't answer. Then he continued, with his hands on her face, 'God made you in my image and likeness, you are His work of art. Now do you love yourself?' Sandra said to me, 'I couldn't say no. It was so pure and wonderful an experience.'

I felt awestruck when she recounted this. I can never remember being more certain of the reality of a genuine encounter with Christ. And on reflection I was amazed at the way spiritual and psychological themes were interwoven

Sandra had made genuine progress, her symptoms of depression were long gone and she was emotionally more robust. She was more stable spiritually. In the next session she finished counselling and she gave me the gift of a book of devotional writings by Thomas Merton.

Images of God

There has been some psychoanalytic research about how images of God develop through childhood and in the later stages of life. Analyst Ana-Maria Rizzuto published a significant book a few years ago. It was called *The Birth of the Living God: A Psychoanalytic Study.* [2] She saw that an infant is born into a family context of shared meanings. Parents have their representations of God and these are shared with their children both consciously and unconsciously. One aspect of this is the parental understanding of the birth: a gift from God? a punishment imposed? a tribulation sent to test faith? or simply a biological accident? Such possibilities colour the developing family myth. After the birth the parents might have a religious ritual to mark the arrival of the child. This might include circumcision, baptism or dedication. Usually there is an element of giving the child a name. As Rizzuto explained, 'It is in this pre-set stage of meanings and private myths that the baby begins his long awakening to himself, to others and to the world.'[3]

The parents are experienced as the first 'thou', to use the term of Martin Buber. This is usually the most significant encounter with a loving person. It is fundamental to the later understanding of God as 'Thou'. I will explore this further through the concept of a self-object.

Another attempt to understand the role of religious experience was made by Donald Winnicott, an English psychiatrist. He used the concept of a 'transitional object' which is equated with the child's 'special' soft toy or blanket. Many, perhaps most, children form some kind of security attachment to such an object. Sometimes the link of breast-thumb-object can be seen. My wife breast-fed our daughter Kym in a terry-towelling dressing gown. Kym then attached to the cuff of her terry-towelling jump suit and then when she grew out of that, we gave her a terry-towelling mouse which she treasured for the next five or six years. Winnicott called such objects transitional because of the eventual loss of interest. He also drew attention to the early symbolic quality of the object. He hypothesized that it represented an intermediate area in which both inner reality and external life contribute.[4] He argued that such a blend of fantasy and reality became the psychological basis of play, art, imagination, creativity and religious experience.

Rizzuto also saw God functioning as a transitional object, 'like jugglers we sometimes call in our god and toss him around, sometimes we discard him because he is too colourless for our needs or too hot for us to handle.'[5] However, God is usually more permanent than the attachment to a teddy bear. This might be due to the respect of parents. The family may speak of Santa Claus, but it is with a 'twinkle in the eye'. When a child is in God's house, he or she is told to sit still and be quiet! The infant child may be bursting with theological interest, 'Does God have a pee-wee? Who made God? Can you see angels?' There is a dynamic interplay of inner fantasy and more mundane external images. The image of God is richly developed long before the child arrives for the first Sunday school lesson!

The child gradually clarifies the distinction between God and his parents. This may relate to the discovery that Mum and Dad are human and not omnipotent. Parents have parents. Meissner has observed that the child will salvage some of his misplaced idealism by projecting it onto an all-powerful and perfect God (who does not have parents).[6] I could continue this trajectory of psychological development, but I think that the more relational quality of religious experience is not adequately captured in such discussions about somewhat static 'images of God'.

Heinz Kohut in his development of 'Self Psychology' as a school of thought in psychoanalysis provides a better way of understanding such dynamics. He has pioneered a new way of understanding early childhood development and this has implications for religious experience.[7] First of all I will need to introduce some key concepts.

Self and selfobject needs

The essence of the self is elusive. It makes itself felt by providing a healthy sense of wellbeing and self-esteem. Alternatively it can be damaged and become a source of fragmentation, anxiety and terrible rage.

Infants need caretaking responses from birth. Mothers usually meet such needs as the primary caretaker, but this is not to deny the contribution of the father, other family members or day-care staff. Kohut understood the meeting of needs in terms of a 'selfobject' relationship. It may appear somewhat impersonal to speak of caretakers as objects, but strictly speaking the selfobject relationship is a function, not a person.[8] The selfobject is the one who meets such a need. And when needs are generally met by parents a balanced, cohesive and vigorous self develops. These needs include:

1. Mirroring needs: to be recognized, valued, appreciated, to feel affirmed and loved. Infants delight in adult smiles, touch, tickles, peek-a-boo games.

2. Alter ego needs: to experience a likeness to the self-object, in effect, 'I am like you.' It is a kind of 'twinship' which I have noticed in the games of young children, such as dressing up in the same clothes.

3. Idealizing needs: to be emotionally connected with an admired person. The distressed infant or child can be soothed by the non-anxious presence, calm voice, enfolding arms e.g. 'Let Mummy kiss your sore and make it better.' It is more than nurture, the effect is on the wholeness of the self.

4. Adversarial needs: to experience the other as a benign opposing force that is supportive while allowing the self to say 'No!' (e.g. in the 'terrible twos'). This confirms a growing sense of autonomy.

5. Efficacy needs: to have an influence on the selfobject. A baby cries and this brings Mother to see what needs to be done.

Selfobject needs do not disappear after infancy, but continue throughout life. For example, the need for teenagers to dress alike is a form of twinship and this is a powerful factor in teenage fashion. The form of the selfobject relationship changes from providing concrete acts such as a reassuring voice and stroking hair to symbols such as art, music, literature, philosophic ideas and religion. The symbols tend to be less personal and more diffuse.

After a busy Sunday morning, feeling 'a bit ragged', I like to come home and listen to the *Pastoral Symphony* or one of the other Beethoven symphonies. The music is soothing which is exactly what a selfobject relationship can provide.

Self Psychology links the failure of selfobject responses through faulty interactions, lack of empathy, and non-responsiveness to damaged states of the self. This can be seen in the language of people who feel very hurt. Words are used such as 'shattered', 'cracked up' or 'damaged'. The following dream from a client gave me some insight into this experience: *A young man returns alone to his flat. He looks at himself in a mirror and finds that his image is laughing at him. He is horrified and smashes the mirror. Then he has a frightening thought, 'Do I still have an image?' He rushes into the bedroom to look in the mirror there. He makes no image in the mirror.* This addresses deep needs for wholeness and substance in the self. The pervading sense of anxiety is profound.

Transference and religious experience

Kohut has described various selfobject transferences in which infantile needs are displaced onto the counsellor. This includes both the residues of past emergency reactions and the experience of reawakened needs in the 'here and now' of the counselling situation. It is my view that such transference dynamics also infuse various kinds of religious experience as illustrated from the writings of the mystics.

1. *Merger transference.* This describes the person's experience of loss of boundaries with the counsellor. It can be seen in the magical belief that the counsellor can 'read minds' and knows everything without being told. There may be only a very minimal recognition that the counsellor is a separate person. I do not equate this state with a regression to symbiotic union since it appears to be more rooted in a profound self-pathology. [9] However, a clear example of the loss of boundaries with God

is found in the writings of Eckhart (d.1372), e.g. 'I discover that God and I are One.'[10]

2. *Mirror transference* is seen in the demand to be recognized, admired and praised. The divine regard for humanity is a central theme of the Christian faith. Creation is 'good' (Genesis 1) and we are created in the 'image of God' (Genesis 1:26) which is a mirroring of some unique aspect of God's nature. The experience of grace is abundant in the writings of St Bernard of Clairvaux (d.1153), 'Easily they love more who realize they are loved more.'[11]

3. *Alter ego transference.* This is seen in the desire to be like the counsellor in appearance, manner, outlook and opinions. Perhaps this is influential in the quest for holiness as seen in the writings of John Wesley. It is obvious in Thomas à Kempis (d.1471) in *On the Imitation of Christ*, 'But they that follow Thee by the contempt of worldly things, and mortification of the flesh, are known to be truly wise.'[12] (cf. Romans 6:1-11).

4. *Idealizing transference.* This is the common positive transference in forming a working alliance with the person. It is present in the admiration and idealizing of the counsellor. Christians believe that God is wise, good, powerful, protecting and loving. I have often experienced the soothing presence of God in a 1662 choral Eucharist. It is part of the normal experience of worship. St Teresa of Avila (d.1582) described a vision of Christ, 'I saw that he was speaking to me, and . . . I was looking upon that great beauty of his, and experiencing the sweetness with which he uttered these words.'[13]

Other needs might be met through different aspects of religious activity. Intercessory prayer might meet efficacy needs. Even agnostics such as Woody Allen can satisfy adversarial needs by refusing to believe in God. After all, he calls himself 'God's loyal opposition.' The real point, however, is that one of the ways religious experience can be understood is in terms of healing the residues of developmental trauma and deficits in caretaking. It is a paradigm for understanding psychological and spiritual growth.

As an illustration: *Johnny grew up with frustrated mirroring needs. His parents responded to moments when he showed pride in his competence with 'Don't be a show-off!' He felt shame and further repressed his needs. His parents were never part of the crowd at his football matches. Nor did they see him act in a school play.* When he got to university, Johnny joined an evangelical Bible study and accepted Christ as Lord and Saviour. He had a profound conversion and discovered that God accepted him unconditionally in Christ. In prayer he found that there was a sense of God's love and he felt more whole. After a couple of years his faith matured and his self-esteem became more solid. Gradually he was able to soothe himself with self talk such as 'I am loved' and 'There is much that I like about myself.' This illustrates a transfer of selfobject function, in this case from God to the self, which Kohut called 'transmuting internalization'. This is seen by Self Psychology as adding to the structure of the self and it is the way that the self matures.

God as Counsellor

I will conclude by suggesting that in Christian counselling there is really only one Counsellor. There is healing in God's presence, whether through a sense of empathy, receptive quietness or gracious acceptance. It is real but difficult to articulate.[14] The understanding of religious experience in terms of selfobject transference provides a useful framework in which to understand the process of growing into spiritual wholeness.

Perhaps I should also add that with some fragile people religious experiences can be destructive of the self. *A young woman raised by an alcoholic single parent has an overstimulated self. She experienced her mother as alternatively neglecting or claustrophobic in her attentiveness. This left her with an unstable grandiosity in which she felt she would be a world famous concert pianist. Unfortunately she had only mediocre ability in music. She was further destabilized by a charismatic experience of 'Baptism in the Spirit'. A regular diet of*

Pentecostal worship tended to make things worse. Maybe it is a question of the right match of self and religious selfobject experience. An understimulated self might find the same environment wholesome.

Some writers in the field of Self Psychology have expressed an appreciation for the healthy role that religious experience can play. Wolf, for example, saw that monastic withdrawal was not away from self-object experience, 'such isolation seems to allow some specially gifted people to experience their relation to religious ideas and figures with an intensity that rivals the most intimate personal self-object responsiveness.'[15] And then it doesn't seem such a big step to God as Counsellor.

Exercise

Reflect on what you would understand to be religious experience. Can you identify aspects of a relationship? How have you experienced healing? What implications would you draw from the kind of counsellor God might be? Do you think this is an appropriate image for the way God relates to us?

To read further

Ana-Maria Rizzuto, *The Birth of the Living God: A Psychoanalytic Study*, The University of Chicago, Chicago, 1979. This is an excellent study of developmental aspects of religious experience. There are some interesting case studies.

Ernest S. Wolf, *Treating the Self: Elements of Clinical Self Psychology*, The Guilford Press, New York, 1988. This is a readable introduction to the concepts of Self Psychology.

PSYCHIATRIC SUPPLEMENT
Ian Harrison

Psychiatry, psychotherapy and counselling

The three fields of psychiatry, psychotherapy and counselling cover a huge area with much overlap in between. They are all notoriously complex and controversial fields and it is even difficult to define each of the terms with any degree of consensus. For example in the field of psychotherapy alone there are now over 460 different varieties or schools.[1] Yet, despite the difficulties, the task of understanding what each field has to offer has become increasingly necessary for a number of reasons.

Firstly, all three fields attempt to address in some way, the large prevalence of psychological problems, or symptoms, in the community. The associated costs of these problems, both in terms of individual suffering and mortality and in terms of the financial cost to the community, are enormous.[2]

Secondly, there is an increasing demand for a more rigorous scientific appraisal or evaluation of the outcome or results of psychotherapy and doubts are being expressed about the effectiveness of certain forms of traditional long-term psychotherapy.[3-5]

Finally, these issues are being raised at a time when there is increasing pressure on governments in a tough economic climate, to spend wisely on treatments of proven value.

Of course considerations such as the cost of a service and value for money are related in the wider context to the demand for greater accountability generally in the professions. In psychiatry, pressure is being brought to bear on the profession to give an account of what it is that psychiatrists do, be it in psychotherapy or biological psychiatry.[4] The question in its simplest form is often one of: What can the consumer (i.e. the patient or client) reasonably expect to improve/change as a result of therapy, be it a symptom or a behaviour; and how can we measure that in a scientifically meaningful way?

In such a climate the task for psychiatry and everyone in the helping professions generally is to continue to ask as much as we can about some very basic recurring questions, such as:

- What is the problem that we are treating and whose problem is it (Diagnosis)?

- Why are we treating the problem?

- When is treatment completed?

- How are we to treat the problem?

- Are the treatments we are using effective? and

- What are the side effects or unwanted effects of those treatments?

The first part of this chapter will address some important questions for us all. In the second part I will be looking more specifically at some of the biological treatments used in psychiatry, particularly focusing on schizophrenia and depression and describing the rationale underpinning the use of medications in these conditions.

Diagnosis: Is there a problem, what is it and whose problem is it?

When faced with a patient or client, especially at the first session, we might well ask: Does this person have a problem or not? Because we are sophisticated, we do not automatically assume that they do.

In fact, it is not unusual for the patient to ask the same question and to fear that they may be wasting our time. In traditional medical and psychiatric practice we might even ask the patient quite directly and openly: What is your presenting problem? Many therapists would be wary of such a direct opening, but nevertheless, sooner or later the question has to be asked: Does this person have a problem or not?

This question is not as easy to answer as one might imagine. Often we may see a person who is nominated as having a 'problem' (the patient, or if the therapist is a counsellor, the counsellee) which turns out to be different from what it seems. For example: a wife's painful back, for which no medical cause can be found, might be protecting her husband and herself from having to face a problem that is more difficult to acknowledge: perhaps the husband's sexual problem of impotence or premature ejaculation. Although the wife presents as having the problem it is really the husband, or more correctly the couple, who have the problem. [6]

Or to give another example, a child's disruptive behaviour might become so unmanageable that a husband has to give up his two or three evenings per week in pastoral care or ministry work in order to stay at home and help his wife supervise their child. Not only does the child's behaviour improve, as we might expect, but the family is also brought closer together, reducing the sense of loneliness and frustration felt by the husband's resentful wife who might otherwise have felt guilty at having to ask her husband to spend less time with the needy of their parish. The result is an increase in cohesion in the family and a restoration of the balance.

In this example, the problem of behavioural disturbance in the child is not so much a problem to be solved, as a tactic that we should stand back and admire. We should wonder at the care and concern and protective instinct that enables the child to engineer such a rescue mission of the otherwise out of control, and perhaps immature, father who does not know when to stop, or when he has done enough, or what is in the best interests of those closest to him.

We could multiply such examples which are prevalent in the field of child and adolescent psychiatry. Rebelliousness and non-conformity in an adolescent is often brought to the counsellor when the real difficulty lies in the parent who is unable to let go of the child emotionally or to give up control over the child's mind and body. In this situation it is the parent who is not able to conform with a natural process of development and allow the adolescent to become independent and develop increased autonomy. If such conflicts are to be resolved successfully, it is often the parents who have to become the patients, so to speak. The important principle is that the person nominated as having the problem is not always the one with the problem.

While it may seem that many problems cease to exist if looked at in this way, it is equally important not to fall into the common, almost opposite, trap of saying that there is no problem and that the patient, or family, can therefore go home happy. In doing this we might miss the point that all major problems are to some degree, at least initially, hidden by lesser problems or even imaginary ones. Very few people announce their worst problem when asked about their presenting problem. [7]

The depressed mother who brings her perfectly healthy baby along to the doctor expressing concern about the baby may well be projecting her own concerns and fears about herself onto the baby. If she is merely told there is no problem, then clearly the situation remains unresolved. All it really means is that the doctor has not been able to diagnose the real problem properly. Of course, the real problem may be difficult to diagnose, but hopefully the woman will continue to take her healthy child to others until her problem is recognized.

It is important to state at the outset that a diagnosis is a very dangerous thing, to be handled with great care. In our increasingly technical and educated world we are apt to deify any high-sounding gobbledegook and expect to be blinded by science. At the very least a diagnosis is a two-edged sword. Even the correct diagnosis in the wrong hands can inflict damage, while conversely, a therapist may conduct a successful therapy without any diagnosis at all. When used proficiently, diagnoses are an aid to treatment and recovery and to that extent can be very helpful. In a few situations an accurate diagnosis may be lifesaving, but in most cases they are a matter of opinion, even a matter of taste, and best filed away with other old and poorly focused snapshots from the past.

There is a wealth of evidence that the reliability of diagnosis, particularly in the field of personality assessment and disorders (even amongst psychiatrists who are presumably well trained to diagnose psychiatric conditions), is sometimes quite poor.[8] Moreover, there is evidence that the interviewer's own personality and style of interaction can have an influence, not only on the proceedings, but also on the eventual diagnosis of personality disorders.[9]

A correct diagnosis hopefully not only leads a therapist in the direction of the right therapy but also warns of the potential problems which might occur in such a patient and of the prognosis (or outcome) that could be reasonably expected from various treatments, be it counselling, psychotherapy or medication. At this point, a diagnosis really becomes a diagnostic assessment and it would normally include a whole range of characteristics, such as the patient's previous level of functioning, coping skills and personality strengths, past history and family history as well as biological, social and cultural factors. Such an assessment, covering the so-called bio-psycho-social factors and ranging over the recent and distant past, bears little resemblance to mere diagnostic labels often bandied about in a pejorative manner.

The important point is that a comprehensive patient formulation or diagnostic assessment has some meaning in guiding treatment and giving some indication (although admittedly it is only a guide) to prognosis.

For the counsellor and psychotherapist, this is especially important in the assessment of a patient's personality and suitability for the various forms of psychotherapy. In many centres, especially over the past thirty years, much information has been gathered in an attempt to classify the problems of personality into various different groups. Each group is assumed to show common patterns of behaviour in terms of the individual's characteristic relationship patterns, expression of emotions, regulation of impulses and social behaviour etc.[10]

In this way, a number of so-called personality disorders have been defined using a number of different criteria. This may in part explain the apparent propensity for patients to be increasingly labelled as having personality disorders of one type or another. Labels commonly used in the 1960s such as immature, inadequate or dependent have given way to currently more popular labels for personality disorders such as borderline or narcissistic personality disorders. Many of our patients have attracted such labels in spite of the many studies showing a wide variation in opinion as to the validity and reliability of such diagnoses.

This leads us to the problem of diagnosis and its relationship to labelling for which psychiatry in particular has been criticized. One of the most damaging ramifications of diagnosis stems from the effect on people when they are labelled. The degree to which we all tend to cling to a label is understandable given the desire we have to make sense of ourselves and the world in which we exist. Labels are seductive and they have a powerful unconscious influence.

Moreover, the earlier a label is applied the more profound its effects. If a young toddler is said to have the same foul temper as his Uncle John, or on the other hand, the same inquisitive mind and placid nature as his Uncle Peter, then you can virtually guarantee that eventually these labels will become reality.

For some patients, the degree to which the label is believed and the adverse effect it has is often in inverse proportion to the amount of time actually spent in the presence of the diagnoser. Labels that are announced to individuals from professors on high (often during a five-minute ward round in a psychiatric hospital) can have reverberating effects ten, twenty or thirty years later, long after more recent and comprehensive evaluations have attempted to correct the diagnosis. Having once been labelled a depressive or a manic-depressive or schizoid or paranoid, how can one ever be able to see the world again except through the glasses that have now been so expertly provided? In many cases labels become self-fulfilling prophesies.

There are, however, some situations where a psychiatric diagnosis is useful. If a patient had severe depression (often termed major depression or endogenous depression), then such a label would be useful to know because appropriate medical treatment should be instituted for an illness that is, in many cases, life-threatening. This cannot be emphasized too strongly. Similarly the adolescent with aberrant behaviour and psychological and relationship problems might be having his or her situation minimized by well-meaning family members or friends when he or she may be suffering from a severe and distressing illness such as acute schizophrenia (schizophreniform disorder).

Why are we treating this problem?

Although we would like sometimes to believe otherwise, not all patients come willingly for therapy. Most come with a great degree of reluctance and ambivalence. Some would not come at all but for the urging and manipulation of their families. Others have been expressly ordered, either by the law or by a spouse who has had enough and is threatening a separation or divorce.

In an ideal world we would only treat a person's problem because they themselves recognized it as a problem which interferes either with their prospects for work or pleasure (what Freud referred to as the ability to love and work), or because it produces in them psychological and emotional pain, even though there may be no visible or outward signs. Since this is not an ideal world, we have to deal with problems that are vague, poorly defined and masked, and patients who are anxious, poorly motivated, resistant or unable to change or not as keen to give up their problem as those around them are to see the problem eradicated.

In fact, all of us at some time or other would answer the above description. Which of us is not poorly motivated for change, and which therapist has not found him- or herself at some point perhaps unwittingly colluding with a patient's problem and fostering resistance?

In general psychiatry there is the possible added difficulty of having to deal with patients whose liberty has been infringed. One of the freedoms we must defend is the right of each person to see the world in his own way and to act according to his own wishes, providing it does not impinge on the rights and freedoms of others.

To give an example; what does it matter if a member of society wants always to wear a hat covered in aluminium foil to ward off controlling rays being beamed from the planet Pluto, or stand outside a service station declaring it to be the only true royal palace? Surely there is no problem in any of that? But what if they stand there day and night, and even in the rain? What if they catch cold and are clearly delusional in their speech, most likely suffering from paranoid schizophrenia? Well so what? That's not a crime. What if they then catch pneumonia and develop a severe fever and remain fixed outside the service station on guard duty? Perhaps they are at risk of death from pneumonia. Are they then condemned to die for their beliefs?

What if they begin to attack verbally the service-station owner as a traitor who has the Queen of England trapped in one of the underground tanks? No crime so far. And what are we to treat? Whose problem is it anyway? Certainly not the man's whose feelings of duty to his Queen far outweigh any personal suffering he might be undergoing. When should we step in and say that we owe this delusional man a duty of care?

What about the girl who declares herself to be fat and overweight when she clearly is very underweight? Perhaps she is suffering from anorexia nervosa and is so thin that she is about to die from malnutrition. We could go on with further examples.

This is a controversial area. There has been a movement of large numbers of patients in recent years out of psychiatric hospitals and into community settings. While generally this is to be welcomed, some of these patients drift out of care and become victims of their own psychological disabilities and subject to exploitation.

Suffice to say that the impingement upon a patient's liberty is not taken lightly these days and there are legal safeguards involving magistrates' hearings and mental health review tribunals to make sure that a psychiatrist's medical judgment is in accord with society's current wishes to protect the freedom of individuals and to ensure that their care can be carried out in the 'least restrictive environment'.[11]

When is treatment completed?

The question of how to determine when a therapy is completed is a very difficult one and is really an extension of the previous question. In fact we could rephrase the question as: Why are we still treating this person? Just as some patients are keen to continue therapy beyond a period when any measurable change is occurring, there are many patients who are all too easily satisfied at having had the minimal amount of attention paid to their problem. They soon find the whole process of therapy or counselling overwhelming, frightening, embarrassing or self-indulgent. On reflection, they come to see their problem as trivial, especially in comparison with 'all the people out there with really genuine problems', people more in need of our help. Such patients will almost urge their therapist to dismiss their case after one or two sessions as no longer being worth their time.

This is a complicated area, described at one stage by Freud, when he wrote of patients who declared themselves cured after a very short number of sessions, long before they could have realistically expected results from his form of therapy. Indeed it was true that they were cured in that their original symptoms had totally disappeared, but only, Freud thought, because they had become so frightened of therapy and particularly of the prospect of examining their unconscious conflicts and repressed or forbidden impulses or wishes (to use Freud's theories) that the fear of therapy outweighed or trumped their original fears. Freud called this a transference cure, a result of the strongly negative (or even the strongly positive) feelings aroused early by the relationship with the therapist or therapy. Given enough time and distance from the therapy, Freud predicted that the patient's original symptoms would return.

This is a difficult issue as a therapist may wish to avoid

pathologizing the person's problem and so may agree with the patient's sentiments and say, yes, you need not be concerned about these problems. Although it is usually not helpful to continue to exhort patients to stay in therapy against their wishes, there is also the danger that the therapist may err in colluding with the patient's fears of therapy, or their low self-worth, or their belief that things have to be fixed up straightaway and that they should be better by now, and so may agree with the patient's suggestion of what would most likely be a premature end to therapy.

In order to answer these questions of what it is we are treating and why, and even for how long, some therapists rely on the technique of having clearly defined goals, using clearly defined symptom measures and even a clearly defined length of treatment (a determined number of sessions) at the commencement of therapy. That way they are in no doubt as to why they are treating the patient, and as the person improves, progress can be clearly gauged by repeated measures. In fact they can even be said to be 'cured' when the predetermined end point is reached.

The question arises though as to what constitutes a 'cure'. It is not unusual for patients to get 'better' very quickly. Having developed a helpful and positive relationship with the therapist, many problems seem to disappear almost spontaneously and the therapist is left wondering what it was that was causing the patient to come for therapy in the first place.

The real question is: Can the patient's improvement be maintained over the long term and after the termination of the therapy? Many studies of short-term therapies, apparently showing success in treating patients with severe problems in quite short periods of time, have inadequate follow-up of the patient's long-term outcome. This is not dissimilar to the visiting evangelist who returns to his home town with the statistics on those who were healed and converted. Little is finally reported about those who relapse into sickness or backslide from their original conversion, be it one month, six months or later.

If the therapist has any doubts about the existence of the patient's original difficulties, inappropriate talk of termination of the therapy will often bring the problem back in focus, sometimes in full force, and often with the therapist being the recipient of the problem as it manifests itself in the relationship with the therapist; i.e. in the transference.

The question of length of treatment is a controversial one and one which many parties will become increasingly interested in as governments, independent insurance companies and health maintenance organizations struggle, at least in mainstream medicine, to contain the costs associated with all forms of therapy be they medical, surgical or psychiatric.

I would like to turn now to the more specific area of biological treatments in psychiatry.

Biological treatments in psychiatry

It is a formidable task indeed to discuss the biological or non-psychotherapy treatments used in psychiatry. Since whole textbooks have been devoted to the subject (e.g. *Physical Treatments in Psychiatry* by Kiloh et al.), any brief attempt is bound to appear cursory and will be fraught with difficulties.[12]

Assuming that the reader has not trained in medicine, then some of the major concepts taken for granted by a psychiatrist will not be familiar. Nevertheless, there is much that can be said and psychiatrists along with other medical practitioners face the problem daily of how to inform their patients of the pros and cons of treatments and the mechanisms of action of the treatments and medications that they are recommending.

In fact there may be some advantage in presuming a limited knowledge on the part of the reader in that the finer and more esoteric points often debated amongst psychiatrists can be avoided entirely. The usual caveat must be made at the outset though, namely that decisions regarding treatment cannot be based on the author's opinions or information given here.

Hopefully in the pages that follow we will be able to come to an understanding of some of the broad principles of biological treatments, including the mechanisms of action of a number of medications, as well as their history. We will also hopefully be able to look at some of the ongoing dilemmas facing biological psychiatry.

Biological treatments in psychiatry have a long history. Just how long is not clear, but what is known is that the syndromes of melancholic depression were discussed in Sumerian and Egyptian literature from 2600 BC.[13] At various times the mind has been assumed to be either an inseparable part of the soul to be prayed or incanted over, or alternatively, as a part of the body to be subject to physical purges, pokings or prescribing. Moreover, since the exact seat of the mind could not be easily determined, the part of the body so prodded could vary from the head to the toe.

Although mental illnesses were commonly attributed to the influence of evil spirits, the medieval period in Europe saw a rise in the influence of the ancient physician, Hippocrates (460–377). His theory that the body was composed of four 'humours' – blood, phlegm, black bile and yellow bile – and that these humours controlled both physical and mental health, began to influence the more sophisticated medieval Europeans. In fact, they were likely to consider these four factors as being as important as the influence of spirits in the causation of mental illness.[13]

In the seventeenth and eighteenth centuries, descriptions of mental illness became more detailed and rudimentary classifications systems were developed. Nevertheless, effective treatments lagged far behind. In fact, most treatments were crude and barbarous, often based on cleaning the system of superfluous material by use of phlebotomies (cutting of the veins), leeches, mineral waters and repeated vomiting.[13]

Over the past forty years, enormous advances have been made in uncovering the biological basis for psychological function. In North America in particular, research into the neurochemical basis of cognitive and emotional functioning, and especially into the disorders of psychological functioning such as schizophrenia and manic-depressive illness (bipolar disorder), has progressed to a considerable degree. Actual areas of the brain can now be demonstrated (using sophisticated scanning equipment) to be responsible for certain cognitive and emotional processes.

This has created the hope that all psychological illness will one day come firmly back into the fold of biological medicine, to be understood virtually as a series of chemical processes. Many would rather be spared that prospect, but the biological hopes are epitomized by Guse whose recent article, 'Biological Psychiatry: Is there any other kind?' espouses the view that counselling and psychotherapy will one day be redundant, if (in Guse's opinion) they are not already so.[14]

Limitations in time and space mean that we have to turn away from this controversy almost immediately but hopefully the reader has an idea of the dilemma.

Once a decision is made to embark on treatment, one immediately has to confront the problem of which treatment. In an ideal world the question is answered quite logically: the best treatment, the one with the best effect and with the least side effects. In fact, in an ideal world it would be the one with a hundred per cent effectiveness and no side effects. However, there is a major problem with biological treatments, not only in psychiatry but in medicine generally, namely the problem of specificity. An extreme example might help to illuminate the problem.

One might be able to remove a patient's neurosis (albeit briefly) by placing him or her under a general anaesthetic. The neurosis is no longer being expressed (though presumably it is still there), but the problem now is that a myriad of other psychological and physical functions are also not being expressed. The treatment has not been specific; indeed it has been highly nonspecific. This difficulty extends in a much more subtle way to current drug treatments. Because of the interconnections of various complex systems in the brain, it is not possible with the medications currently available to affect only one neurochemical system in isolation from the many others.

In treating a mental disorder, we first need to know the area of the brain (or the neuronal system or nerve tracts) that is responsible for the symptoms or lack of function observed and then we attempt to influence the area or tract of nerve fibres that control those disordered functions. This assumes that the functioning of the cells inside these nerve tracts are disordered and that it is possible to correct this. Even at the outset, one can see that the aim in biological therapy is far more ambitious than merely sedating someone; from merely making them 'more calm'. A patient may well become 'calmer' than they were prior to treatment, but hopefully the treatment is more specific and has more to offer than mere sedation.

Moreover, this says nothing of the sort of psychosocial considerations that have to be considered and the psychotherapy that needs to be employed as a part of any treatment offered in biological medicine or psychiatry. In order to fulfil the purpose of the chapter, however, we must take an artificially reductionist view, but hopefully the reader will be aware that no biological treatment can occur without the proper use of accompanying psychosocial therapies. In fact, some of these psychosocial treatments, for example, those used in the treatment of schizophrenia, are highly specific and are tailored to the particular condition and its manifestation in the individual and in the wider family or social setting.[15, 16]

Before we can go much further, however, we need to understand some basic principles of neurobiology and the structure and function of nerve cells. The best place to begin is by looking at a nerve cell.

A NERVE CELL

Figure 6 shows a longitudinal cross-section of a nerve cell in a line of what may be a series of many millions of cells, with the 'action' occurring from left to right.

The important parts to note are: 1 The nucleus. 2 The synthesis of neurotransmitters. 3 The vesicles of neurotransmitters awaiting. 4 The transmitter release into 5 the synaptic cleft. 6 The postsynaptic receptors leading to 7 the transmission of the impulse. 8 The metabolism of some neurotransmitter and 9 the reuptake of neurotransmitter substance through the presynaptic receptor.

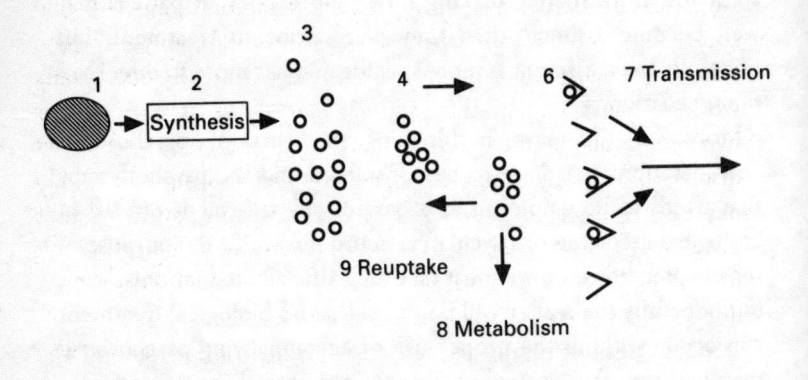

In looking at the nerve cell (above) we must remember that we have already stripped it of much of its complexity and that such a schematic and mechanical view does not adequately represent the fluidity of the system. It does, however, help us to understand some of the principles of biological treatments.

Let us assume that the function of the nerve is to produce a steady, regular amount of chemical (or neurotransmitter substance) which is then transported down the central axis of the cell and finally deposited into the synaptic cleft between the two nerve cells at point 5. Let us also assume that the neurotransmitter substance then hits up against the wall of the next nerve cell 6 (the postsynaptic wall), binds with a matching receptor 7 and, after activating that receptor, (which causes the transmission of the impulse and further chemical events in the next cell), then 'falls' back into the synapse where it is either broken down by an enzyme 8 or taken back up into the nerve cell by the reuptake mechanism on the presynaptic wall 9 to be used again.

Given that we have nominated nine points of interest in this nerve, we can see already that there are at least nine points at which this system could potentially go wrong, and also presumably, a number of points at which we could, in theory at least, manipulate the system to put it back closer to how we assume it 'should' be.

Of course, we do not really know how it should be. Rather, all we know is that some drugs reduce symptoms and working backwards from that point it is a slow process of finding out which systems are being affected (and how) by these drugs. By continually working backwards in this way we can arrive at a theory or hypothesis about how the original system must have been disordered. Having stumbled upon an effective drug and having developed a model of how the drug works, we are now in a better position the second and third time round because we can now look for a drug that might have similar properties to the first drug, but not so many of its disadvantages or side effects.

Space does not permit us to go into great detail or to cover the wide range of biological treatments used in psychiatry but if we look at just two major illnesses, that of Schizophrenia and Major Depression, we can consider some of the important principles, presumed mechanisms and problems of biological treatment.

The biological treatment of schizophrenia

In attempting to understand the problem of schizophrenia, a theory has been put forward for many years that the chemical problem underpinning the disorder is an excess of the neurotransmitter, dopamine.[17] Dopamine operates as a transmitter of the nerve impulse when it is released from the nerve cell endings into the synaptic cleft in the dopamine tracts. Subsequent research has found that drugs which are effective in alleviating, or in some cases, eliminating the symptoms of schizophrenia (or psychosis generally) have the ability to bind with, and block, the dopamine receptors on the postsynaptic wall (at point 6 of Figure 6). Not surprisingly these antipsychotic drugs are called 'postsynaptic receptor blockers' and they have remained the most effective biological treatment of schizophrenia since the 1950s.

Before we come back to Figure 6, a brief historical aside may be useful as it indicates the way in which treatment breakthroughs often occur by chance, and also the problems of nonspecificity of biological treatments.

Chlorpromazine was the first antipsychotic drug widely used for the treatment of schizophrenia in the 1950s. Prior to its use in schizophrenia, it was originally marketed as an antihistamine. This leads us to the important point regarding specificity, namely, that postsynaptic receptor blockers don't just block the dopamine postsynaptic receptors: they also block other receptors in the brain which leads, in each case, to either a wanted or unwanted effect. Unwanted effects are not surprisingly referred to as side effects. In blocking histamine receptors, the antipsychotic drugs have antihistamine properties, leading to drowsiness as a side effect. This brings us back to our history.

In the 1940s the major problem confronting surgery was that of surgical shock. Dr Henri Laborit, a French surgeon, was interested in this problem which was thought to be caused by the release of histamine. The French drug company Rhone-Poulene began marketing chlorpromazine in 1951 with the suggestion on the label 'for use as a general anaesthetic'. In 1951 Laborit first used chlorpromazine and discovered that it reduced his patient's postoperative anxiety and the need for larger doses of anaesthetic.[12]

Laborit urged his psychiatric colleagues at the Val de Grace hospital to try chlorpromazine with their patients and he published an article in 1952 suggesting a role for chlorpromazine in psychiatry. Subsequently, a colleague, Dr Hamon, successfully treated a patient with severe manic-depressive disorder using small doses of chlorpromazine. By 1955 the use of chlorpromazine in the treatment of schizophrenia was accepted worldwide and it led to a reversal of the trend towards increased hospitalization of people suffering from schizophrenia. The number of psychiatric in-patients in the USA fell from 560,000 in 1956 to 300,000 in 1971. The length of stay was also reduced from sixty-six per cent of patients staying longer than two years before World War II to only ten per cent staying longer than this in 1960.[12] Although a number of dopamine-blocking drugs have been developed and used since the 1950s, Chlorpromazine is still one of the major medications used in the treatment of schizophrenia.

How do antipsychotic drugs work?

Turning aside from any theories about the potential causes of schizophrenia, and assuming that the symptoms are finally produced by a chemical disorder or imbalance, then the obvious question is: What is the nature of the chemical problem in schizophrenia? If we look at Figure 1 we are faced with a number of possibilities. Are the nerve cells making too much dopamine? Is the dopamine leaking into the synaptic cleft too easily? Or is the dopamine being produced normally and are there, instead, too many receptors on the postsynaptic wall? The postsynaptic receptors act like bull's-eyes on a dartboard. Naturally if your dartboard has thirty bull's-eyes you'll be more likely to score a bull's-eye than if it has twenty, ten or one. It may be, however, that there is no abnormality in the number of postsynaptic receptors and since the postsynaptic receptors are the last link in a long chain or process, one can see immediately that the use of antipsychotic drugs to block the postsynaptic receptors may be a very crude way of trying to modulate the system – rather like shutting the gate when the horse has bolted. Moreover, it is based on an assumption that there is an excess of the dopamine chemical in the dopamine system. Recent evidence suggests that this general assumption about dopamine is not necessarily correct.[17, 18]

What if, instead, there is something wrong with some other system earlier on down the track (from direction A), a system which feeds into and amplifies the dopamine system? It would therefore be more precise to alter or block that system. On the other hand, perhaps some later system is at fault, a system which takes its input from the dopamine system (direction B). A theory put forward in the 1980s by Weinberger postulates that the dopamine system is itself operating normally, but that it is not being properly inhibited by another inhibiting neurone system that may be damaged or absent.[19]

At this point we now need to make another shift in our focus. This time moving from the micro, chemical events occurring between nerve cells to the broader, macro relationship between different areas of the brain connected by bundles of nerve fibres we need to consider the relationship and functioning of different lobes of the brain, especially the frontal lobes (at the front of the brain) and the temporal lobes (at the side) and the midbrain (deeper in the brain).

Weinberger's theory begins by noting that increased levels of stress lead to increased stimulation of the dopamine system at its origin deep in the midbrain, an area just above the top of the spinal column. Beginning in this area, and on each side of the brain, the dopamine pathways branch out in two directions to give input to the *frontal* lobes and the *temporal* lobes. Stimulation of the dopamine tract leading to the frontal lobe aids in attempts at mastery of the stressful situation by activating various cognitive functions which are situated in the frontal lobe. This activation is considered advantageous and enables one to think about how best to handle and cope with the stress.

Not only is the frontal lobe activity normally increased as a result of stress, but so also is the activity in the temporal lobe, leading to a state of hyperalertness. This too may also be of some advantage. However, what seems to be important in the temporal lobe is that other fibres are also normally stimulated at the same time, to act in an opposing way on the temporal lobe to inhibit and dampen down the hyperalertness produced by the midbrain-to-*temporal*-lobe system to manageable levels. Without this dampening down, the midbrain-to-*temporal*-lobe system is left unopposed and the hyperalertness can easily develop into sensory overload, misperceptions and hallucinations. According to Weinberger, in schizophrenia these inhibitory fibres are not active, presumably due to damage either pre- or postnatally or because of genetic factors.

Any theory of schizophrenia needs to explain two important clinical observations. Firstly, the onset of severe forms of schizophrenia occurs classically in the late teens and early twenties. To account for this, Weinberger argues that the fibres inhibiting the midbrain-to-*temporal* pathways do not normally become myelinated (or activated) until late in the second decade of life, presumably in response to sexual maturation. Prior to that time they are presumably not required and so their absence is not noted until they are required to come on line.

Secondly, patients with schizophrenia have two sets of almost independent symptoms. The first set of symptoms involve the more dramatic and bizarre symptoms of delusional thoughts, hallucinations, disordered speech and sentence construction and strange behaviour. These symptoms are thought to be due to an *increase* or overactivity in the midbrain-to-*temporal*-lobe system. These symptoms (sometimes referred to by convention as positive symptoms) can be reduced or in some cases eliminated by dopamine-blocking drugs. The other set of symptoms involve deficits in normal personality functioning such as reduced socialization and withdrawal, reduced speech and poverty of thought, poverty of emotion, poor motivation and reduced personal care and hygiene etc. These symptoms are called negative symptoms and are thought to be due to a *deficiency* or underactivity of dopamine in the midbrain-to-*frontal*-lobe system.[18, 20]

So, not only is there thought to be a lack of inhibition of the midbrain-to-temporal pathway, (leading to dopamine overactivity) but evidence also suggests that the pathway coming from the midbrain to the frontal lobe is underactive and perhaps interrupted in some way. The question arises as to the potential sites of damage which could account for the two virtually opposite phenomena.

Weinberger suggests that the damage may be somewhere along the midbrain-to-frontal-lobe tract, or in the frontal lobe itself and that the size and extent of the lesion could determine the severity of the symptoms. Unfortunately more recent research has yet to confirm the above theory.

Figure 7 shows this situation schematically. One can see that the midbrain-to-frontal-lobe pathway (1) is interrupted at its terminal end and this also interrupts the inhibitory pathway which leads back to the temporal lobe. The midbrain-to-temporal-lobe pathway is left functioning normally, but unopposed.

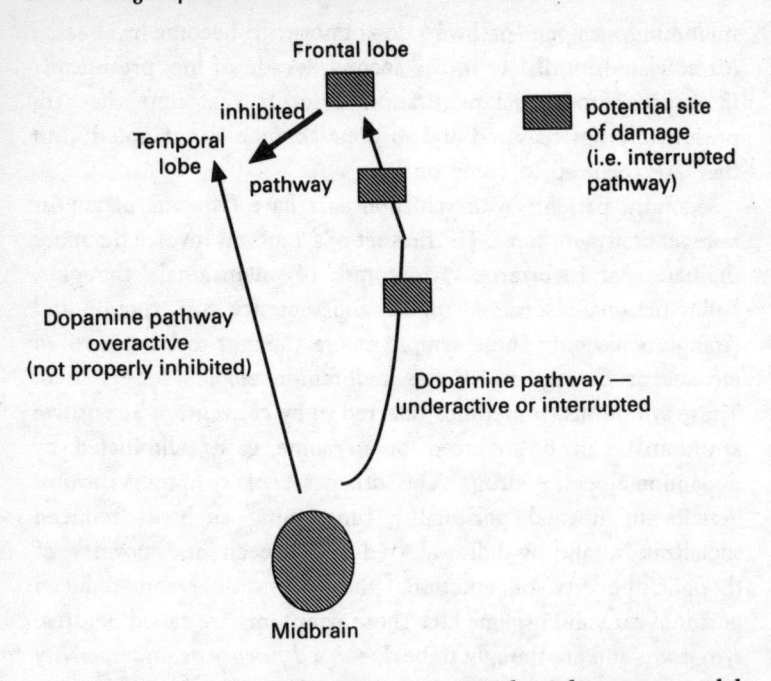

Of course, the above representation is only a theory or model of the anatomical and neurochemical basis of schizophrenia. Many of the pieces of the puzzle remain missing and the most likely scenario is that further information derived from more sophisticated research using noninvasive, brain-imaging tools will end up modifying such a model beyond recognition. Nevertheless, it serves as a good example of the current stage in attempts to understand major psychiatric illness at a biological level.

One of the major difficulties in the treatment of schizophrenia with dopamine blocking drugs is perhaps already apparent if we consider the above theory, namely that the dopamine blocking drugs will block or aggravate further any deficiency in the midbrain-to-frontal-lobe pathway and potentially exacerbate the negative symptoms. This can, in fact, be the case and for this reason doses are hopefully kept at the minimum level that will control the positive symptoms.

Before ending this section we should reiterate that the treatment of schizophrenia, while it involves as much biological sophistication as possible, is not an entirely biological affair. Its management encompasses a number of psychological and social strategies, involving both the individual and the family. This includes aspects of problem solving and the modification of communication patterns, especially if the communication contains components high in what has been termed, expressed emotions.[15, 16]

Side effects of antipsychotic drugs

Perhaps we have gravitated too much into the treatment of schizophrenia, but before we leave we must discuss some of the important side effects and adverse effects of antipsychotic drugs. We have mentioned sedation due to blockage of histamine receptors and the reduced motivation and drive caused by frontal-lobe-dopamine blockage.

Unfortunately there are two other pathways in the brain where dopamine is used as the neurotransmitter. This is unfortunate as the dopamine-blocking drugs will block dopamine receptors wherever they are found, not just in the area that we wish. One of these pathways, the nigro-striatal pathway is essential for the control of fine movement. In elderly people this pathway can be affected by neuronal loss leading to the condition known as Parkinson's disease. Treatment with antipsychotics can cause a chemically induced form of Parkinson's disease. While this condition is reversible upon ceasing medication, this is not always a feasible option and patients taking antipsychotics often have to take medication used for the treatment of Parkinson's disease, e.g. the anticholinergic drug benztropine (Cogentin), to control the Parkinsonian side effects.

The symptoms of Parkinson's syndrome include a tremor or shaking of the limbs (usually the hands) and reduced movement and rigidity. This leads to the commonly observed rigid stance, stooped shoulders and non-swinging of the arms on walking which characterizes the appearance of patients taking antipsychotics without adequate amounts of anti-Parkinsonian medication. Some antipsychotic drugs have a strong anticholinergic side effect which means that benztropine (an anticholinergic) may not be necessary. On the other hand some antipsychotics have almost no anticholinergic effects and so are more noted for their Parkinsonian side effects.

Somewhat related to the Parkinson's syndrome is an acute form of muscle spasm, the so-called dystonic reaction which can occur at any time but particularly in young patients exposed for the first time to potent antipsychotics. The most common form is a sudden or increasing stiffness and spasm in the neck, but other muscles including the back, jaw and eye can be affected. The symptoms are quickly reversed with anticholinergic medication (benztropine) but they can be frightening and distressing if patients are not warned about the possibility in advance. Some psychiatrists prescribe routine anticholinergics in the first few days of treatment to prevent dystonic reactions.

Another side effect, akathisia, is the inability to sit still. Patients taking antipsychotics will often pace up and down or continue to move their legs in a jittery fashion when standing or seated. This distressing side effect can even occur at low doses of medication where it is experienced as a subjective feeling of restlessness. Unfortunately, it responds only partially to benztropine and other medications.

Perhaps the most damaging of all side effects are those that are irreversible, including a form of retinal damage caused by long-term, high-dose (greater than 800 mg per day) use of thioridizine (Melleril). Awareness of this side effect means that high doses of this drug are no longer prescribed. Another irreversible side effect is known as tardive dyskinesia. This is a syndrome of involuntary movements involving any part of the body, but usually the face, lips and tongue. While it mostly occurs in patients who have been treated for many years (often beginning after decades of treatment), it has been known to occur with only brief exposure to antipsychotics. It is often reversible if discovered in its early stages and the medication ceased, but again, the cessation of medication is not always an easy step to take.

Other side effects include lowering of blood pressure

(particularly on standing or waking in the morning) weight gain, increased burning or redness of the skin when exposed to the sun, and sexual dysfunction. As mentioned previously, anticholinergic receptor blockade occurs with some antipsychotics leading to dry mouth, constipation, blurred vision and urinary hesitancy. These will be discussed under the section on depression as antidepressants are more renowned for their anticholinergic side effects.

Before what began as a brief note becomes something rather longer, we should turn to a discussion of depression, including the treatment modality of ECT.

The biological treatment of depression

While the situation with regard to depression is also quite complicated, we can use the above principles to discuss its treatment. We must also note at the outset two important points regarding depression which seem almost contradictory. Firstly, that the majority of depressions can be successfully treated by psychological means without recourse to medications, and secondly, that severe (endogenous) depression is often a serious illness with a high complication rate, not the least being a fifteen per cent lifetime risk of suicide.[20]

Returning to our discussion of the biology of severe depression, the model neurone in Figure 1 remains the same, although we are now talking about different nerve tracks in different areas of the brain which use different neurochemical substances, namely, serotonin and noradrenaline. Both of these naturally occurring chemicals have been implicated in the biology of depression.

Logically we should begin with the question: How does severe depression develop? This is a difficult question requiring an examination of a multitude of factors not all of which are biological. Even if we restrict ourselves to the biological realm, we still cannot answer the question with any certainty, but we can talk about how the depression manifests itself in terms of disordered functioning at a chemical and cellular level. The standard theory begins by saying that there is a deficiency of either or both of two substances, serotonin and noradrenaline.

Assuming there was a deficiency of neurotransmitter output from the neurone, we can see by examining the neurone in Figure 1 that we could attempt to increase the transmitter substance in a number of ways. Nevertheless, this requires a more detailed knowledge of the mechanisms surrounding the synaptic cleft than was necessary for the discussion of schizophrenia.

Once liberated into the synaptic cleft, the neurotransmitter substance may bind with the postsynaptic receptor and/or it may be either taken back up into the releasing neurone to be repackaged and released again, or it may be broken down into its building block substances by an oxidase enzyme, the so-called monoamine oxidase, and the breakdown products then excreted via the bloodstream. If we assume that certain forms of severe depression occur as a result of a deficiency of neurotransmitter in the synaptic cleft then we can see that there are a number of potential mechanisms for increasing the amount of neurotransmitter.

Firstly, to allow a greater amount of time for the neurotransmitter to act in the synaptic cleft one could try to block its reuptake by interfering with the reuptake mechanism which is found on the presynaptic wall. Secondly we could block the monoamine oxidase system so that the neurotransmitter is not broken down so quickly. In either case there would be a net increase in the amount of neurotransmitter remaining in the synaptic cleft.

Of course, these chemically induced blockages can never be complete or total but even if they involved a change of only a few per cent, it may be significant enough to have a therapeutic effect. You may have already guessed that one group of the most commonly prescribed antidepressants are in fact reuptake blockers, while another group comprise the monoamine oxidase inhibitors (or MAOIs). Together these two classes of drugs have been the mainstay of treatment for severe depression over the past thirty years.

The history of the discovery of antidepressants makes for no less interesting reading than that of schizophrenia. There were, in fact, two quite different antidepressants discovered in the same year of 1957.[13] The first, iproniazid (a MAOI) was initially used in the treatment of tuberculosis. It was noticed that many patients' moods improved, in some cases quite dramatically, when taking this substance. This was even so amongst those patients whose actual tuberculosis had not shown any improvement. There was, 'a return of vitality, a desire to leave the hospital and a general increase in social interest in subjects who for years had shown little interest in life'.[12]

Iproniazid was actually the first monoamine oxidase inhibitor (MAOI) and within a year of the first published results, more than 400,000 patients had been treated with the drug. Other MAOIs were soon synthesized and introduced and as iproniazid was shown occasionally to cause non-infectious hepatitis, its use declined and later ceased.

The tricyclic antidepressant, imipramine, was originally trialled as an antipsychotic because of some similarities in its structure to chlorpromazine. (Tricyclic refers to its three-ringed structure.) Because of its different effects it was tried on patients with severe (endogenous) depression and found to be very effective in improving mood. Although other tricyclics have since been developed and are in widespread use imipramine remains the benchmark by which other antidepressants are measured in terms of their safety and efficacy.

How do antidepressants really work?

In returning to our model neurone, we must add a further dimension to our understanding concerning depression. It is known that although one can experience side effects straight away after ingesting antidepressants, unfortunately the beneficial effect is rarely felt before some ten to fourteen days have elapsed from the time of commencing treatment. This is a puzzling phenomenon as one would expect that if there were an immediate increase in the neurotransmitter in the cleft, there would be a correspondingly rapid improvement in mood and a reversal of the other symptoms associated with severe depression such as early-morning wakening, anorexia, weight loss, reduced energy, impaired concentration, anhedonia and morbid self-deprecation.

In fact it can be demonstrated that there is an immediate increase in neurotransmitter substance, but to understand why the clinical improvement does not occur for some one to two weeks, we have to look more closely at the silent member of our system, the postsynaptic receptor. You will remember that the postsynaptic receptors are like numerous bull's-eyes on a dartboard.

Faced with increased bombardment from the neurotransmitter, the postsynaptic receptors can only imagine that there is something going haywire in the system and, like any sophisticated biological system, they will attempt to correct this imbalance, in this case by reducing their own numbers. Their reasoning is that since there is now more neurotransmitter, there is less need for receptors. The receptors, which are positioned in or on the receptor wall (the membrane of the cell) are withdrawn into the cell, broken down and the hole repaired with non-receptor substance. This defensive process is known as down-regulation.

This down-regulation of the postsynaptic receptors is a much slower process than the artificially, medication-induced up-regulation of the neurotransmitters. Without going further into the details, what we know from pathological studies is that the time-lag in clinical improvement in depression corresponds to the time it takes for the down-regulation of the receptors to become fully effective.

One might be tempted to think that the two processes would cancel each other out but this leads to the most surprising aspect of the theory of depression, namely that the postsynaptic receptor component of the system may be the site of the original disturbance. It may be that the symptoms of severe depression are a result of increased receptor populations on the postsynaptic wall rather than due to any changes in the neurotransmitter amount or its regulation.

One theory of electroconvulsive therapy is that it causes the disruption, breakdown or withdrawal of excessive populations of postsynaptic receptors which have presumably sprung up over the period prior to the onset of depression. If these receptors are working normally (a fact not fully known), then depression may even be due to an increase in the overall transmission in the neuronal system. This is the opposite of the assumption that we originally started with, namely that depression is a result of a reduction in transmission which needed increasing. This paradox of the antidepressants causing an increase in neurotransmitters, with the ultimate result being a reduction in receptors and a reduction in transmission, is still the subject of research.

There is an important point that we should make before we leave this section, namely that antidepressants, while they reverse the symptoms of the depression, may not actually have any effect on the underlying course, or natural history, of the episode of depression. Regardless of whether the original disturbance is one of post-synaptic receptor overpopulation or changes in neurotransmitter amounts, these are assumed to be under the control of genetic influences and to occur as part of the expression of the gene code. Of course, this rather biological view can be modified by the presumption that environmental and interpersonal events can also effect gene expression but the point is that once precipitated, a depressive episode can often continue for three to six, to twelve months or even longer. Most severe episodes of depression continue for at least six months and for this reason it is often recommended that antidepressants continue to be taken for at least six months after the patient has improved.

In the days prior to effective antidepressant therapy, patients with severe forms of depression, often referred to as melancholia, would almost always develop a remission in their illness after a sufficient length of time. Patients would sometimes be hospitalized in this time or cared for at home by a nurse, and provided they were able to be kept from suicidal behaviour or wasting away, they would most often recover spontaneously. Even today we can only presume that many people with moderate to severe depression are never treated with antidepressants but instead endure a period of major depression until their previous state returns.

Side-effects of antidepressants

Using a similar principle of classification to the one used in the section on antipsychotics, the major side effects of antidepressants can be divided into groups based on their effect on various receptors. Sedation is a common side effect and can be useful if sleep disturbance has been a feature of the depression and if most of the dose is taken at night. Some of the antidepressants, particularly the monoamine oxidase-inhibitor group, can have a mildly activating effect which can cause a difficulty in falling asleep. For this reason patients are often advised to take these medications in the morning and at lunchtime.

The anticholinergic side effects which occur with the traditional tricyclic antidepressants are similar to those of some antipsychotics, namely: dry mouth, constipation, blurred vision, urinary retention and, rarely, acute glaucoma. The urinary retention is a particular problem in the treatment of elderly men with depression who also may have prostatic enlargement, and this can result in acute and complete obstruction of the bladder outflow requiring temporary catheterization.

The cardiac effects of tricyclics require particular caution, especially in the elderly or those with a history of ischaemic heart disease or arrhythmia. The effects include postural hypotension caused by the blockage of alpha receptors in the walls of the arterial system. Alpha and beta receptors control blood pressure and many antihypertensive medications are based on the effect on these receptors. Tricyclics can dampen down the normal correcting responses to changes in posture. This can create a sensation of light-headedness on standing and in the elderly it can lead to fainting, particularly on rising out of bed in the morning. It goes without saying that any fall in an elderly person can create major problems and one of the well-known complications of antidepressants is that of fractured hips from falls due to postural hypotension.

Tricyclic antidepressants can also cause weight gain and sexual dysfunction such as erectile impotence, decreased libido and inability to attain orgasm. It should be stressed that overdoses of tricyclic antidepressants can be fatal and this makes their prescription problematic in the setting of severe depression.

A particular difficulty with the monoamine oxidase-inhibitor class of medication is the so-called 'cheese reaction'. The difficulty arises because the naturally occuring monoamine oxidases are found not only in the brain but also in the lining of the gastrointestinal tract, where they protect the body from absorbing pure monoamines found in certain foods. In fact, the monoamines are usually broken down in the lining of the intestinal tract by the oxidase before they can be absorbed into the bloodstream. A particularly dangerous monoamine, tyramine, is able to act in a similar way to adrenalin in the bloodstream if it is absorbed unaltered from the diet. It causes a marked increase in blood pressure leading to a throbbing headache and, in some cases, particularly the elderly, this can lead to a cerebral haemorrhage.

Tyramine is found in certain foods such as cheese, red wine, broad beans and foods prepared using the process of spoiling. These foods have to be avoided entirely, along with some common medications which have monoamine-like components (e.g. certain cough mixtures). Patients are provided with a comprehensive list of foods to avoid and instructions about the dietary precautions. For patients who are not in the habit of eating such foods the restrictions are not onerous. For others, however, the disadvantages mean that another medication has to be chosen. Even after stopping the medication it remains bound to the oxidase enzymes for up to two weeks and so the precautions have to be continued in that period.

Newer antidepressants

Of the newer, so-called 'second-generation' antidepressants, mianserin (Tolvon) has the advantage of very few anticholinergic or cardiac side effects. It is very useful in elderly males with prostatic enlargement and in those with cardiac arrhythmias or ischaemic heart disease. It is also much less likely to be fatal in overdose.

More recently, a newer, reversible monoamine oxidase inhibitor, moclobemide (Aurorix) has become available. It does not require the dietary restrictions of the older MAOIs. The reason is that the inhibition is reversible, meaning that the oxidase enzyme in the intestinal lining will give up the moclobemide and bind with any tyramine which may be present. In this way the tyramine is processed normally. Many patients find this medication much more acceptable because they do not have to follow any dietary restrictions and, like other MAOIs, it is not sedating. It also does not have the sometimes severe anticholinergic side effects of the tricyclics. It can, however, cause sleep disturbance and a mild headache (usually in the first few weeks).

Another newer antidepressant fluoxetine (Prozac 20), a selective serotonin reuptake blocker, is notable for its lack of anticholinergic side-effects, sedation or weight gain. It can, however, cause nausea, anxiety and insomnia. A reported association between fluoxetine use and increased suicidality and violence has not been borne out in larger studies.[21] In the USA fluoxetine at present accounts for nearly thirty per cent of all antidepressants prescribed by psychiatrists in private practice.[22]

The use of antidepressants in other psychiatric conditions

We should conclude this section by noting that antidepressants have a role in a quite diverse range of conditions for which they have been shown to have a beneficial effect. These include more minor depressions (although this is a controversial issue) and severe anxiety states such as panic disorder, agoraphobia and post-traumatic stress disorder. There are also cognitive and behavioural treatments for these conditions and medication is usually only used in combination with these treatments. This holds true even for severe depression where medication would usually be later combined with the various forms of psychotherapy such as supportive, cognitive or interpersonal psychotherapy after the medication has improved the patient's overall condition.

Antidepressants can block panic attacks and they can reduce obsessions and compulsions. They have been found useful in eating disorders and they can help reduce phobic states. Many patients with these conditions are at risk of using other medications such as minor tranquillizers, e.g. Valium and Serepax which have a much greater potential for dependency (addiction).

Lithium

The usefulness of lithium, a naturally occuring salt, was discovered somewhat fortuitously by an Australian, Dr John Cade, working in Melbourne in the 1940s. Using experimental animals he discovered that uric acid combined with lithium had beneficial calming effects. Initially he was mainly interested in the uric acid but needed to use lithium to make the uric acid soluble so that it could be injected. He found a beneficial effect but was surprised to find later, through a series of elimination trials, that it was in fact the lithium alone which had been responsible for the beneficial effects.

He tried lithium salts on ten patients who had been chronically hospitalized for many years. Within weeks, most of the patients were able to be discharged virtually cured of the condition and Cade published the world's first account of lithium treatment in the *Australian Medical Journal* in 1949. [23]

Despite an initial lack of acceptance, (particularly in America where it seemed for a number of decades that patients were much more likely to be diagnosed as having schizophrenia than manic-depression), it has now taken a place as one of the leading biological treatments in psychiatry, particularly in preventing relapses in severe manic-depressive illness (bipolar disorder).

How lithium works is unknown, though there are many theories. Most patients with bipolar disorder find a beneficial effect from lithium once the lithium level in the blood (serum) is within a known therapeutic range, normally between 0.6-1.2 mmol/l. For this reason monitoring of the serum level is helpful, although this is not the only reason for measuring the amount of drug in the serum. Because of the wide range of individual differences in absorption and metabolism of lithium, the amount in the serum can vary quite markedly between different patients taking the same oral dose.

A major problem with lithium is its potential for toxicity at serum levels not greatly above the therapeutic range. This means that there is very little margin for error in lithium dosage and hence monitoring of the lithium level needs to be carried out regularly. Lithium toxicity is serious and can be fatal. The side effects of lithium include tremor, nausea, diarrhoea, weight gain, thirst and the passing of larger than normal amounts of urine. These side effects are often dose-related and even a slight reduction in dose can cause a considerable drop in side effects.

The psychodynamics of prescribing

Before finishing the subject of biological treatment it is perhaps appropriate to say something about the psychodynamic (or unconscious) meanings that the prescribing of medication can have. These meanings can be considered from the point of view of the factors operating in both the patient and the doctor.[25] We are all familiar with the placebo effect and the effect of warm and kindly encouragement on the part of the prescribing doctor. The expectations of an improvement with medication often affects one's feeling of wellbeing and so can contribute to improvement.

To be considered efficacious, however, a medication has to be shown to have a superior effect to placebo alone, in treatment trials where patients are usually divided into a group receiving the medication and a separate group receiving placebo only. It is the job of the statistician to show that the improvement in the treatment group is so marked as to be beyond a chance effect. The effect of the drug is then considered to be statistically significant.

This has taken us a little away from our point, however, which is that the giving and taking of medication is imbued with many and varied meanings at multiple levels in the psyches of the participants concerned, and this needs to be considered by the sophisticated therapist.

For some patients the desire for medication is strong and in part it can represent a pattern from earlier developmental stages of childhood. Indeed, according to some models of the mind it would represent or evoke a memory of the taking of the breast in times of distress. This deep pattern of response becomes unconscious for most of us, but in times of stress it is not too difficult to see the sense of comfort that one might derive from the feeling of being fed by the powerful mother-type figure of the therapist and his or her tablets. This situation may especially occur in the depressed patient; indeed it is not an inappropriate response and it has some protective value in bolstering hope, at least temporarily until functioning improves.

Similarly the dependent patient may wish for a more concrete demonstration of the therapist's power and potency (rather than just words) and, particularly when improvement has stalled and both the therapist and patient are called on to face painful feelings, the temptation can be quite strong to turn away from these feelings and to prescribe a medication without there being a legitimate biological rationale. For the patient who has difficulty evoking the memory of important attachment figures when they are no longer present, even the physical presence of the bottle of tablets can represent a thread of attachment and a lifeline to the therapist.

Prescribing can represent a frustration on the part of the therapist or even a fear and a wish not to have to face the angry and demanding aspects of the difficult patient. Perhaps the patient is seen as being bad by not getting better or perhaps the therapist feels impotent. His talking and listening have not helped, neither have his suggestions or advice or counselling. What can he do to restore his feeling of power and usefulness? It is at this point that the temptation to prescribe can be overpowering. If the therapist is sufficiently able to monitor and reflect on his behaviour, however, the desire to prescribe can be useful if seen as a barometer or indicator that certain things may be being left unsaid or unexplored between the two participants in the therapy.

In the ideal world or the perfect therapy, issues that are arising in therapy, be they thoughts and feelings of a threatening, fearful, sexual or shameful nature, and which are preconscious should be explored or brought into consciousness by the therapist's interpretations. Most psychotherapies are based on the belief that all sorts of benefits and improvements in functioning flow from this basic procedure. These models of therapy then propose that problems occur when an awareness of these feelings or thoughts is resisted, and rather than being talked about in the therapy, they may instead be 'acted-out' in all sorts of ways. It is at this point then that we need to understand that the prescribing and the swallowing of medication can be one form of 'acting-out' behaviour.

The issue of control is an important one. For many hostile or paranoid patients the prescribing of medication is experienced as an aversive, controlling influence, and they will often reject prescribed medication, whatever its rationale. For some patients medication will represent the warmth and closeness with the therapist, while for others it will represent a desire for a savage and punitive attack upon the self or a need for control or drowning out of feelings in much the same way as an individual may abuse alcohol.

The point to understand is that, apart from all else, there are unconscious and non-logical motivations for the prescribing and taking of medication, some of which neither the psychiatrist nor the patient will be aware of at the time. It is not unusual for biological therapy to be instigated as an unexplored or unacknowledged desperation measure.

Electro-convulsive therapy

The mention of electroconvulsive therapy (ECT) usually provokes images of the worst aspects of antiquated psychiatric institutions. Most people find it hard to believe that ECT is still a valid treatment in the 1990s. Indeed, it is hard to understand how a treatment can conjure up such barbaric images and yet still have a place in modern therapy. Unfortunately, the simple fact is that psychiatry has yet to find a treatment for severe, incapacitating depression that is as effective as convulsive therapy. In fact, many studies have shown ECT to be more effective and safer than tricyclic antidepressants, especially in the elderly where the risks of antidepressants increase markedly, although other studies have not verified this and the question still remains unclear.[24]

Of course, it would be easier if ECT were not so effective or safe. ECT is a very time-consuming, labour-intensive and costly treatment. If there were a more effective treatment, ECT could be relegated to the museum, psychiatry's image would certainly improve and there would be relief in the minds of potential patients and their relatives. Some countries have banned ECT, but this means that their citizens are being denied a choice in their psychiatric care. Some patients with very severe depression are treated with tricyclic antidepressants for long periods of time when they would be far better off being treated (more effectively) with electroconvulsive therapy.

There is also much confusion about what ECT is and how it works. The term electroshock therapy is an unfortunate one because it implies, at least to those who are unfamiliar with the treatment, a brutal attack upon the brain. It makes one wonder whether the patient is being made better, or less depressed, by being shocked or frightened much in the same way that depressed patients had cold water thrown over them in previous centuries. The irony is that convulsive therapy actually helped bring about the end of real 'shock' therapies.

Even the more accurate term of electroconvulsive therapy still gives the impression that it is the electricity which is the active ingredient, that in some way the electric current has an activating effect. The use of electricity, however, is merely a refinement of the earlier technique and one designed to make the treatment safer.

Movies such as *One Flew over the Cuckoo's Nest* portray ECT as a form of punishment or mind control, and the more recent exposure in New South Wales of the treatment of psychiatric patients with the discredited, so-called 'deep sleep therapy' has added to the confusion about the legitimacy of ECT. It may be useful at this point to examine some of the history of convulsive therapy.

The belief that convulsions might influence the course of mental illness dates back to at least the eighteenth century. In 1785 Oliver treated a patient with large doses of camphor taken orally to induce a seizure with an apparent improvement in his mental state. The beneficial, and often dramatic effect of fits continued to be reported. Muller in 1930 noted that two patients with catatonic schizophrenia, who spontaneously developed fits, were cured.[12]

Some erroneous notions soon developed, however, such as the idea that schizophrenia and epilepsy were mutually exclusive and that a patient therefore could not have both illnesses together. Just to show how strongly this idea was held, in 1932 Nyiro and Jablonsky transfused epileptic patients with blood from patients with schizophrenia in the hope of curing their epilepsy. Perhaps not surprisingly, the results were very disappointing.[12]

The problem soon became one, firstly, of how to induce a seizure safely in order to take advantage of the possible benefits of seizures, and, secondly, to determine which patients or which illnesses might benefit most from convulsive therapy. Meduna in 1934 experimented with camphor oil, injected intramuscularly, to produce fits and later with another substance (Metrazol) which worked more rapidly. The problem with camphor oil was its lack of predicability, with patients having literally to sit and wait for up to two hours for the convulsion to occur. Their anxiety not surprisingly developed to extremes. In 1936 Meduna reported that of forty-three schizophrenics treated, nineteen were cured and seven improved. Various other substances were used to induce convulsions in the late 1930s but in 1938 Cerletti and Bini introduced the method for inducing convulsions electrically.[12]

The use of electricity alone for therapeutic purposes dates back to Roman times with the use of the torpedo fish, which could discharge up to 50 amps, for the treatment of headaches. Following the development of electric condensers, the therapeutic use of electricity became more widespread. An enthusiastic adherent was John Wesley who in 1759 observed, 'I doubt not but more nervous disorders would be cured in one year by this single remedy than the whole English Materia Medica will cure by the end of the century.'[13] As the authors of *Physical Treatments in Psychiatry* point out, this must have been the evangelist rather than the scientist speaking.[12]

Since the 1940s there have been major advances in the techniques used for ECT. The four most important advances according to Kiloh et al, were the use of anaesthetics to ensure the patient was asleep before the procedure began, the use of muscle relaxants to avoid damage to limbs, the use of one-sided placement of the electrodes on the scalp to lessen short-term memory disturbance and the use of machines which continuously adjust voltage to the patient's individual resistance so that a maximum (fixed) current was not exceeded and memory impairment reduced.[12]

As mentioned earlier, it is perhaps unfortunate that ECT remains such an effective treatment for the more severe forms of depression. Certainly the initial enthusiasm for its use in schizophrenia has waned and it is now used only rarely for that condition. Because of the dramatic improvements that can be seen in severe depression and because of the increased safety of the procedure, it was perhaps used too freely in recent decades for the treatment of milder, chronic (or neurotic) depressions. The treatment is now almost entirely reserved for severe depression, particularly for patients who have ceased taking adequate amounts of fluid (and who might otherwise need intravenous fluids), those with medical conditions where tricyclic antidepressants would be contraindicated, those with extreme suicidality and those who have failed to respond to an adequate trial of antidepressants. Of the patients resistant to the effects of medication, a large number will later respond to a course of ECT.

Even if ECT is more effective, many would wonder about the possibility of profound side effects and damaging consequences. There are side effects of both the anaesthetic and the seizure. Headache is reported in about ten to fifteen per cent of patients but the most common side effect is that of short-term memory disturbance whereby recent events are not recalled. This has been shown to improve after the cessation of ECT and some sophisticated studies using psychometric testing six to twelve months after ECT have not shown any difference in memory function in those that have had ECT compared with those who have had tricyclics.[12]

Of course, no treatment should ever be given unless the benefits outweigh the risks of the original condition. Much of the controversy surrounding psychiatric treatments generally occurs because the risks of the various conditions, left untreated, are not fully appreciated. For example, the lifetime risk of suicide in patients with recurrent, severe depression is very high, perhaps up to fifteen per cent. This is thirty times the rate seen in the general community.[20]

Of course, one can never accurately predict whether a person will in fact engage in suicidal behaviour, although there are some well-known risk factors. It is not always a wish for relief that drives a depressed person to attempt suicide. In cases of severe depression, one's thinking can become so distorted that the sufferer can come to believe that they are the cause of their family's or even their community's problems and that if they had any shred of decency left they would kill themselves so that everyone else would be better off. Depression can be a very dangerous illness.

Some problems in treating religious patients
I would like to finish with a brief discussion of this important topic. There are a number of things to consider, but I think there are three main points. The first is obvious.

Many Christians have a suspicion of psychiatry and psycho-therapy. This is understandable and as it should be. Since the general population has doubts about psychiatry, one would hope that Christian people would be even more discerning. Some therapists hold a great sway over their patients and some hold quite strong opinions concerning social, ethical and religious issues which they are not backward in announcing and promulgating. Some hold that religious beliefs are neurotic, while others think they are fine as long as it is their own religion or belief system that you are talking about. Most psychiatrists, however, will keep religious matters to the periphery unless they feel that it is central to the issues being dealt with.

The solution? It is not too difficult for Christians to work out whether a particular therapist is going to respect and understand the importance of their beliefs and most patients will leave a therapist who does not seem to be able to empathize with them.

Nevertheless, the issue of referral and choice of therapist presents some difficulties as it is a requirement that a referral to a specialist in psychiatry be made by another medical practitioner. Usually this is done on the suggestion of the patient's general practitioner who may recommend a psychiatrist whose abilities he is familiar with. Quite commonly, however, patients will themselves initiate a referral to a psychiatrist without going into much detail as to why they are seeking referral and sometimes suggesting a particular psychiatrist who has been recommended to them by relatives or friends.

Some counsellors will also, on occasions, advise their clients to seek psychiatric opinion or management if the case appears complicated or if the client is not responding well to counselling. At such times they may even suggest a psychiatrist known to them who may or may not be a Christian. In this way the patient may arrive at the psychiatrist via a number of different routes and with various spoken and unspoken expectations.

For some Christians it seems to be an issue as to whether seeking psychiatric help represents a failure in exercising sufficient faith. That is a question that must be determined according to the individual's own understanding of Scripture. Where major mental illness is concerned I cannot personally see the difference between mending a fractured limb and mending a neurochemical pathway. Psychiatry in its field is just as valid as orthopaedics in its own. Admittedly the issue is certainly more grey when you move into the area of psychotherapy.

A major problem that I see with some Christian patients, however, is that having decided to consider psychotherapy as a treatment option for their difficulties, there often appears to be a feeling that whatever the consequences, they will be swift, dramatic and far-reaching. Some Christians, particularly if they have arranged to see a Christian psychiatrist, have expectations, of immediate and comprehensive results which can be unrealistic.

Another problem that can occur, admittedly with less mature patients, is due to their inability to tolerate the frustration inherent in sessions of a fixed duration and frequency. Such patients have often had many lengthy counselling sessions with their minister or pastor, often at odd hours or late at night, and they then do not understand that in the world of secular therapy, sessions begin and end at a given time even if the therapist is a Christian.

The resentment experienced by the patient in both these situations can be dealt with either by explaining the reality of the situation early in the consultations or by interpreting the patient's idealized hopes and wishes concerning the way in which the therapy will be conducted. This needs to be done early at the first sign of the emergence of negative feelings towards the therapist.

This does not mean that a counsellor should not respond to an individual's problems or crises late at night or at difficult, inconvenient times, but rather that a counsellor should be alert to the need to provide definite structure as well as avoiding setting up expectations which eventually cannot possibly be met.

NOTES

Introduction

1 E. Kennedy, *On Becoming a Counsellor: A Basic Guide for Non-Professional Counsellors*, Seabury Press, New York, 1977, p.x.

Chapter 1

1 Gary Collins, *Christian Counselling:* A Comprehensive Guide, rev. ed., Word Publishing, Milton Keynes, England, 1989, pp. 16-17.

2 The Big Umbrella, quoted in G. Collins, *Christian Counselling*, p. 22.

3 A reasonable overview is J. Kovel, *A Complete Guide to Therapy*, Penguin, Harmondsworth, 1976.

4 E.g. *Competent to Counsel*, Baker, Grand Rapids, Michigan, 1971.

5 E.g. L. J. Crabb Jr, *Effective Biblical Counselling*, Zondervan, Grand Rapids, Michigan, 1977, and Marshall Pickering, London.

6 *Healing Adventure*, Logos, Plainfield, NJ, 1969.

7 *The Transformation of the Inner Man*, Logos, Plainfield, NJ, 1982.

8 Cf. Ray S. Anderson, *On Being Human*, Eerdmans, Grand Rapids, MI, 1982.

9 *See* Don S. Browning, *Religious Thought and the Modern*

Psychotherapies, Philadelphia, Fortress Press, 1987, p. 1.

10　*See also* J. D. Crossan, *The Dark Interval: Towards a Theology of Story,* Argus Communications, Texas, 1975.

11　*The Evangelical Faith,* Vol. 1, Eerdmans, 1974, pp. 92–100.

12　M. Jordan, *Taking on the Gods: The Task of the Pastoral Counsellor,* Abingdon, Nashville, 1986, p. 18.

13　*See* A. MacIntyre, *After Virtue: A Study in Moral Theology,* Duckworth, London, 1981.

14　*ibid.,* p. 29.

15　Henri Nouwen, *The Living Reminder,* Seabury Press, New York, 1977, p. 76.

16　Wayne Oates, *The Presence of God in Pastoral Counselling,* Word Books, Waco, Texas, 1986, p. 23.

17　Charles V. Gerkin, *The Living Human Document,* Abingdon Press, Nashville, 1984, p. 56.

18　*ibid.,* p. 62.

Chapter 2

1　D. Geldard, *Basic Personal Counselling: A Training Manual for Counsellors,* Prentice Hall, Sydney, 1989, p. 13.

2　For example, R. R. Carkhuff, *Helping and Human Relations,* vol 1 and 2, Hold, Rinehart and Winston, Inc., New York, 1969.

3　Gerard Egan, *The Skilled Helper: A Model for Systematic Helping and Interpersonal Relating,* Brooks/Cole Publishing Co., Monterey, California, 1975, and later editions.

4　Gerard Egan, *You and Me: The Skills of Communicating and Relating to Others,* Brooks/Cole Publishing Co., Monterey, California, 1977, p. 117.

5　*War and Peace,* vol 3, Heron Books, London, no date.

6　D. Geldard, *Basic Personal Counselling,* Prentice Hall, Sydney, 1989, p. 32.

7　M. Gelder, D. Gath and R. Mayou, *Oxford Textbook of Psychiatry,* second edn, Oxford University Press, Oxford, 1989, p. 696.

8　See D. Geldard, *Basic Personal Counselling,* pp. 21–22.

9　*ibid.,* p. 8.

10 Gerard Egan, *The Skilled Helper*, p. 93.
11 *ibid.*, p. 96.
12 D. Geldard, *Basic Personal Counselling*, p. 10.
13 G. Weinberg, *The Heart of Psychotherapy*, St Martin's Press, New York, 1984, p. 183.
14 D. Geldard, *Basic Personal Counselling*, p. 55.

Chapter 3

1 Gerard Egan, *The Skilled Helper*, p. 135.
2 *ibid.*, p. 172.
3 *ibid.*, p. 178–179.
4 J. A. Kottler and D. S. Blau, *The Imperfect Therapist*, Jossey-Bass, San Francisco, 1989, p. 154.

Chapter 4

1 Ira Tanner, *Healing the Pain of Every Day Loss*, Winston Press, Minneapolis, Mn, 1976, p. 3.
2 John Bowlby, *Attachment and Loss: Attachment*, Vol. 1, Penguin Books, Harmondsworth, England, 1971; *Attachment and Loss: Separation*, Vol. 2, Penguin Books, Harmondsworth, 1975.
3 *See* E. Lindemann, 'Symptomatology and the Management of Acute Grief', *American Journal of Psychiatry*, 1944, No. 101, p. 141.
4 E. Kübler-Ross, *Questions on Death and Dying*, Macmillan, New York, 1984.
5 An interesting study on the place of culture and even historical period on how the grief process is understood is M. Stoebe, M. M. Gergen, K. J. Gergen, and W. Stroebe, 'Broken Hearts or Broken Bonds', *American Psychologist*, vol. 47, no. 10, pp. 1205–1212.
6 *An Australian Prayer Book*, AIO Press, Sydney, 1978, p. 594.
7 C. S. Lewis, *A Grief Observed*, Faber and Faber, London, 1961, p. 7.

8 *Totem and Taboo* (1913), in the Standard Edition, vol 13, Hogarth Press, London, 1955, p. 65.

9 R. S. Sullender, *Grief and Growth*, Paulist Press, New York, 1985, p. 56.

10 Quoted in F. Mcnab, *Life After Loss*, Millennium, Newtown, NSW, 1989, pp. 246.

11 J. W. Worden, *Grief Counselling and Grief Therapy*, Routledge, London, 1983, p. 28.

12 The loss of a child is a very intense and in some ways a special case in grief. See N. Kohner and A. Henley, *When a Baby Dies: The Experience of Late Miscarriage, Stillbirth and Neonatal Death*, London, Pandora Press, 1991. See B. A. Stevens, 'When a Child Dies'. *Church Scene*, (Feb. 5, 1988), pp. 5-6.

13 Charles Dickens, *Great Expectations*, Heron, London, first published 1861, p. 341.

14 *Diagnostic and Statistical Manual of Mental Disorders*, 3rd Edn. American Psychiatric Association, Washington, DC, 1980. *see* p. 333.

15 J. W. Worden, *Grief Counselling and Grief Therapy*, p. 66. The four categories of abnormal grief are suggested by Worden as well.

16 Bible, New Revised Standard Version, World Bible Publishers, Iowa Falls, 1989. All biblical quotes are from the NSRV.

17 Derek Kidner, *Wisdom To Live By*, Intervarsity Press, Leicester, 1985, p. 60.

18 Bruce D. Rumbold, 'The effects of loss and separation', *Australian Ministry*, 3/4, (Nov 1991), p. 11.

19 Bruce Wilson, 'The God Who Suffers', *St Mark's Review*, Vol 140, (Summer, 1990), p. 31.

Chapter 5

1 This term was first used by Franz Alexander, cf. F. Alexander, 'The Dynamics of Psychotherapy in the Light of Learning Theory', *American Journal of Psychiatry*, (1963), 120, pp. 440-448.

2 *The Oxford Textbook of Psychiatry*, p. 695.

3 *Doing Psychotherapy*, Basic Books, New York, 1980, p. 11.

4 Weinberg, *The Heart of Psychotherapy*, p. 126.

5 Other structural matters might include times of sessions, who is expected to be present and fees.

6 Ronald R. Lee, *Clergy and Clients: The Practice of Pastoral Psychotherapy*, Seabury Press, New York, 1980, p. 39. This is an excellent book for what is involved in assessment.

7 *Diagnostic and Statistical Manual of Mental Disorders*, 3rd edn revised, Washington, DC, American Psychiatric Association, 1987.

8 Joseph Sandler, et al., *The Patient and the Analyst*, International Universities Press, New York, 1973, p. 30.

9 Weinberg, *The Heart of Psychotherapy*, p. 131.

10 *The Oxford Textbook of Psychiatry*, p. 696.

11 Geldard, *Basic Personal Counselling*, pp. 76–77.

12 *ibid.*, p. 79.

13 *See* R. Bandler and J. Grinder, *Reframing: Neuro-linguistic Programming and the Transformation of Meaning*, Real People Press, Moab, 1982.

14 Storr, *The Art of Psychotherapy*, p. 25.

15 Weinburg, *The Heart of Psychotherapy*, p. 81.

16 For an excellent discussion of 'emergency psychology', or what is appropriate in such situations *see* D. S. and L. Everstine, *People in Crisis: Strategic Therapeutic Interventions*, Brunner and Mazel, New York, 1983.

17 A good case can be made for giving advice when the counsellor may be aware of relevant research, but only when there is a significant involvement of both parties in the decision-making process, *see* B. Fischoff, 'Giving Advice', *American Psychologist*, (April, 1992), 47/4, pp. 577–588.

18 J. Mann, *Time Limited Psychotherapy*, Harvard University Press, Cambridge, MA, 1973, p. 50.

19 *The Oxford Textbook of Psychiatry*, p. 697.

20 I. Yalom, *Love's Executioner and Other Tales of Psychotherapy*, Penguin, London, p. 35.

21 M. F. Basch, *Practising Psychotherapy: A case book,* Basic Books, New York, 1992, p. 23.

22 S. Freud, *Dora: An analysis of a case of hysteria,* Collier Books, 1963, New York, p. 138.

23 Basch, *Doing Psychotherapy,* p. 104.

24 E. Kennedy, *On Becoming a Counsellor,* Seabury Press, New York, 1977, p. 188.

25 B. A. Stevens and M. E. Arnstein, *Psychological and Emotional Disorders in Rehabilitation Casework,* ACT Institute of Technical and Further Education, Canberra, 1990, pp. 34-35.

Chapter 6

1 DSM III-R, pp. 222-223. The revision DSM IV is expected to be out soon.

2 *The Oxford Textbook of Psychiatry,* p. 236.

3 John Maltsberger, *Suicide Risk: The Formulation of Clinical Judgment,* Universities Press, New York, *see* pp. 1-3.

4 D. P. Phillips and L. L. Carstensen, 'Clustering of Teenage Suicides after Television News Stories about Suicide', *The New England Journal of Medicine,* vol. 315, no. 11, pp. 685-689.

5 For statistics *see* 'Suicides, Australia 1961-1981', *Australian Bureau of Statistics,* Canberra, 13 April, 1983.

6 G. Weinberg, *The Heart of Psychotherapy,* p. 266.

7 I have only mentioned the competing theories, *see* almost any textbook on introductory psychology for more details.

8 Eds. E. McGrath, G. Kieta, B. Strickland and N. Russo, Washington, DC, American Psychological Association, 1990.

9 *The Oxford Textbook of Psychiatry,* a marked improvement in 71 per cent of cases, p. 255.

10 One of the pioneers of rational thinking as a basis of a more satisfying life was Albert Ellis, *see* A. Ellis and R. A. Harper, *A Guide to Rational Living,* Hollywood, CA, Wilshire Book Co., 1961.

11 D. Burns, *Feeling Good: The New Mood Therapy,* S&W Information Guides, Melbourne, 1980, p. 39.

12 *Beating the Blues: A Self-help Approach to Overcoming Depression,* Doubleday, Sydney, 1991.

13 E.g. *The Christian Counsellor's Manual,* Baker, Grand Rapids, Michigan, 1973.

Chapter 7

1 For a general discussion *see* David Hechler, *The Battle and the Backlash: The Child Sexual Abuse War,* Lexington Books, Lexington, 1988.

2 Wendy Maltz, *The Sexual Healing Journey: A Guide for Survivors of Sexual Abuse,* HarperCollins*Publishers,* New York, 1991, p. 31.

3 'Adult Survivors of Childhood Sexual Abuse', *Clinician's Research Digest,* 10/7, July, 1992, p. 5.

4 Karin C. Meiselman, *Incest: A Psychological Study of Causes and Effects with Treatment Recommendations,* Jossey-Bass Publishers, San Francisco, 1978, p. 3.

5 Meiselman, *Incest,* pp. 333-334.

6 Peter Horsfield, 'The Gerasene Demoniac and the Sexually Violated', *St Mark's Review,* No 152, Summer 1993, p. 4.

7 *See* Estella Weldon, *Mother, Madonna, Whore: The Idealisation and Denigration of Motherhood,* Free Association Press, London, 1988.

8 *See* P. M. Cole and F. W. Putnam, 'Effect of Incest on Self and Social Functioning: A developmental psychopathology perspective', *Journal of Consulting and Clinical Psychology,* 1992, 60, pp. 174-184.

9 *DSM III,* p. 271.

10 For a family approach to treating incest *see* T. S. Trepper and M. J. Barrett, *Systemic Treatment of Incest: A Therapeutic Handbook,* New York, Brunner/Mazel Publisher, 1989. I found the idea of apology sessions interesting, *see* pp. 135-150.

11 Judith L. Herman, *Father-Daughter Incest,* Cambridge MA, Harvard University Press, 1981.

12 *See* the important article by Elizabeth F. Loftus, 'The Reality of Repressed Memories', *American Psychologist,* vol. 48, no. 5, May 1993, pp. 518-36.

13 R. Rohr, 'The Holiness of Human Sexuality', *Sojourners*, October, 1982, p. 14.

14 *See* the recent publication, David K. Sakheim and Susan E. Devine, *Out of Darkness: Exploring Satanism and Ritual Abuse*, New York, Lexington Books, 1992.

15 S. P. Bank and M. D. Kahn, *The Sibling Bond*, Basic Books, New York, 1982, p. 176. The younger the victim the more damaging and confusing the experience.

16 Robin Norwood, *Women Who Love Too Much*, New York, Pocket Books, 1985.

17 S. P. Bank and M. D. Cahn, *The Sibling Bond*, p. 177.

18 We also need to address the unfortunate, but not uncommon, situation in which the clergyperson is the abuser. This has a damaging effect on the victim's spiritual trust, spiritual sense of self and leaves the person feeling ravaged or abandoned by God. P. Horsfield, 'Sexually Violated', p. 4.

Chapter 8

1 For a historical review *see* C. B. Broderick and S. S. Schrader, 'The History of Professional Marriage and Family Therapy', pp. 5-32, in *Handbook of Family Therapy*, eds. A. S. Gurman and D. P. Kniskern, Brunner and Mazel, New York, 1981.

2 L. von Bertalanffy, *General Systems Theory: Foundations, Development, Applications*, rev edn, George Braziller, New York, 1968. Also H. Werner, *The Comparative Psychology of Mental Development*, International University Press, New York, rev edn 1957, first published 1948.

3 For a collection of his papers *see* M. Bowen, *Family Therapy in Clinical Practice*, Jason Aronson, New York, 1978.

4 *See* N. A. Ackerman, *Treating the Troubled Family*, Basic Books, New York, 1966.

5 E.g. M. White, 'Couple Therapy: 'Urgency for Sameness' or 'Appreciation of Difference', *Dulwich Review*, Summer 1987, pp. 11-13. A collection of more recent papers is D. Epston and M. White, *Experience, Contradiction, Narrative, and Imagination*,

South Australia, Dulwich Centre Publications, 1992. Also M. Arnstein, 'An Overview of Three Models of Marital Therapy', *The Australian and New Zealand Journal of Family Therapy*, vol. 9 no. 3, 1988, pp. 151-158.

6 I am not aware of any distinctly Christian approach to marriage or family counselling.

7 Anon., 'Toward the Differentiation of a Self in One's Own Family', ed. J. Framo, *Family Interaction*, Springer, New York, 1972.

8 M. E. Kerr, 'Theoretical Base for Differentiation of Self in One's Family of Origin', ed. C. E. Munson, *Family of Origin Applications in Clinical Supervision*, Hawthorn Press, New York, 1984, p. 9.

9 M. E. Kerr, 'Theoretical Base', p. 11.

10 M. E. Kerr, *Family Evaluation: An Approach Based on Bowen Theory*, W. W. Norton and Company, New York, 1988, p. 57.

11 E. Friedman, *Generation to Generation*, Guilford Press, New York, 1985, p. 42.

12 *Age* (Melbourne newspaper), 3 May 1989.

13 E.g. in the 12th-century French court of Eleanor of Aquitaine, D. Jansen and M. Newman, *Really Relating*, p. 21.

14 R. A. Johnson, *The Psychology of Romantic Love*, Arkana, London, 1983, p. 54.

15 *See* H. Hendrix, *Getting the Love You Want: A Guide for Couples*, Schwartz and Wilkinson, Melbourne, 1988, pp. 41-42.

16 Sam Keen has said: 'Love in its three epiphanies - romance, marriage, sex - is a dying God.' *The Passionate Life: Stages of Loving*, Gateway Books, London, 1985, p. 3.

17 R. A. Johnson, *The Psychology of Romantic Love*, p. 193.

18 This is seen in the literature on adult children of alcoholics, e.g. C. Black, *It Will Never Happen To Me!* M.A.C., Denver, Colorado, 1982, and the Australian book L. Byrski, *Under the Influence: Growing Up in Alcoholic Families*, Collins Dove, Melbourne, Vic., 1987.

19 The popular book by Robin Norwood explores this, *Women Who Love Too Much*.

20 Hendrix, *Getting the Love You Want*, p. 29.

21 In the more recent book by Harville Hendrix, *Keeping the Love You Find*, in Pocket Books, New York, 1992, he develops an interesting developmental perspective and has some exercises to help the reader to determine the stage at which they were wounded: attachment, exploration, identity, competence, concern or intimacy.

22 Hendrix, *Getting the Love You Want*, p. 43.

23 M. and B. Kelsey, *Sacrament of Sexuality*, Amity House, New York, 1986, p. 242.

24 Hendrix, *Getting the Love You Want*, p. 77.

Chapter 9

1 The birth order of children is significant in many ways, W. Tolman, *Family Constellation: Its Effects on Personality and Social Behaviour*, 2nd edn, Springer, New York, 1969.

2 The classic study of violence towards children is by Alice Miller, *For Your Own Good: The Roots of Violence in Child Rearing*, trans. by H. and H. Hannum, Virago Press, London, 1987. An Australian book to help women in violent families, T. Roxburgh *Taking Control: Help for Women and Children Escaping Domestic Violence*, Greenhouse Publications, Elwood, Vic., 1989.

3 'More emphasis needs to be placed on the positive elements of family-of-origin material.' Munson, *Family-of-Origin Applications*, p. 70.

4 An excellent treatment of this theme with feminist insight is M. Walters, B. Carter, P. Papp and O. Siverstein, *The Invisible Web: Gender Patterns in Family Relationships*, Guilford Press, New York, 1988.

5 V. Pillari, *Scapegoating in Families*, Brunner/Mazel, New York, 1991.

6 See R. C. Aylmer, 'Bowen Family Systems Marital Therapy', in *Clinical Handbook of Marital Therapy*, eds. N. S. Jacobson and A. S. Gurman, The Guilford Press, New York, 1986, pp. 107–148.

7 B. Stagoll and M. Lang, 'Climbing the Family Tree: Working

with Genograms', *Australian Journal of Family Therapy*, vol. 1, no. 4, 1980, p. 163.

8 For a more complete treatment of family and marriage evaluation, *see* M. Kerr and M. Bowen, *Family Evaluation*, pp. 282–338.

9 K. McAll, *Healing the Family Tree*, Sheldon Press, London, 1982.

10 'Couples Therapy and Marriage Contracts', *Handbook of Family Therapy*, pp. 85–130.

11 P. Guerin, Jnr, L. F. Fay, S. L. Burden and J. G. Kautto, *The Evaluation and Treatment of Marital Conflict: A Four-stage Approach*, Basic Books, New York, 1987.

12 A good book by Australian authors is B. Montgomery and L. Evans, *Living and Loving Together: A Practical Manual for Better Relationships*, Viking O'Neil, Ringwood, Vic., 1989.

13 H. G. Lerner, *The Dance of Anger*, Harper and Row, New York, 1985, p. 56.

14 Guerin, *Marital Conflict*, p. 150.

15 T. Fogarty, 'Systems, Concepts and the Dimensions of the Self', in *Family Therapy*, ed. P. J. Guerin Jnr., Gardner Press, New York, 1976, pp. 144–153.

16 Guerin, *Marital Conflict*, p. 191.

17 Jansen, *Really Relating*, p. 167.

18 *ibid.*, p. 217.

19 Kerr, *Family Evaluation*, p. 193.

20 S. Shapiro, *Manhood: A New Definition*, G. P. Putnam's Sons, New York, 1984, p. 59.

21 Guerin, *Marital Conflict*, p. 249.

22 *ibid.*, p. 248.

23 D. Granvold, 'Structured Separation for Marital Treatment and Decision-making', *Journal of Marital and Family Therapy*, vol. 9 no. 4, 1983, p. 404.

24 *ibid.*, pp. 407–408.

25 *Helping Your Child Through Separation and Divorce*, Dove Communications, Blackburn, Vic., 1981, p. 23.

26 Guerin, *Marital Conflict*, p. 251.

27 For guidance on this and other related issues, C. Chan and R.

McBain, *Divorce: An Australian Men's Guide,* Richmond, Vic., William Heinemann, 1985.

28 Shapiro, *Manhood,* p. 136.

29 Bruce Fisher, *Rebuilding: When Your Relationship Ends,* Impact Publishers, San Luis Obispo, 2nd edn, 1992. Also the 'eventual' challenge of remarriage and the possibility of blended families, *see* Joy Conolly, *Step-families: Towards a Clearer Understanding,* Corgi Books, Balmain, NSW, 1983.

Chapter 10

1 H. Hendrix, *Getting the Love You Want.*

2 A psychodrama variant of this exercise is to mirror the body posture and movement as well.

3 'Chronic Anxiety and the Defining of a Self', M. E. Kerr, *The Atlantic,* Sept, 1988, p. 53.

4 M. Kerr, *Family Evaluation,* p. 139.

5 *See* the discussion in M. Kerr, *Family of Origin Applications,* pp. 29-30.

6 *See* Annette Lawson, *Adultery: An Analysis of Love and Betrayal,* Oxford University Press, Oxford, 1990. Also the recent book by Emily M. Brown, *Patterns of Infidelity and Their Treatment,* Brunner/Mazel, New York, 1991.

7 M. Hunt, quoted by A. P. Thompson, 1982, p. 142.

8 Guerin, *Marital Conflict,* p. 64.

Chapter 11

1 H. Lerner, *Dance of Anger,* p. 44.

2 M. Kerr, *Family Evaluation,* p. 72.

3 Guerin, *Marital Conflict,* p. 47.

4 Quoted in the *Canberra Times,* 30.4.88, p. 31.

5 M. Kerr, *Family Evaluation,* p. 74.

6 *Brain Sex,* Mandarin, London, 1989, p. 127.

7 H. Lerner, *The Dance of Intimacy,* Harper and Row, New York, 1989, p. 104.

8   *ibid.*, p. 112.

9   H. Lerner, *Dance of Anger*, p. 27.

10 H. Lerner, *Dance of Intimacy*, p. 7.

11 *ibid.*, p. 35.

12 S. Freud,*Dora: An Analysis of a Case of Hysteria*, Collier Books, New York, 1969.

13 J. Gleick, *Chaos: Making of a New Science*, Cardinal, London, 1988; and B. Stevens, 'Chaos: A challenge to refine systems theory', *Australian and New Zealand Journal of Family Therapy*, Feb 1991, pp. 23–26.

14 A book for women in abusive relationships is Susan Forward, *Men Who Hate Women and the Women Who Love Them*, Toronto, Bantam Books, 1986.

15 An early book on this is D. Bowskill and A. Linacre, *The 'Male' Menopause*, Pan Books, London, 1976. A more recent exploration is H. Formaini, *Men: The Darker Continent*, Heinemann, London, 1990.

16 I have not discussed the treatment of sexual difficulties in the marriage relationship. I consider this to be the therapeutic role of a specialist and recommend referral. A book which discusses this area with practical guidelines is *Integrating Sex and Marital Therapy*, eds. G. R. Weeks and L. Hof, Brunner/Mazel Publishers, New York, 1987. Also the Australian sex-therapist W. Williams, *Man, Woman and Sexual Desire*, Williams and Wilkins, Adis, Sydney, 1986.

17 D. Stoop and J. Masteller, *Forgiving Our Parents, Forgiving Ourselves*, Servant Publications, Ann Arbor, Michigan, 1991, pp. 169–179.

18 Friedman, *Generation to Generation*, p. 169.

19 S. Shapiro, *Manhood*, p. 167.

Chapter 12

1   For example Carl Rogers, *Carl Rogers on Encounter Groups*, Harper and Row, New York, 1970. Also Eric Berne, who formulated Transactional Analysis, *see* his *Principles of Group Treatment*, Oxford University Press, New York, 1966.

2 *See* I. D. Yalom, *The Theory and Practice of Group Psychotherapy*, 3rd edn, Basic Books, New York, 1985, p. 12. This is a classic text which I have used extensively in this chapter.

3 There is an opportunity to develop more sensitivity to body language, e.g. Allan Pease, *Body Language: How to Read Others' Thoughts by Their Gestures*, Camel, Avalon Beach, NSW, 1981; and W. Lamb and E. Watson, *Body Code: The Meaning in Movement*, Routledge and Kegan Paul, London, 1979.

4 Yalom, *Group Psychotherapy*, p. 89.

5 *ibid.*, p. 22.

6 S. Rutan and W. N. Stone, *Psychodynamic Group Psychotherapy*, Macmillan, New York, 1984, p. 39.

7 'The therapist will look for something in the present transaction that makes the patient's experience at least understandable from his or her point of view.' M. Gill, 'The Interactional Aspect of Transference: Range of Application', in *The Transference in Psychotherapy*, ed. E. A. Schwaber, International Universities Press, New York, 1985, p. 95.

8 Yalom, *Group Psychotherapy*, p. 310.

9 *ibid.*, p. 41, Cf. R. Michels, 'Transference: An Introduction to the Concept', in Schwaber, *Transference*, pp. 13-19.

10 *See* James Mann, *Time Limited Therapy*, Harvard University Press, Cambridge, MA, 1973.

11 Yalom, *Group Psychotherapy*, p. 125.

Chapter 13

1 Nathaniel Branden, *The Psychology of Self-Esteem*, Bantam Books, New York, 1969/1987, p. 109.

2 Josh McDowell, *His Image, My Image*, Here's Life Publishers, San Bernardino, CA, 1984, p. 31.

3 *Psychology of Self-Esteem*, p. 141.

4 R. L. Bednar, M. G. Wells, S. R. Peterson, *Self-Esteem: Paradoxes and Innovations in Clinical Theory and Practice*, American Psychological Association, Washington, DC, 1989/1991, p. 102.

5 *ibid.*, p. 108.

6 *ibid.*, p. 157.

7 Trish Nove, *A Training Manual on Assertiveness Skills for Community Educators and Health Professionals*, NSW Dept of Health, Greenwich, NSW, no date of publication, p. B39.

Chapter 14

1 *See* Robert Johnson, *Inner Work: Using Dreams and Active Imagination for Personal Growth*, Harper and Row, San Francisco, 1986.

2 A-M. Rizzuto, *Birth of the Living God*, The University of Chicago, Chicago, 1979.

3 *ibid.*, p. 183.

4 D. Winnicott, *Playing and Reality*, Tavistock, London, 1971, p. 2.

5 A-M. Rizzuto, *Birth of the Living God*, p. 180.

6 *See* W. W. Meissner, *Psychoanalysis and Religious Experience*, Yale University Press, New Haven, 1984.

7 *See* M. Kohut, *The Analysis of the Self*, International Universities Press, New York, 1971 and *The Restoration of the Self*, International Universities Press, New York, 1977.

8 Ernest S. Wolf, *Treating the Self*, Guilford Press, New York, 1988, p. 52.

9 Howard Bacal and Kenneth Newman, *Theories of Object Relations: Bridges to Self Psychology*, Columbia University Press, New York, 1990, p. 232.

10 *The Fire and the Cloud*, ed. D. A. Fleming, Geoffrey Chapman, London, 1978, p. 172.

11 *ibid.*, p. 86.

12 *ibid.*, p. 190.

13 *ibid.*, p. 223.

14 This assumes the existence of God. If this is a problem then the role of fantasy objects can be examined. See Howard Bacal and Kenneth Newman, *Theories of Object Relations*, p. 252-255.

15 E. S. Wolf, *Treating the Self*, p. 53.

Psychiatric Supplement

1   H. Omer and P. London, 'Metamorphosis in Psychotherapy: End of the Systems Era', *Psychotherapy*, 25/2, (1988), pp. 171-179.

2   D. A. Regier, et al, 'The NIMH Epidemiologic Catchment Area Programme', *Arch. Gen. Psychiatry*, Vol 41, (1984), pp. 934-941.

3   G. Andrews, 'The Evaluation of Psychotherapy', *Current Opinion in Psychiatry*, Vol 4, (1991a), pp. 379-383.

4   — 'The changing nature of psychiatry', *Australian and New Zealand Journal of Psychiatry*, Vol 25, (1991b), pp. 453-459.

5   — 'Psychotherapy: From Freud to Cognitive Science', *The Medical Journal of Australia*, Vol. 155, (1991c), pp. 845-848.

6   J. Ellard, *Psychiatry for the Non-Psychiatrist*, Reprinted from Modern Medicine by Geigy Pharmaceuticals, 1975, p. 5.

7   T. B. Karasu, *Wisdom in the Practice of Psychotherapy*, Basic Books, New York, 1992, p. 17.

8   G. Gorton and S. Akhtar, 'The Literature on Personality Disorders 1985-1988: Trends Issues and Controversies', *Hospital and Community Psychiatry*, 41/1, (1990), p. 39.

9   B. Brandchaft and R. Stolorow, 'The Borderline Concept: Pathological Character or Iatrogenic Myth? Paper delivered at Conference on Borderline States at Univesrity of California, (1981).

10 DSM-III-R (1987).

11 New South Wales Mental Health Act.

12 L. G. Kiloh, J. S. Smith and G. F. Johnson, *Physical Treatments in Psychiatry*, Blackwell, Melbourne, 1988.

13 K. M. Moriarty, et al., 'Psychopharmacology: An Historical Perspective', *Psychiatric Clinics of North America*, Sep; 7/3, (1984), pp. 411-433.

14 S. B. Guse, 'Biological Psychiatry: Is there any other kind?', *Psychological Medicine*, Vol 19, (1989), pp. 315-323.

15 I. R. H. Falloon, 'Family Stress and Schizophrenia', *Psychiatric Clinics of North America*, 9/1, (1986), pp. 165-182.

16 M. J. Goldstein, 'Psychosocial (nonpharmacologic) Treatments for Schizophrenia, *Review of Psychiatry*, Vol 10, (1991),

chapter 6, pp. 116-135. American Psychiatric Association, Washington.

17 K. L. Davis, et al., 'Dopamine in Schizophrenia: A review and reconceptualization', *American Journal of Psychiatry*, Vol 148, (1991), pp. 1474-1486).

18 K. F. Berman and D. R. Weinberger, 'Functional Localization in the Brain in Schizophrenia', *Review Of Psychiatry*, Vol 10, (1991), Chapter 2, pp. 24-59.

19 D. R. Weinberger, 'The Pathogenesis of Schizophrenia: A Neurodevelopmental Theory', *Handbook of Schizophrenia*, Vol. 1, (1986), Chapter 18, pp. 397-406.

20 K. Hawton, 'Assessment of Suicide Risk', *British Journal of Psychiatry*, Vol. 150, (1987), pp. 145-153.

21 G. F. Johnson, 'New Antidepressants', *Modern Medicine of Australia*, (April, 1992), pp. 88-89.

22 M. Olfson and G. L. Klerman, 'Trends in the Prescription of Antidepressants by Office-based Psychiatrists', *American Journal of Psychiatry*, Vol. 150, (April, 1993), pp. 571-577.

23 J. F. Cade, 'Lithium Salts in the Treatment of Psychotic Excitement', (1949), reprinted *Australian and New Zealand Journal of Psychiatry*, Vol. 16, (1982), pp. 129-133.

24 A. Rifkin, 'ECT Versus Tricyclic Antidepressants in Depression: A review of the evidence', *Journal of Clinical Psychiatry*, 49/1, (1988), pp. 3-7.

25 R. Spielman, Psychodynamic Aspects of Prescribing Medication, *The Australian Journal of Psychopharmacology*, (May 5, 1991), pp. 6-7.

INDEX